In Memory of

Dr. Richard Weber Bailey
1926-2000

This clear and accessible introduction describes the history and the character of the Orthodox Churches of the Christian East from the accession of the Emperor Constantine in 312 to the present day. It includes the various national Orthodox Churches – both Chalcedonian and non-Chalcedonian – and also the Church of the East and the Greek Catholic Churches. There are both common traditions shared by these Churches but also different and sometimes divisive local characteristics. The distinctive Orthodox approaches to the themes of liturgy, theology, monastic life and spirituality, icons, popular religion, mission, politics and the issues which divide East and West are discussed in turn. A final chapter presents the response of the Churches to their new freedom following the collapse of Communist governments and the prospects for the future. An understanding of other Church traditions can open up fresh ways of looking at our own faith.

JOHN BINNS is Vicar of Great St Mary's, The University Church, Cambridge. He has been involved for many years in ecumenical projects, as Vice-Chairman of the Fellowship of St Alban and St Sergius; Chairman of the St Matthew's Children's Fund, Ethiopia; and a director of the Institute for Orthodox Christian Studies, Cambridge. Dr Binns is the author of *Cyril of Scythopolis: The Lives of the Monks of Palestine* (with R. Price, 1992), *Ascetics and Ambassadors of Christ* (1994), and *Great St Mary's: Cambridge's University Church* (with P. Meadows, 2000).

An Introduction to the
Christian Orthodox Churches

JOHN BINNS

CAMBRIDGE
UNIVERSITY PRESS

PUBLISHED BY THE PRESS SYNDICATE OF THE UNIVERSITY OF CAMBRIDGE
The Pitt Building, Trumpington Street, Cambridge, United Kingdom

CAMBRIDGE UNIVERSITY PRESS
The Edinburgh Building, Cambridge CB2 2RU, UK
40 West 20th Street, New York, NY 10011-4211, USA
477 Williamstown Road, Port Melbourne, VIC 3207, Australia
Ruiz de Alarcón 13, 28014 Madrid, Spain
Dock House, The Waterfront, Cape Town 8001, South Africa

http://www.cambridge.org

First published 2002

Printed in the United Kingdom at the University Press, Cambridge

Typeface Sabon 10/13.5 pt   *System* LATEX 2$_\varepsilon$ [TB]

A catalogue record for this book is available from the British Library

ISBN 0 521 66140 4 hardback
ISBN 0 521 66738 0 paperback

Contents

List of illustrations and maps

Illustrations
Between pages 144 and 145

Maps

Preface

The use of the word Orthodox in the title of this book requires some definition since it is a word which, while it has a clear meaning, has been used in a bewildering and contradictory variety of contexts. It is derived from two Greek words: *orthos*, meaning straight or right and hence correct, and *doxa*, meaning originally opinion (from the verb *dokein* or seem), but also glory or worship. So in the context of religion it is a claim that you are right – in contrast to your opponents who are wrong; and it is also often associated with being conservative since rightness implies adherence to the tradition of the past and wrongness suggests an innovative deviation. The word can be used in all religious contexts: for example, Orthodox Jews, as opposed to Reformed or Liberal, and modern Protestant Christians who call themselves orthodox in contrast to liberals.

The Church in its formative years met in a series of Councils to define what was orthodox as opposed to what was heretical. Division occurred especially after the Council of Chalcedon (451). Those who supported its decisions (Byzantine Greeks, and then later Russians and other East European Churches) called themselves Orthodox – and still do – while those who opposed the Council (among them Copts or Egyptians, and Syrians) also called themselves Orthodox – and they still do too. Then, a few centuries later, the next major controversy to divide the Church occurred, which was between West and East. The Christians of the East continued to call themselves Orthodox – but now in contrast to Western Christians, who came to call themselves Catholic. This usage became increasingly accepted, and by 1600 it was possible to speak of the Orthodox Church and to mean the Greek or Eastern Church. It is in this sense that the word Orthodox is used in this book.

This book discusses both the Orthodox Churches in communion with Constantinople and also the Orthodox Churches that opposed the definitions of the Council of Chalcedon. In addition, two other Churches are described, neither of which can correctly be referred to as Orthodox, but which share many historical and other traditions with the Orthodox Churches and exist alongside them. These are the Church of the East, which had its centre in what is now Iraq, and the Greek Catholic or Uniate Churches, which accepted the authority of the Pope and so are Catholic and which exist in parts of Eastern Europe and in the Middle East. Any discussion would be incomplete without them.

All these Churches are found in the eastern parts of the Christian world, and therefore are sometimes called the Eastern Churches. This is misleading for two reasons: first, because the Orthodox emphasise that they follow the one Christian faith which is common to the whole Christian Church that covered both East and West for well over a millennium; and, second, because, during the last century many Orthodox Christians have migrated to the West and have established strong roots in Western society. Both for most of its history and in its present state, Orthodoxy is a world-wide Church, even though its institutions were formed in the eastern part of Christendom.

So the title Orthodox is used to refer to several Churches which have, from time to time, been in conflict over doctrinal and other matters. So I seldom use the term 'the Orthodox Church', and prefer to refer to 'Orthodox Churches', qualifying this with rather cumbersome adjectives like Chalcedonian or non-Chalcedonian. In spite of the fact that there are serious divisions within them, they share common roots, historical experiences and cultural expressions. The purpose of this book is to try to understand both the shared ways of living and expressing the Orthodox faith, and also the distinctiveness of different traditions within Orthodoxy. This will be done through selecting some significant themes, which form the headings of the chapters. These are preceded by a survey of the variety of Orthodox Church life, which also introduces some of the themes to be dealt with later, and are followed by a necessarily impressionistic discussion of a rapidly changing contemporary situation.

As for the tricky question of which form of proper names to use, I have tried to be as clear as possible, using the form of a name most likely to be familiar. This can lead to some inconsistency: so, for example, Sergius of Radonezh but Sergei Bulgakov. Even though my choices may jar on the reader from time to time, I hope that it will at least be clear who is being referred to.

Acknowledgments

As a student I once attended a series of mission sermons by Metropolitan Antony Bloom of the Russian Orthodox Cathedral in London. He presented a vision of faith at once open and compassionate, but also demanding and uncompromising. It was an introduction to a tradition which has continued to shape and renew my own understanding and faith. To the example of Metropolitan Antony, I must add many others who have generously shared their own experiences and insights – which lie behind the ideas of this book. I must especially acknowledge the help and encouragement of friends and colleagues in several countries. In Serbia, I am especially grateful to Bishop Stefan (Boca) of Žiča; Fr Radomir Bulatović, a fellow-student many years ago and self-appointed language teacher at the Orthodox Theological Faculty in Belgrade; the monks of the monastery of Kaona, Fr Teofilo Stanimirović (now deceased) and Fr Milutin Knežević; and also to Fr Vladimir Vukašinović, Fr Ieronim Močević and Alexander Popović. Then there are those who helped to explore the Ethiopian theological tradition: Fr Colin Battell OSB, Fr Berhanu Bisrat, Deacon Mesfin Tsige, Dr Anthwan Mikhail Yacoub and Clive Oppenheimer. I am also grateful for the support and hospitality of Archbishop Mar Eustathius Matta Roham, Fr Stephen Griffiths, Fr Dale Johnson, Fr Abdullah Tafas and his son Jihad, in Syria and Turkey; Canon John Peterson and Yizhar Hirschfeld, in Jerusalem; and Alexander Kyrlezhev, in Moscow. In England I have valued working with colleagues in various ecumenical ventures, especially Bishop Basil (Osborne) of Sergievo and Deacon

Stephen Platt; and, like so many others, I have learnt much from Bishop Kallistos (Ware) of Diokleia.

I am especially grateful to those who have read the manuscript and provided much helpful advice and comment: Fr John Chryssavgis of Holy Cross Theological College, Brookline, Massachusetts; Marcus Plested and Fr John Jillions of the Institute for Orthodox Christian Studies in Cambridge; and the late Christopher Hookway, who read and commented on an early version of this book during the last months before his death. I hope they are not too shocked by what I have written, and will recognise that, even when it makes mistakes and misjudgments, it seeks only to understand and make sense of what is complex and often confusing. I am also very grateful to Philip Oswald, who provided the image on the front cover, and the pictures of the dome of the Haghia Sophia and of the monk planting a tree; and to Martin Palmer and the Circa Picture Library, for the picture of the child receiving communion.

The book is dedicated to my family, first and foremost to Sue, my wife, who has always encouraged me to read, travel and soak in the atmosphere of Orthodox Christianity; and also to William and Sally; and to our friends Fr John and Shanta Lee, who have given me more than they would guess in many different ways.

Map 1. The Chalcedonian Orthodox Churches

Showing the national boundaries of present-day local Churches, including the unrecognised Churches of the Ukraine and Macedonia

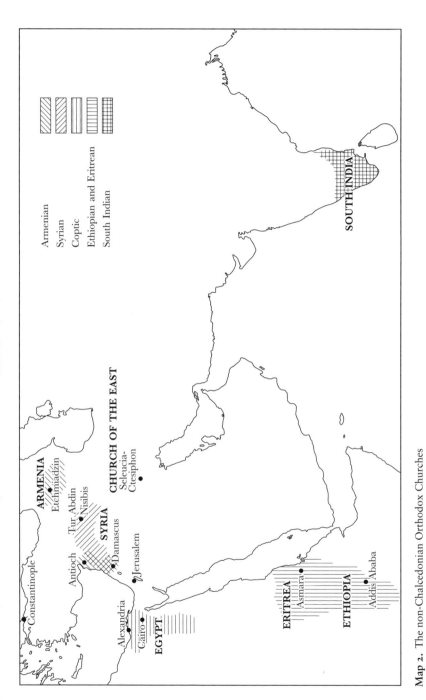

Map 2. The non-Chalcedonian Orthodox Churches

The Churches are located to the east and south of the medieval Byzantine Empire, with further centres in Ethiopia and India. The members of the Church of the East are now few in number

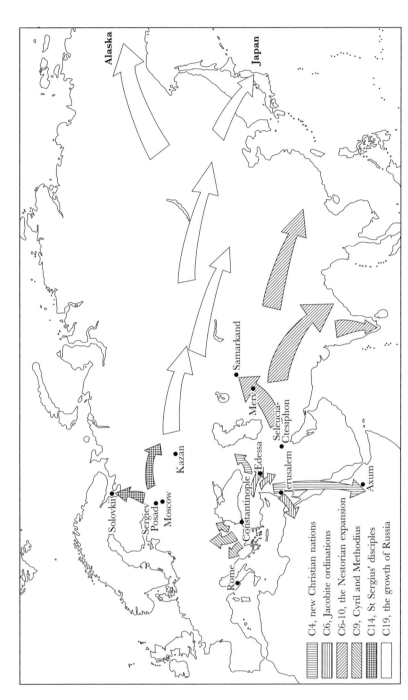

Map 3. The expansion of the Eastern Church

Alaska

Japan

Solovki

Sergiev Posad

Moscow

Kazan

Samarkand

Merv

Seleucia-Ctesiphon

Edessa

Jerusalem

Constantinople

Rome

Axum

C4, new Christian nations

C6, Jacobite ordinations

C6-10, the Nestorian expansion

C9, Cyril and Methodius

C14, St Sergius' disciples

C19, the growth of Russia

Introduction: identifying Orthodoxy

A WALK DOWN STRAIGHT STREET

Straight Street in Damascus is the only road to be named in the Bible (Acts of the Apostles 9.11). We are told how the zealous Jew, Saul, was taken here after his experience on the road to Damascus, led by the hand, temporarily blinded by the light of God's presence and bewildered by the voice which spoke to him. A disciple called Ananias healed him of his blindness and baptised him. After a few days in Damascus, Paul left to begin his extraordinary career of preaching the gospel of Christ and sharing in setting up the infant Christian Church. Straight Street, the main street of the city, then a broad thoroughfare lined by columns, could be reckoned to be the cradle of the Church.

You can still walk down Straight Street. It is not as wide – nor as straight – as it was in Paul's day, but it is still one of the main streets of the old walled city of Damascus. It is lined with shops, bends a little, and is noisy and crowded. Today you are likely to approach it from the side of the modern city centre, and, about halfway down, you find an alleyway which leads to the marbled church and mansion that is the residence of His Beatitude Patriarch Ignatios IV, the Greek Orthodox Patriarch of Antioch and All the East; then a little further along is another smaller sideturning which leads to the less imposing church and residence of His Holiness Moran Mor Ignatius Zakka I Iwas, the Syrian Orthodox Patriarch, also of Antioch and All the East. On the other side of the road is the church of the Greek Catholic, or Melkite, Patriarch Maximos V Hakim, and he too is Patriarch of Antioch.

The three Patriarchs of Antioch who reside in the Street called Straight are not the only bishops to hold this title. Some thirty miles to the west is the Lebanese capital, Beirut, and here are a further two occupants of this see: the leaders of the Antiochian Syrian Maronite Church (usually known simply as the Maronites), and of the Syrian Catholic Church. There used to be a sixth Patriarch of Antioch, of the Latin Catholic Church, but this title is no longer used.

This variety becomes even more evident in the life of the parishes of the interior of Syria. To the east of the country is the Syrian diocese of the Gezirah, and here I once spent a day visiting homes in the Syrian Orthodox parish of Nasra'a with Fr Louis, the parish priest. He told me that there were in the parish 300 Syrian Orthodox families, 130 Armenian Catholic, sixty Syrian Catholic, five Syrian Protestant, four Armenian, three Assyrian Church of the East, and two Chaldaean. The Syrian Orthodox priest knows them well and many of them attend his church.

The life of the Christian communities in Syria shows clearly that there is not one single Eastern Orthodox Church, nor one doctrinal tradition which can be called Orthodoxy. The varied composition of the ecclesiastical life of modern Syria provides clear demonstration of the division, complexity, richness and turbulence of the history of the Christianity of the East. The Christians of Syria are conscious both of the diversity of Church life and also of their shared culture and history. Since they form a minority within a predominantly Muslim state, they are more conscious than some other Christians of the tradition which binds them together. So here we are vividly aware of both the unity and diversity that is a marked feature of the Christian life of the East.

This diversity is less apparent in other areas. Both Russia and Greece, for example, are self-consciously Orthodox and, what is more, Byzantine Orthodox countries. From this perspective, the history of Orthodoxy is identical with the history of one Church tradition. Since the West is usually more aware of Church life in these countries, it is easy to understand Orthodoxy mainly in these terms.

This book takes the Syrian experience as a starting-point. It recognises that the Orthodox Churches originate from a common background which has shaped the nature of the life of the Churches. It also seeks to show the differing forms of Christian living which have developed through a turbulent history. The turbulence is suggested by the fact that none of the five Patriarchs of Antioch has been able to remain in his episcopal see, since the ancient city of Antioch is now called Antakya and falls within the boundaries of modern Turkey, a city with numerous mosques but no living churches.

Damascus is the place where Paul's change of life began; and Antioch, about 200 miles to the north, is the place where the name 'Christian' was first used (Acts 11.26). From here the Church spread east, west, south and north. From the perspective of this book, these two ancient cities have a central place in the Eastern Christian world. To the north and south lie the two largest Orthodox Churches. To the east extends the greatest – but finally temporary – missionary expansion of the Church. To the west is the cultural and theological source of Orthodoxy. These Churches of Russia, Ethiopia, the East and Constantinople will all be discussed in the course of this book.

BYZANTINE ORTHODOX CULTURE

Although the city of Constantinople lies at the western side of the territory of the Christian East, it has had a decisive influence on the history of all the Orthodox Churches. The evolution of Eastern Christianity is bound up with the life of the Byzantine Empire. It developed either within the structures of the Empire or else just outside and in reaction against it. In modern usage the word Byzantine conjures up images of either an evocative and exotic oriental civilisation, or a labyrinthine and impenetrable bureaucracy. In any case Byzantium is, for most Westerners, remote both geographically (as lying beyond the territories of Europe) and historically (as a part of pre-modern medieval times). It requires an effort of imagination to grasp the importance and the attractiveness of the idea of the universal Christian Empire or to comprehend the formative influence of Byzantine civilisation on the life of the Church.

Any grasp of the nature of Orthodox Christianity has to begin with a recognition that it was nurtured and shaped in the Eastern Roman Empire, often called Byzantine, with its capital in the great city of Constantinople. This Empire understood itself to be continuous with the classical Roman Empire, and in the Middle East today Greek Orthodox are usually referred to as Rum (or Roman) Orthodox. It also saw itself as universal, appointed by God to govern the Christian world, and so those unfortunate enough to be outside this great society had to live awaiting the civilising benefits of Roman and Christian rule. Among the events that led to the formation of the Eastern Empire was the conversion of the Emperor Constantine to Christianity. The significance of this event may be exaggerated since the Church was widespread before the Emperor's conversion and paganism continued to be influential after it. The Emperor's new faith nonetheless gave the Christian Church a new status within the Empire, and inaugurated a new stage in the history of the Church. As a result, the Christian Church was set on-course to become the official state religion, a far cry from the revival movement within Judaism initiated in rural Palestine by the prophet Jesus of Nazareth. The conversion of Constantine had an impact nobody could have guessed at the time. As a result, this book begins its account of the life of the Eastern Churches at this point in history, three centuries after the life, death and resurrection of the founder, and refers to the events and personalities of the first centuries of the history of the Church only in passing.

Byzantium – named after its mythological founder, Byzas the son of the sea-god Neptune – was a Greek settlement founded in the seventh century BC at the place where the Bosphorus opens into the Sea of Marmara, between the Mediterranean and the Black Sea, where there is a natural and easily defended harbour. It caught the attention of the Emperor Constantine, who selected it as the site of the new capital city of the eastern part of the Roman Empire. The Emperor began to build here in 325, and five years later the new capital was dedicated with the name of Constantinople – the City of Constantine. It remained as the imperial capital for more than a thousand years, a city of unparalleled wealth, prestige and piety. The Empire over which it presided fluctuated in size. It reached its largest extent under the Emperor Justinian (527–65), when it included most of Italy, the Balkans as far north as modern Hungary, Egypt, Asia Minor, Syria and Palestine, the North African coast, and even parts of Spain. This massive tract of territory was reduced in size, at first gradually and then drastically, when in the seventh century the Arab armies overwhelmed the Eastern provinces of Syria, Egypt and Palestine, then swept on towards Constantinople. But although Syria and Egypt were not reconquered, the Byzantine Empire regained the ascendancy in Asia Minor and remained a formidable power at least until the Crusades in the eleventh century. In 1204 disaster struck, when the capital city of Constantinople itself was conquered by the Western armies of the Fourth Crusade. The Crusaders had unfortunately decided that the intrigues and rivalries of a Byzantine imperial succession dispute and the tempting prospect of booty made the Christian city of Constantinople a more attractive and attainable objective than the (then) Muslim city of Jerusalem (el Quds, as it was known to the Arabs). This was a decisive moment, starting a process of retrievable decline in both the power of the Byzantine Empire and also in the relations between the Eastern and Western parts of the Church. In 1261 the city was recaptured by Michael VIII Palaeologus (1259–82) but, in spite of a cultural resurgence under the Palaeologan dynasty, the Empire never regained its former glory and seemed to limp on painfully until 1453, when, on one of the catastrophic days of Christian history, the great city of Constantinople fell to the Turkish army of the Sultan Mehmet II.

Constantinople was bigger, more populous and richer than any other city in the early Christian world. It was dominated by three huge centres of public life. The hippodrome was nominally a stadium for chariot races, but in practice was far more than that. It was the place of assembly for the people of the city, and housed demonstrations of military might, triumphal processions welcoming returning victorious armies, public meetings and demonstrations, festivities and games, and all kinds of civic celebration. Next to it stood the Sacred Palace, entered through the *Chalke* (or 'Brazen') vestibule decorated with statues and frescoes, leading to the reception hall or Tribunal of Nineteen Couches, in which banquets were held, and then on to a mass of chambers, churches and palaces. Within this maze of magnificence the Empress Theodora, the wife of Justinian, was able to maintain a monastery of dissident Monophysites, including the former Patriarch Anthimus, who disappeared into the safety of the Palace for twelve years – everyone assuming he was dead – until he emerged after the death of the Empress, and this at a time when the Empire was officially Chalcedonian. The third great centre was the Great Church of the 'Immortal Wisdom of Christ', or *Haghia Sophia*. Originally built in 360 by Constantius, the son of Constantine, it was destroyed in 404, rebuilt, then destroyed again in a popular revolt called the Nike rebellion in 532, then immediately rebuilt and dedicated in 537. This is the building which stands today.

It was the Great Church of the Empire, in which the Patriarch and Emperor celebrated the liturgical feasts together. The liturgy of the Chalcedonian Orthodox Church evolved in this building and was exported to other Church centres, displacing local forms of worship. The scale of the liturgical life is hinted at by the reforms of Patriarch Sergius, who, in 612, decided that things were getting out of control, and reduced the number of clergy who served at the Haghia Sophia to a mere 80 priests, 150 deacons, 40 deaconesses, 70 subdeacons, 160 readers, 25 cantors and 100 doorkeepers. 'Harun ibn Yahya, an Arab visiting the city in the ninth century, was amazed at the lavish magnificence of the liturgy on feast days, and described processions from the Palace of over 50,000 sumptuously dressed attendants preceding the Emperor.[1] There were numerous churches and monasteries as well.

Little wonder that the representatives of the Prince Vladimir of Kiev reported their impressions of attending the liturgy at the Great Church in the tenth century with open-mouthed amazement. 'We knew not whether we were in heaven or earth for surely there is no such splendour or beauty anywhere upon earth. We cannot describe it to you. We cannot forget that beauty.' The worship of the church of Haghia Sophia demonstrated the wealth, the artistic and architectural brilliance, the size and scale of the Empire, and the centrality of faith and worship.

Although there was a flourishing intellectual life based on the University, which was founded in 425 and at its height was staffed by over thirty professors, Constantinople evolved into a city of monks, with the extraordinary claim made by the eleventh-century Patriarch John of Antioch that, during the iconoclast controversy which had taken place a couple of centuries before he was writing, the population of the city was divided equally between monks and laity.

The city was a combination of a New Rome, succeeding to the old as capital of the Empire; a New Jerusalem, appropriating relics from around the Empire, such as the Virgin Mary's robe and belt, to enhance its monopoly of sacred fullness; and a New Athens, as a centre of Greek learning and culture. Its rise coincided with the decline of the Western Roman Empire, which fell in 410 – just ninety years after the founding of Constantinople. Its decline and fall, beginning with the conquest by the Crusaders in 1204 and being prolonged painfully over the next two centuries, coincided with the rise of the Universities of Western Europe and the growth of new Western European nations. Then its final – and from a Christian point of view, tragic – loss to the Ottomans in 1453 took

---

[1] From A. Vasiliev, *Seminarium Kondrakovianum* v, cited in P. Sherrard, *Constantinople, Iconography of a Sacred City* (London 1965), p. 73.

place as the Renaissance and Reformation were transforming Western Europe. So the most creative periods of Western Christianity succeeded those of Eastern Christianity. As a result, from an Eastern viewpoint, Western Church life tends to have a novel, changing and impermanent character, since it largely evolved after Constantinople fell. From an Eastern point of view, Protestantism followed on inexorably from Papacy, since both share in the error of having diverged from the authentic tradition of the East, and as a result both share a restless, intellectual, individualistic form of the Christian faith. Roman Catholicism and Protestantism are sad examples of heretical divergence from the universal truth of the apostolic faith developed, articulated and faithfully preserved in Constantinople and those Churches in communion with it. By contrast, a Western observer tends to think that Orthodoxy froze in 1453, and has failed to adjust to the post-medieval world.

During the period of the Byzantine Empire, the Orthodox Church was formed, with its doctrine defined at Councils convened by the Emperor, its liturgy that of the city of Constantinople which came to be used throughout the Empire, its ecclesiastical art being the iconography of the Byzantine Empire, and its culture shaped by the monastic tradition which was nurtured in the capital and on Mount Athos. This is not to suggest that Orthodoxy is a Byzantine invention. Like all Churches its roots lie in the events described in the New Testament. Indeed, it can be argued convincingly that the culture of the Eastern Churches is far closer to the world of the New Testament than that of the West, and, further, that Western civilisation appropriated and adapted a faith which is Eastern in origin and character. But the life of the Orthodox Church evolved and developed in distinctive ways during the millennium of Byzantine rule, so that it can be seen as the Byzantine form of Christianity.

The impact of the Byzantine Empire lived on long after the once impregnable walls of Theodosius protecting the city had been breached. It has been said that the Orthodox Church is the Church of Byzantium which has survived the Empire by five hundred years.[2] Certainly it is the institutions of the Byzantine Church that continue to provide cohesion and community among the scattered Churches of the Orthodox East.

The vastly greater numbers of adherents of Byzantine Orthodoxy, the developed formulation of its theological traditions, and the accessibility

---

[2] A. Schmemann, *The Historical Road of Eastern Orthodoxy* (London 1963), p. 199.

of its music, art and liturgy should not lead us to ignore the Eastern and Orthodox Churches which fell outside the Empire and spoke different languages – Coptic, Syriac, Armenian and others. Byzantium had an influence on these too, however. This happened partly through shared linguistic and cultural traditions that flourished both within and beyond the boundaries of the Empire, and partly through the negative influence of being a dominant political power, which smaller groups reacted against and seceded from. So in the chapters that follow we will explore both common patterns shared by the Eastern Churches, and also recognise points of divergence.

Evaluations of the contribution of the Byzantine Empire to Christianity vary. For many, it was a creative and life-giving cultural synthesis of a Hebrew religious awe and a Greek search for philosophical truth. For these, the task facing the Church today is to leave behind the centuries of political subjection to Ottoman or Communist rule and of intellectual dependence on Western theology and philosophy, and to recover the vitality and creativity of the Byzantine centuries. A modern Greek theologian, Christos Yannaras, has said that the way to health of the Church is to recognise the cultural greatness of Byzantium and to present a Hellenistic corrective to Western individualism. Others fear that a desire to recreate the spirit of Byzantium will result in a rigid conservatism and an identification of the Church with a specific cultural form, while the task of the Church is to present the apostolic faith to modern generations, in the West as well as the East. Alexander Schmemann, the former dean of St Vladimir's Seminary in New York, admitted in his posthumously published journals to a deep distaste for all things Byzantine.[3] Whether the Byzantine Empire is seen as a highpoint of Christian civilisation or as merely one relative cultural form of a universal faith, the significance of the millennium of Byzantine civilisation in shaping the Orthodox Church must be acknowledged.

[3] See C. Yannaras, *Philosophie sans rupture* (Geneva 1986), p. 7. A. Schmemann, *The Journals of Father Alexander Schmemann 1978–1983* (New York 2000), is an example of an unusually frank criticism of a Byzantinist approach.

2

Description: a map of Orthodoxy

We began by walking down Straight Street and encountering three Patriarchs, all presiding over the territory of Antioch, once an important city of the Byzantine Empire and the capital of the diocese of Oriens, which consisted of the eastern part of the Empire. These leaders provide a convenient way of approaching a description of the Churches since each comes from one of the three main families of Churches. The largest of these groups or families is that of the Byzantine or Chalcedonian Orthodox, accounting for the vast majority of Eastern Christians; they are the Churches of the Eastern Roman Empire and those which emerged out of Byzantine missions. They are (mostly) in communion with the Patriarch of Constantinople. Then there is a group of churches called the Oriental Orthodox, which thrived in the areas to the east of the Byzantine Empire. These are sometimes called non-Chalcedonian or pre-Chalcedonian Churches, since their separation took place after they declined to accept the doctrinal decisions of the Council of Chalcedon (451). The name Monophysite has been used, but seems less acceptable when applied in the present day since it associates these Churches with more extreme forms of Monophysite teaching that have been judged to be contrary to Orthodox teaching. The third family are the various Eastern Churches that accept the authority of the Pope of Rome, which are known as Greek or Eastern Catholics. Like Monophysitism, the title Uniate, which was once generally used, acquired a derogatory tone in the course of the last century, now that the existence of Eastern Catholics has come to be seen as an obstacle to the unity of the

Churches. The Churches that make up these groups will be discussed in turn.

THE CHALCEDONIAN ORTHODOX CHURCHES

The Chalcedonian Orthodox Church is in fact a group or family made up of several national or 'local' Churches. Since there is no central organisation but rather a loose federation of Orthodox Churches, independent churches tend to be formed in response to local needs – such as a newly constituted nation-state, or a mission Church which has developed sufficiently to become independent. A new Church should be given its independent status by the Mother Church on which it previously depended, and then recognised by the Patriarchate of Constantinople, as senior bishop, and by other national Churches. There are two levels of independence. An 'autocephalous' Church is self-governing in all respects, and selects and consecrates its own leadership. An 'autonomous' Church has a lesser degree of independence, and must obtain the blessing and agreement of the Mother Church in order to consecrate its head. The movement towards independence may be erratic, with a Church recognised by one Church but not by another. There are currently sixteen autocephalous Churches. These are the Churches of Constantinople, Alexandria, Antioch, Jerusalem, Russia, Serbia, Romania, Bulgaria, Georgia, Cyprus, Greece, Poland, Albania, Czech lands and Slovakia, and America (which is not recognised by Constantinople). And there are a further five autonomous Churches – not all recognised by all Churches – which are the Churches of Sinai, Finland, Japan, China and Estonia. In addition a number of other Churches exist but are considered to be uncanonical, or irregularly established, and these may become recognised in due course if their status is accepted by the other Churches. The shape of world Orthodoxy is constantly shifting as the external organisation of the Churches develops to accommodate new political and social realities. Somehow, in spite of the diverse and decentralised nature of Church organisation, the Orthodox Churches maintain a strong sense of unity based on sharing in a common faith.

Five patriarchates and one catholicosate

The origins of Church ordering lie in the administration of the Eastern Roman Empire. This is shown by the way that the Church has borrowed secular language to describe ecclesiastical ordering. The Roman Empire was divided into administrative units which were called 'dioceses', of which there were five in the Eastern Empire: Egypt, Oriens (or 'the east', mainly Syria), Thrace, Pontus and Asia. The word 'bishop', in Greek *episkopos*, simply means 'overseer' or 'inspector', and could be used in contexts other than the ecclesiastical to refer to any kind of supervision. The senior bishop in each diocese was known as the Metropolitan, as bishop of the see in the *Metropolis*, or principal city. More senior than the Metropolitan Bishop was the Patriarch. This title, with its implication of paternal care and authority and also its Biblical overtones, was first used in legal and administrative documents in the sixth century, probably in the Metropolitan (now Patriarchal) diocese of Antioch. It was used to recognise the honour and precedence given to those bishops of regional or diocesan capitals. This adaptation of the Church to the imperial administrative structures shows the non-theological nature of Church ordering, and helps to explain why new local Churches have been able to develop through history, as national and other groupings have struggled to achieve an independent political existence.

The five major episcopal sees of the Empire have a recognised priority which remains to this day, even though they are no longer the largest or most influential of the Orthodox Churches. In the Byzantine period they had the right to consecrate other bishops within their areas of jurisdiction, and to be consulted over matters of doctrine and Church order, but they did not have authority within the see of another bishop. The five were listed in canon 26 of the Council of Chalcedon (451). They were Rome as the ancient capital of the Empire; Constantinople or New Rome as the capital of the eastern part, which thus came to preside over three dioceses of Asia, Pontus and Thrace; Alexandria, the metropolitan city of the diocese of Egypt; Antioch, in the diocese of Oriens; and Jerusalem, which was added to the list by virtue of being the city in which Jesus Christ lived and died. This arrangement came to be known as Pentarchy, or the authority of five, and was confirmed at the Council of Constantinople in 869–70 and formulated by Patriarch Peter III of Antioch in the eleventh century. By this time political developments had already begun to eclipse the significance of four of the Patriarchates: Rome was increasingly absorbed by the different priorities of the West, while Alexandria, Antioch and Jerusalem were in territories ruled over by the Arab dynasties. The formulation of this tradition is a witness to the importance attached to the Roman Empire as the expression of the universal Christian Church.

Patriarch John IV of Constantinople, known as the Faster (582–95), was the first to use the title Ecumenical (or Universal) Patriarch. Pope Gregory I of Rome (590–604) indignantly responded that there was no universal bishop and that he, Gregory, although acknowledged as first bishop, was nothing more than the servant of the servants of God – a title still used by the Popes. But John based his claim on the fact that the city over which he presided was the capital of the Empire and therefore was the Ecumenical or Universal City. As the power of the city grew, so did that of the Patriarch. From being a suffragan to the Metropolitan Bishop of Heraclea in 330, he was made second in honour after Rome at the Council of Constantinople in 381, and so, after the schism between East and West, he has become, by default, the senior bishop in the Chalcedonian Orthodox world. His prominence grew as Arab advances reduced the power of the other three Patriarchates. Perhaps surprisingly, the capture of Constantinople by the Turks in 1453 led to a further increase in his power. He was given judicial as well as spiritual authority over all Christians in the Ottoman Empire, and as a result his area of jurisdiction was extended from the small area to which the Byzantine Empire had been reduced to the huge territory covered by the Ottoman Empire. This led to the situation whereby the Muslim Ottomans became the promoters of the power of the Ecumenical Patriarch at the expense of national Churches such as Serbia and Bulgaria. The Patriarch wore the imperial double-headed eagle of Byzantium on his vestments to show that he personified the continuation of Byzantine authority.

The power of the Ecumenical Patriarch disintegrated with the rise of nationalism in the nineteenth century. He was faced by an awful dilemma: whether to encourage the stirrings of Greek nationalism, and the establishment of a Hellenic Christian state in Greece; or whether to support the Ottoman Empire, which was the source of Patriarchal authority, and which was uncomfortably close to the Patriarchal residence at the Phanar in Istanbul. Whatever he did he would be the loser. In 1821, revolution broke out in the Peloponnese. The Ecumenical Patriarch Gregory V found himself forced by the Ottoman authorities to excommunicate the revolutionaries, which he did on Palm Sunday. But this action failed to appease the angry Turkish rulers, who, just one week later, dragged him from his church while he was celebrating the

Easter liturgy and hanged him from the gate of the Patriarchate. Here he hung, still in his vestments, so that those who entered had to push past the swinging body, until his corpse was secretly removed a week later and taken eventually to Odessa in Russia, where it was given an honourable burial. The gate on which his body was hanged remains closed to this day.

Since then the situation of the Patriarchate in Turkey has continued to deteriorate. In 1921 the Greeks invaded Turkey, and briefly recaptured Constantinople. But then as the new Turkey became established, there were exchanges of Greek and Turkish populations, and anti-Greek feeling grew among Turks, especially after the partition of Cyprus in 1974–5. The Orthodox population within Turkey has shrunk to under 2,000 residents, although the Patriarch retains jurisdiction over parts of Greece, including the islands of the Dodecanese, Crete, some regions of north-east Greece and the monastic republic of Mount Athos. The main significance of the Patriarchate today is its international authority, since the Patriarch presides over the Churches of the diaspora, in Western Europe, America and Australasia. There are 5,255,000 people under his jurisdiction, of which a tiny proportion live inside Turkey, where once the Eastern Christian world had its centre.[1]

Since the number of Orthodox in Turkey has shrunk so alarmingly and since Turkish law requires the Patriarch to be a citizen of Turkey, it must be doubtful whether the Orthodox community will be able to produce suitable candidates for this position. If this proves impossible, the dramatic prospect of the Ecumenical Patriarchate moving from the ecumenical city presents itself. It must be hoped that permission is given by the government to re-open the Patriarchal Academy on Halki (in Turkish, Heybeliada) which was closed in 1971, but is kept in good order awaiting the day when pupils will return. This could nurture future candidates for the episcopate and patriarchate.

The Patriarch of Constantinople has much prestige but little power. The precise nature of his authority is not agreed by all Orthodox, and

---

[1] No reliable statistics are available. The membership figures given are based on those submitted by the Churches themselves to the World Council of Churches (WCC), with some correction. I am grateful to Alexander Belopopsky of the WCC for this information. Also valuable is R. Roberson, *The Eastern Christian Churches, a Brief Survey*, 3rd edn (Rome 1990), which is updated on the Internet web-site http://www.cnewa.org/ecc-introduction.htm.

the Patriarch of Moscow has developed as an alternative authority, especially within the Slav-speaking nations. The Ecumenical Patriarch would claim four powers: first, to be a court of final appeal for any case in the Orthodox world; second, to summon the leaders of local Churches to a joint Council; third, to have jurisdiction over Orthodox who live outside the territory of national Churches; and, fourth, to give consent to the setting up of new independent or autocephalous Churches.

The three Patriarchates of the East are Alexandria, Antioch and Jerusalem. These great cities of the Empire fell to the onslaught of the Arabs in quick succession – Antioch in 636, Jerusalem in 638 and Alexandria in 642. Apart from brief periods of Crusader rule and, in the case of Antioch, a return to Byzantine government from 969 to 1084, these Patriarchates have remained under Muslim rule since then. The Churches are relatively small but very different in character, and are now exhibiting signs of vitality and growth.

The Patriarchate of Alexandria declined quickly due to the growth of the Coptic non-Chalcedonian Orthodox Church, and as a result the Patriarch spent long periods residing in Constantinople. In 1846 he returned to Egypt, and in addition to his small Church in Egypt, he has jurisdiction over the growing and vibrant Orthodox Churches of Africa. Here Orthodoxy has exercised an attraction for African Christians, since it is recognised to be an ancient Christian Church which is not associated with the European colonial powers. In 1946 a group of Ugandan Orthodox under a priest called Reuben Spartas was received into the Patriarchate of Alexandria. Then a community in Kenya, who had developed a relationship with Archbishop Makarios III of Cyprus, became Orthodox. In 1997 a mission was established in South Africa which is receiving large numbers of local Orthodox groups. There are also new and growing Churches in West African countries. While numerically insignificant in Egypt, and with only 280,000 members in the whole continent of Africa, the huge territory under the jurisdiction of Alexandria contains many vibrant and growing Orthodox Churches.

Antioch and its hinterland were, in the period of the Empire, more diverse in culture and language, with large Greek centres set in the mainly Syriac countryside. So, while in Egypt the Chalcedonian Church declined, in Syria both the Chalcedonian and non-Chalcedonian Churches flourished, both led by Patriarchs of Antioch. The city of Antioch itself has changed hands several times, with, for a while, a Latin Patriarch installed by the Crusaders. Since the fourteenth century the Patriarch has resided in Damascus, and the state of Syria remains the centre of the Church's life. The Patriarchate of Antioch has had to adapt itself to a religiously diverse society, and it now has a more open relationship with other Churches than is the case elsewhere. Over the last few years, it has re-established communion with the Syrian Orthodox Church, and complete re-union under one Patriarch is discussed. Some point out that the Patriarchate of Antioch never formally separated from the Roman Catholic Church, and they hope for continued improvement in ecumenical relations. Of its 3 million adherents, the majority live in the diaspora, with many congregations in the USA, some of which use a Western liturgy, and also conduct an active mission especially among college campuses. In England, the Church has provided a welcome for converts from the Church of England after that Church decided to ordain women to the priesthood, and an English-speaking deanery has been established. In Syria it has responded to the largely Arab race of its members: since 1898 the Patriarchs have been Arabs rather than Greeks, and Arabic is the liturgical language. There is a large theological academy, dedicated to St John of Damascus, at Balamand in the Lebanon. Among Orthodox Churches today it represents an open ecumenical approach to inter-Church relationships and also a focus for Arabic-speaking Orthodoxy.

Jerusalem is not far from Damascus, but the tradition of its Patriarchate contrasts dramatically with that of Antioch. The Patriarch and bishops are Greek, and its clergy are drawn from the monastic Brotherhood of the Holy Sepulchre, formed in the sixteenth century to care for the Holy Places. Its membership of 260,000 is almost entirely Arab, from Israel, the West Bank and Jordan, and there is an underlying tension between the Greek hierarchy and the Arab faithful. It is traditional and conservative in its theological stance. In common with other Churches in modern Israel, it is declining in numbers. Its future health depends on whether the Greek hierarchy will become open to the needs and aspirations of the Arab members, and on political stability for the Arab population.

Another ancient Church founded during the period of the Byzantine Empire was the Church of Georgia, in the Caucasus. Its foundation is closely associated with that of neighbouring Armenia, and both became Christian states in the early fourth century, Georgia slightly later than

Armenia, traditionally in 326. There have been strong connections with Jerusalem, and the foundation of the Church is attributed to a slave girl called Nino, who, according to some traditions, came from Jerusalem, and who converted Mirian, king of Kartli or East Georgia. The first church was built at the old capital of Mtzkheta, where there is still a seminary. Originally part of the Patriarchate of Antioch, the Church became autocephalous at the end of the fifth century under a Catholicos or Catholicos Patriarch. Unlike neighbouring Armenia, the Georgian Church accepted the decisions of the Council of Chalcedon, and so these neighbouring Churches have drifted into different 'families'. A Georgian Christian literary tradition was based not only on the nation-state of Georgia but on communities in Jerusalem and the surrounding desert monasteries, and later on Mount Athos. In 1801 Georgia was occupied by Russia and its Church was absorbed into the Russian Church. Its independence was restored in 1917, although its autocephalous status was not recognised by Constantinople until 1991. It suffered under Communist persecution, which left only fifty churches open in the 1980s. Today there are 3 million Christians out of a total population of 4.6 million.

Other greek churches

Four other Churches have Greek origins. They were established in widely different periods and under different circumstances. All of them are presided over by an archbishop.

The oldest is the Church of Cyprus, which gained independence from the Patriarchate of Antioch in the fifth century with its claim to ancient origins enhanced by the discovery of the relics of the apostle Barnabas. It has suffered throughout its history from foreign dominance as a rapacious succession of invaders – Crusaders, Knights Templars, Venetian, Ottomans and British – all in turn took control of the island. Under Archbishop Makarios III (1950–77) Cyprus gained political independence, and the archbishop was elected president. Tensions emerged, leading to a *coup* against the government and invasion by Turkish forces in 1974. Today slightly over a third of the island is under Turkish control, and as a result around 200,000 Greeks have been displaced. Many religious sites, for example the monastery of the Apostle Andrew on the northeastern tip of the island, have passed out of Orthodox control. Most of those who left went to Great Britain, and as a result the Greek Orthodox archdiocese of Thyateira in Britain has a strongly Cypriot character. Like many displaced communities, the Greek Cypriots long to return and as a result of this dream are concerned to retain their Greek ethnic identity. Greek Cyprus is firmly Orthodox and the Church has 600,000 members. It is said that a higher proportion of its population are monks than in any other country.

The next in chronological order is the tiny Church of Sinai, with less than a thousand members. It consists of the monastery of St Catharine, which was founded by the Emperor Justinian I (527–65). The monastery is strongly fortified and has therefore been able to preserve its collection of some 4,000 manuscripts and large numbers of icons, some dating from before the iconoclast controversy. There are references to the Abbot being also bishop of the diocese from the seventh century, but the foundation of the autonomous Church took place in 1575. As well as the monks, the archdiocese of Sinai includes a small number of Orthodox living on its property in Cairo and elsewhere.

A much more recent foundation is the Church of Greece. Although the Orthodox Church is sometimes – incorrectly – spoken of as the Greek Orthodox Church, the independent Church on the Greek mainland is relatively new, although the Greek language and culture have shaped the whole of the Eastern Church. The Church of Greece came into being during the nationalist struggles of the nineteenth century, was set up as an independent Church in 1833, and gained recognition from the Ecumenical Patriarchate in 1850. Its boundaries are not quite coterminous with those of the modern Greek state since some areas remain under Constantinople. In its infancy the state of Greece was guided by Western European nations, and its first king, Otto of Saxe-Coburg, a Catholic, was appointed in 1832 at the Treaty of London. The constitution of the Church was drawn up by, among others, Georg von Maurer, a Lutheran, under the influence of German Lutheran and Russian models. The University of Athens was set up in 1839, based again on Western styles of higher education. Greece is the only Orthodox country to be a member of the European Union, and combines generally good relations with the West with a deeply rooted Orthodox culture. It is estimated that around 95 per cent of the population is Orthodox, a total of over 10 million members, and the Church retains a strong influence in political life. Churches in the cities are generally well attended, and many are forced to celebrate the liturgy twice on a Sunday in order to accommodate the large numbers of worshippers. The Church is closely connected to the state, which pays the wages of the clergy and forbids proselytising by any other Church. The refusal of rights to minority religious groups has been condemned by the European Court of Human Rights.

Finally, the Albanian Church should be included since it consists of both Greeks and Albanians. The state of Albania gained independence in 1912–13, and the first bishop of an Albanian Church, Fan Noli, who was consecrated in America in 1908, was also the prime minister for a few months in 1924. The Church declared its autocephaly in 1922, and this was recognised by Constantinople in 1937. Before the Communist regime was established over 20 per cent population was Orthodox, but by 1970 all churches had been closed. After the end of Communism the Patriarch of Constantinople appointed a new Metropolitan and three other Greek bishops. Since then the Church has taken care to serve both nationalities, with two Greek bishops resigning in favour of Albanian replacements. The Church is seen as a model example of a local rather than an ethnic Church, able to transcend national division.

Slav orthodox churches

By far the largest group of Orthodox Churches from a numerical viewpoint are the Slav Churches of Eastern Europe and Asia. Total numbers of Chalcedonian Orthodox are estimated, conservatively, at 175 million. Of these the Russian Church, with a membership of over 100 million (depending on how membership is defined), and the Romanian Church, with over 20 million members, together comprise around two-thirds of all Chalcedonian Orthodox. This group of Orthodox Churches emerged out of a remarkably successful missionary initiative in the ninth century led by the brothers Cyril and Methodius, which in time led to the establishing of autocephalous Churches in Bulgaria, Serbia and Russia.

While there is evidence for Christianity in Russia at least from 867, the foundation of the Church is dated to 988, after the embassy of Prince Vladimir of Kiev, whose members were so struck by their attendance at the liturgy of the Great Church of Haghia Sophia. As a result the Prince was baptised, taking his people with him into Orthodox Christianity. The celebration of the millennium of this event in 1988 was the beginning of a new freedom for the Church after the period of Communist government – although Ukrainians pointed out that Kiev is not in Russia at all but in the Ukraine.

About halfway through its history the Church gained its independence from Constantinople. It became autonomous in 1448, just before the fall of Constantinople, and then in 1589, Patriarch Jeremias of Constantinople visited Moscow seeking support for the struggle of his Church under Ottoman rule. He was entertained lavishly but it became clear that he would not be permitted to leave until he agreed to instal Metropolitan Job of Moscow as Patriarch. And so the Patriarch of Moscow became the only Orthodox Patriarch independent of Muslim domination. From this beginning the Russian Orthodox Church grew rapidly, developing into an alternative centre of authority to Constantinople. The phrase 'Moscow, the Third Rome' is sometimes used, but its ambitions to dominate the Orthodox territories were not seen as a claim to re-create the Roman Empire.

The Church has suffered from a wider variety of political subjection than those in other places. First, Russia was conquered by the Mongol invaders, from the fall of Kiev in 1240 to the Battle of Kulikovo in 1380 (although the Mongols were tolerant of the Church); then, second, there was the absolutist and Westernising state control of Peter the Great and his successors, which lasted from the abolition of the Patriarchate in 1700 to the Council of the Church in 1917; and, finally, the atheist Communist regime from 1918 to 1988 set out to eliminate the Church. The last was a period of persecution of the Church of a length, a ruthlessness and a thoroughness unparalleled in Christian history. So apart from a few heady months towards the end of 1917, the Russian Church has had little experience of living in freedom from some form of political control until the present day.

Russian Christianity has both excited and disappointed observers. It has produced little original theology, but a rich literature of devotional classics. Its saints, among them Seraphim of Sarov (1759–1833) and Silouan Antonov of Mount Athos (1866–1938), are, unusually for saints of the Orthodox Churches, well known in the West as well as the East. It has also produced the most famous icon painter of all time, Andrei Rublev (c.1360–c.1430), and church music which is suffused with emotion and feeling. For many in the West, Russian spirituality and culture have become vividly known through the novels of the nineteenth century, of Lev Tolstoy and Fedor Dostoevskii, who both write out of strongly Christian – but not, in the case of Tolstoy, Orthodox – perspectives. The religious creativity of the Russian people is found not in academic theology, but in painting, literature, music and, above all, in the spirituality of monks and ascetics, who have all been rooted in the life of the people of Russia. There is a spontaneity and popular character to Russian religion resulting from its roots in popular culture rather than the official leadership of the Church.

A striking feature of the Church is its capacity to nurture a variety of extremes, and to be divided by controversy. Usually hermits and the monks of larger communal monasteries co-exist happily, but in Russia there was, in the sixteenth century, a conflict between the two styles of monastic life, represented by the groups known as Possessors and non-Possessors. Then in the following century a more serious schism, or *Raskol*, broke out between reformers and conservative Old Believers, a split which was never healed. There are still significant communities of Old Believers in modern Russia. The nineteenth century produced a creative series of mission ventures which gained huge tracts of the East and even of America for Orthodoxy, but also a stagnation in the central administration of the Church, which was held in the stifling grip of state control. It is perhaps against this background that we might understand the confusing mixture of extreme right-wing nationalism and anti-Semitism on the one hand, and an open liberalism on the other, which is found in the modern Russian Church and which Western observers often find hard to understand. The leadership is often criticised for its caution, for not speaking out against anti-Semitism or extreme nationalism, and also for acting against individual liberal-minded clergy. We should avoid the assumption that the Church should conform to the standards of modern liberal democracies, which have emerged from a Western historical tradition. The decisions and actions of the Patriarch and bishops of the Church which we hear of suggest a cautious but calculated guidance of a many-sided Church community along a middle path of compromise.

The Russian Church grew out of the life and culture of the Byzantine Empire, but then lived through a series of different historical experiences and developed its own cultural tradition. This combination of Byzantine roots and Russian history has contributed to the distinctiveness of the Russian Church, and will be discussed further in the chapters that follow.

Other Slav nations also became Orthodox. Among them is Serbia, which emerged into nationhood and prominence during the declining years of Byzantium. The first archbishop of Serbia was Sava (1175–1225), the son of the king Stephen Nemanja, whose creative influence on the Serbian Church is such that Serbian Christianity is often referred to as *'Svetosavlje'*, or, to translate awkwardly, Saint-Sava-ism. A Patriarchate of Serbia was established in 1346, suppressed in 1459 (by the Ottomans), restored in 1557, suppressed again in 1766, and finally re-established in 1920. The Serbian Church has lived through a bewildering variety of experiences: a glorious – if short-lived – medieval kingdom which covered most of the Balkans and even threatened Constantinople; and then domination by a succession of alien rulers – Ottomans (from 1459 to 1878), a Nazi Croat regime called the Ustaše (under which up to a million Serbs were killed in concentration camps), then a Communist-style government (from 1945 to 2000). From this historical experience has arisen a longing to re-establish a Christian Serbian state which has been one of the factors that has contributed to the recent wars in the states of the former Yugoslavia. The church has 8 million members.

Bulgaria was also a powerful state in the Byzantine period, at times threatening the Empire. The ninth-century khan, or prince, Boris, wavered between Byzantine Orthodoxy and Roman Catholicism, but settled on Orthodoxy, which he realised would allow a greater measure of autonomy to the Church. Later the raids of the Bulgarians on Byzantine lands led the Emperor Basil II (976–1025) to carry out a series of ruthless campaigns which gained him the nickname of Basil the Bulgar Slayer, and after that the kingdom ceased to exist, being absorbed into the Empire. Later, during the Ottoman period, the Church was governed by the Ecumenical Patriarch. With the development of a nationalist Bulgarian identity in the nineteenth century, the Turkish authorities set up an independent Church, under an exarch, but this was not recognised by Constantinople until 1961, although a Patriarch of Bulgaria had been elected eight years earlier. Bulgaria has nurtured a variety of religious movements, especially those with a spiritual emphasis. In the tenth century a priest called Bogomil (the Slavonic equivalent to the Greek Theophilos) taught an extreme spiritual version of Christianity which rejected everything material, including the incarnation, sacraments and icons. This dualist heresy spread through the Balkans, becoming especially strong in Bosnia. In the fourteenth century the north of the country became a centre for Hesychast prayer, from where it was disseminated to other Slav areas. Since the late nineteenth century, the Church has been divided by schisms of various kinds. The Church is similar in size to the Church of Serbia, also with around 8 million members.

After Russia, Romania boasts the largest Orthodox Church, claiming the allegiance of around 90 per cent of the population, amounting to over 20 million members. In fact Romanian is not a Slavonic but a Romance language related to Latin, spoken by Dacian tribes who were part of the Roman Empire before the arrival of the Slav peoples in the sixth and seventh centuries. There is archeological evidence of Christian communities in the third century – a source of considerable pride for Romanian Christians. Romania is considered here as one of the Slavonic Churches since it lay within the range of the missions of Cyril and Methodius, and used Church Slavonic as its liturgical language until the seventeenth century. The Romanian language was introduced into the Church gradually, with a text of a complete Romanian Bible printed in 1688. There are three provinces: Moldavia, Wallachia and Transylvania. Transylvania was part of the Austro-Hungarian Empire from 1687 to 1918, and so has Roman Catholic and also strong Greek Catholic influences, but Moldavia and Wallachia, which evolved as separate entities in the fourteenth century, were autonomous provinces within the Ottoman Empire, and were able to maintain their Orthodox allegiance, free from some of the penalties imposed in other parts of the Ottoman realms. The Church was declared autonomous in 1865, and a Patriarch was elected in 1925. Under Communism there was a complex relationship between Church and state, but the Orthodox Church remained dominant, contributing to national aspirations. Since the fall of the Communist President Ceaucescu in 1990, the Church has shown many signs of vitality. Monasticism is thriving, with many new monasteries being built. The church – like the nation – has a comparatively open attitude to the West. It is active in the ecumenical movement, maintaining for example a prominent role in the World Council of Churches. This is a reflection of the positive involvement of Western nations and groups within Romania, and the country's sense of occupying a position between East and West.

There are several other national Orthodox Churches. In the Czech lands and Slovakia, the Orthodox Church (now with 100,000 members) was given independence, or autocephaly, by Russia in 1951, but this was not confirmed by Constantinople until 1998. Then in Poland there is a mixed group of Orthodox from different nationalities who formed a Church that proclaimed its independence in 1922, and has a membership of 1 million. The Orthodox Church in Finland became a national Church after the country became independent in 1918, and gained autonomous status under Constantinople. The Finnish Church celebrates Easter on the same date as Western Christianity, in contrast to all other Orthodox, and shows signs of being more open to modern influences. With 56,000 members, it is the second largest Church in Finland, although still accounting for only a small proportion of the population.

These Churches are part of the Orthodox world of Eastern Europe and the Middle East, and are dominated by the great political and cultural influences of Constantinople and Moscow – of Greek and Slavonic. To them must be added the two Far Eastern Churches of Japan and China, established through the missionary activities of Russians expanding eastwards in the eighteenth and nineteenth centuries. They received autonomy from Moscow in 1957 (China) and 1970 (Japan). The Churches are small, and in the once mighty Russian trading centre of Harbin in Mongolia, a centre of commercial life and the seat of an archbishop in the nineteenth century, less than ten Orthodox remain. There is no information available about the state of the Orthodox Church in China. Its membership is estimated at 10,000 and it has no presiding bishop. The Church of Japan is larger, with 30,000 members.

The west

In the twentieth century the political map of Europe went through convulsive changes. The stability of the Orthodox world, dominated by the successive great and long-lived empires of the Byzantines, the Ottomans and the Russians, has been replaced by a volatile and, for those involved, disorienting process of change. The last century has witnessed the First World War, the rise of modern Turkey, the Bolshevik Revolution, the Second World War, the extension of Communist government into Eastern Europe, the emergence of militant Islam, and then the rapid collapse of Communist government and the rise of new nations. All this has amounted to a period of breathtaking change.

One consequence is that Orthodoxy has been scattered by emigration and become a world-wide church, a process known as the *diaspora*, from the Greek word meaning 'scattering'. There have been, for several centuries, some Orthodox communities in the West. The first Orthodox missionaries in America were a group of Russian monks who arrived on Kodiak Island off the coast of Alaska in 1794, although there were Orthodox even before then in the form of fur traders who had intermarried with local people. From this small beginning, the Church spread. A bishop was consecrated for America in 1840, and then a new episcopal seat of a Russian missionary diocese was established in San Francisco in 1872. To the east of the continent a parish for members of several Orthodox nations was founded in Galveston, Texas in 1862. From the 1900s, immigrants from Eastern Europe and the Middle East arrived in large numbers.

The first Orthodox parish in England was founded by Greeks in London in 1677, in what is still called Greek Street. This church remained open for only seven years, and was then given to the French Huguenots. After the Greek revolution of 1821, Greek merchants started to settle in England and parishes were founded in London and Manchester. Notable waves of immigration took place after the Second World War, and then after the partition of Cyprus in 1974. In 1998 there were 209 Orthodox places of worship. Of these just over a half are Greek Orthodox, which form easily the largest ethnic group.

Of the Orthodox communities in the West, the most complex and divided was the Russian. Large numbers fled the Bolsheviks after 1919. They included some of the most creative theologians in Russia, who have become enormously influential among Western theologians, through the Orthodox Theological Institute of St Sergius in Paris and then St Vladimir's Seminary in America. The Russian émigrés were faced with the problem of how to relate to the Patriarchate of Moscow, clearly the head of the Church but unable to exercise effective leadership because of the extremely difficult situation he found himself in under a militantly atheist Communist government. Possible options were unquestioning support for the Patriarch, immediate rejection, and gradual disassociation – and different groups took each option, leading to a series of tragic schisms within this remarkable community.

The Paris community was led by Metropolitan Evlogii, the Patriarch's exarch, who remained loyal to Moscow as long as possible. These Russians accepted the Moscow Patriarchate until 1927, when the Metropolitan was required by the Church in Moscow to commit his clergy not to take part in any political actions. In 1929 Evlogii visited England and took part in prayers for the persecuted Christians of Russia. This was seen by the Soviet regime in Russia as a political act and, under government pressure, the Patriarch of Moscow asked Metropolitan Evlogii to resign. Instead, he, and most of the Paris community, sought the protection of the Patriarch of Constantinople. Some, including the theologian Vladimir Lossky, remained loyal to Moscow.

The supporters of the monarchy naturally refused to have anything to do with a government that had been responsible for the assassination of the Tsar. Since the Patriarch was forced to express loyalty to the Communist authorities, he was inevitably seen as their associate. After the 'White' monarchist armies, so-called in contrast to the Red Communist forces, were defeated in the Civil War of 1919–21, large numbers of royalists arrived in Europe. The Serbian Church offered hospitality, and a Council presided over by the conservative Metropolitan Antonii Khrapovitskii was held in Sremski Karlovci in 1921. This set up as an autonomous administration, which moved to New York after the Second World War. Known variously as the Russian Orthodox Church Outside Russia, or the Russian Orthodox Church Abroad, or the Synodal Church, it has remained staunchly conservative, traditional and monarchist, and recognises neither the Moscow Patriarchate, tainted by collaboration with atheist Communism, nor the Ecumenical Patriarchate, because of liturgical and doctrinal innovation. Attempts to achieve reconciliation between this Church and the Moscow Patriarchate following the end of Communism have failed, and it has gained the allegiance of some parishes inside Russia, forming a community known as the Free Russian Orthodox Church. In practice this has acted as an alternative Church for Russians who dislike or are disciplined by the Moscow Patriarchate. Its strength lies in its firm adherence to the old traditions and some remarkable and saintly bishops, among them John Maximovich (1896–1966). Its rejection of the ecumenical movement has influenced many to follow its example.

Another Church which emerged from the Russian Church is the Orthodox Church of America. The actions of the Russian Church in Moscow became less and less relevant to Russians living in America, as did the conservative monarchism of the Russian Orthodox Church Outside Russia. Eventually in 1970 the Metropolia – so-called because it was under a Metropolitan – was granted autocephaly by Moscow and became the Orthodox Church of America. This church is recognised only by the Moscow Patriarchate, although it includes among its members some of the best-known Orthodox theologians working in the West.

The Orthodox Churches in the West are growing steadily, not only as a result of further immigration, but from a steady stream of conversions as well. The natural conservatism of Orthodoxy has proved attractive to many Westerners in a period when Western churches have adapted and changed to accommodate themselves to a modern and increasingly secular society, becoming increasingly liberal in theology and ethics. Converts are especially attracted to the larger Russian and Greek Churches. It is estimated that there could be as many as 25 million members of the Orthodox Churches in the West. By far the largest number are in the USA, where there are around 5 million. There are also large numbers of Orthodox in Australia, Argentina, Germany, Canada, Brazil, Chile, Great Britain, France and many other countries, in approximately that order. They are now divided among several jurisdictions, with, at the time of writing, forty-eight bishops in five jurisdictions in the USA alone. Faced by this confused situation many people hope that the Orthodox Church in the West will overcome its national divisions and form itself into a Church rooted in the new community, using the language of the host nation and engaging in mission within it. Others value the link which the diaspora Churches retain with the home Church. The Oriental Orthodox Churches also have significant Church communities resident in Western countries.

The political, social and cultural fragmentation of the twentieth century has been mirrored in the Churches, producing a number of challenges for the Orthodox community. This process has resulted in a large number of Church groups which have become separated from the family of canonical Chalcedonian Orthodox Churches.

Several conservative groups have removed themselves from communion with the Ecumenical and other Patriarchs. These are opposed to two developments in the last century. The first cause of dispute concerns the calendar. Until the twentieth century Orthodox Churches had used the old Julian calendar, which is thirteen days behind the calendar as reformed by Pope Gregory XIII in 1582. A Council held in 1923 proposed the adoption of a slightly modified form of the Gregorian Western calendar. Since then most Orthodox Churches have adopted the new calendar, with the exception of the Russian, Jerusalem and Serbian Churches. Other conservative groups have also refused to use the new calendar, and formed separate Churches in Greece, Romania and Bulgaria. Both calendars are therefore in use in Orthodox churches, and sometimes dates are given with the addition 'NS' (New Style) or 'OS' (Old Style) to show which calendar is being used. In addition to the calendar, conservative groups tend to be opposed to any kind of involvement in the ecumenical movement.

Divisions of a different kind have resulted from the nationalist movements which have set up new states. The same aspirations that produce a new nation also encourage a new Church. The new states are mostly in the western part of the former Soviet Union, and consist of territory that has changed hands in the course of the century. The situation is further complicated by political and personal rivalry and ambition. The most confused situation is found in the Ukraine, where there are three Orthodox Churches – one Russian and two Ukrainian – and one Greek Catholic Church. Here disputes over the ownership of church buildings and other property have led to violence and tension between the different communities. Hopes of a single Ukrainian Orthodox Church seem unlikely to be realised in the near future. Another difficult area is the former Yugoslav Republic of Macedonia. Here there is only one Church, but it is small and remains unrecognised by any of the Orthodox Churches. The ecclesiastical confusion in many places offers the Patriarch of Constantinople an opportunity – not always taken – for creative support and reconciliation among opposing groups.

NON-CHALCEDONIAN ORTHODOX CHURCHES

In 1099 Jerusalem fell to the Crusaders. This, we know, was a momentous event. It restored the Holy Places to Christian rule; it was an early success for the Western expansionist initiative of the Crusades; and it was part of the process which led to irreconcilable alienation between East and West. From the Islamic viewpoint it was a serious loss of territory. The defeated Muslims made an urgent request for support to the Abbasid Caliph al-Mustazhir (1094–1118) in Baghdad. The caliph thought about the situation and decided to refer the delegation to the Sultan Barki-Yaruq. He, in his turn, gave it further consideration but did nothing. But for the Abbasid rulers, viewing the world from Baghdad, the loss of Jerusalem – so significant for the Muslims of the area – seemed of little significance, certainly not worth a military campaign. Their lack of interest is a reminder of the perhaps obvious point, but one which is often easy to overlook, that our outlook on our faith is shaped by who we are and where we come from. If you are a Western Christian, or even a Chalcedonian Orthodox, the non-Chalcedonian Churches of the East can seem small, distant and different. But they represent an old and authentic tradition of Christianity. They are to be found beyond the eastern and southern fringes of the Byzantine Empire, and exist in a different geographical, linguistic and cultural world from either Western or Byzantine Orthodox Christians. They, like the Abbasid caliphs of Baghdad, are a long way from the West.

The Syriac language is the dialect of Aramaic that was spoken in the once important cultural centre of Edessa (today Urfa, in southern Turkey). It is close to the language spoken by Jesus, and is the vehicle of a Semitic culture, with a poetic tradition, a love of rich and imaginative imagery, but also with a precision which preserved and passed on Greek philosophical ideas to the Arab philosophers who in their turn passed them on to the Western Christian philosophers of the medieval period. It has been said that there are three languages of ancient Christianity: Latin, the language of the Empire and of government; Greek, the language of the New Testament and of most early preaching; and Syriac, the language of Jesus and the Semitic world of the Bible. Syriac is the language of the Church of the East and the Syrian Orthodox Church, and thus of the South Indian churches. Furthermore it was Syrians who evangelised Ethiopia. Links were also established between Syria and Egypt, where Coptic, which descended from the language of ancient Egypt, was spoken.

In a class of its own among the Churches of this Eastern or oriental world is a Church which is today small but which once came close to displacing Islam as the dominant faith of the continent of Asia. This is the Church of the East, or, to use its full modern title, the Apostolic Catholic Assyrian Church of the East, sometimes referred to as the Nestorian Church. Its origins lie in the eastern part of Syria, around Edessa and Nisibis (today Nuseybin in Turkey). When, in the fourth century, the Persian Empire expanded westwards into Syria, the Christians of this region found that they had become part of the Persian – instead of the Byzantine – Empire. They moved east and south towards the capital of the Persian Empire at Baghdad. The head of the Church, to be called the Catholicos, had his seat at Seleucia-Ctesiphon, on the Tigris, south of contemporary Baghdad. In 484 this Church in the Persian Empire adopted a two-nature, or dyophysite, Christology. It accepted as orthodox the Patriarch of Constantinople Nestorius (428–31), who was condemned at the Council of Ephesus of 431, and has sometimes been happy to be called Nestorian. But there are different degrees of Nestorianism and the teaching of the Church should be not be seen as heretical.

From its base on the Tigris, it rapidly expanded eastwards, into India and China. In 1318 the Church had 30 metropolitan bishops and 700 suffragan dioceses. The period of their influence was described by the Coptic scholar, Aziz Atiya, as 'one of the most enlightened chapters in Christian history, sanctity and scholarship'.[2] They were influential in the Mongol court, and it is tantalising to speculate on what would have happened if the Mongols had adopted Nestorian Christianity as their state religion, rather than Islam, as eventually happened. Had they done so the influence of the Church of the East would have been maintained and extended through Asia, but instead it was rapidly and thoroughly eliminated from all areas except a part of northern Iraq. Later, in the nineteenth century, it was encouraged by friendly contacts with Anglican missionaries and actively supported the Allies during the First World War. This had further disastrous consequences, as the hoped-for support from the West did not materialise and the Nestorians were displaced from the homeland by Kurds and other ethnic groups.

By custom, the Patriarchate is hereditary, descending from uncle to nephew. Today the church is divided into two groups. The larger part was led by Patriarch Mar Shimun XXIII, who was consecrated in 1920 at the age of eleven, was deported from Iraq in 1944, settled in the USA, where he was assassinated in 1975 by a young Assyrian for reasons which remain unclear. His successor, Mar Dinkha IV, was consecrated at a synod held in Alton Abbey in England and now lives in Chicago. The smaller and more conservative group is called the Ancient Church of the East, and its Patriarchate is in Baghdad. In 1945 the larger Church was reduced to only four bishops, but the number has now grown to twelve, and it has an estimated 365,000 members, of which a third live in Iraq. Both parts have friendly relations with Western Churches, especially the Roman Catholic Church, and it is to be hoped that its small size does not lead to the absorption of this ancient Church by its larger Catholic partner.

Also with its roots in eastern Syria is the Syrian Orthodox Church, which is one of the three Patriarchates encountered in Straight Street. This Church is one of five (or six, if we include the recently founded

---

[2] A. Atiya, *A History of Eastern Christianity* (London 1968), p. 241.

Eritrean Orthodox Church) Churches which are variously called non-Chalcedonian, or pre-Chalcedonian, or Oriental Orthodox. The name Monophysite, like that of Nestorian in the case of the Church of the East, is still sometimes used but is better avoided, since it implies a heretical understanding of Christ's humanity. The reasons for the division between these Churches and the Churches described in the earlier part of this chapter are political and cultural as well as doctrinal. From 1960 a series of discussions both official and unofficial have examined the differences between Chalcedonian and non-Chalcedonian Orthodox, and have agreed that the differences in doctrine concern the language used to express the faith rather than the faith itself. This has led to warmer relations and to the beginnings of a restored communion between the two groups of Orthodox. Communion has been officially restored in Syria, and unofficially in other areas. Some of the Chalcedonian Orthodox Churches, especially Russia and Serbia, are hesitant, but the reconciliation of Churches that have been divided since 451 is one of the triumphs of the modern ecumenical movement.

The non-Chalcedonian Churches are to be found in the areas to the east and south of the Byzantine Empire on the one hand, and to the west of the area of influence of the Church of the East on the other. The heartlands of these Churches remain in Armenia, Syria, Egypt, South India, Ethiopia and Eritrea, although changes in the political map and migrations have dispersed the Churches more widely. While having their roots in the Christianity of the eastern Mediterranean, they have developed in a different political environment from the Chalcedonian Churches, and in a non-Greek and non-Slav cultural atmosphere.

Armenia is the northernmost of the group. It is proud to claim to be the first Christian nation. King Trdat (298–330) was converted some time before 314, when Gregory the Illuminator was consecrated as bishop, and, although it is difficult to be precise about this date, Armenians consider that their Church was founded in 301. On this reckoning, the conversion of the king of Armenia pre-dates the conversion of Constantine by several years. Its inclusion among non-Chalcedonian Churches is partly accidental, since there were no Armenian representatives at Chalcedon, and as a result the decisions of the Council were ignored rather than opposed. It drifted out of contact with the Byzantines, attaching itself to Syrian anti-Chalcedonians in 506. Most of Armenia was conquered by the Persians, and this encouraged the development of a national language with its own distinctive script. Armenians have spread through the Middle East, and as a result there are now four ecclesiastical jurisdictions: at Ejmiacin, or Etchmiadzin, near Yerevan in the Republic of Armenia, which is the undisputed spiritual centre of the Armenian people; at Jerusalem, where the community is much diminished in size and functions mainly as a pilgrimage centre; at Constantinople, now hugely reduced following genocidal massacres by the Turks in 1915–22 (in which around one and a half million Armenians lost their lives); and Sis, based in Antelias in the Lebanon, which cares for sizeable numbers of Armenians in the Middle East. The setting up of the Republic of Armenia, in place of the former Soviet Republic, has provided a base for the Armenian Church. The republic is currently economically and militarily successful, and the Church there is developing. About a third of the 10 million Armenians live in Armenia.

The Syrian Orthodox Church is sometimes called the Jacobite Church after one of the greatest missionaries of all time, Jacob bar-Addai or James Baradaeus. During the middle years of the sixth century he travelled around the eastern parts of Syria and set up an ecclesiastical structure, consecrating clergy who formed the hierarchy of the Church. The heartland of the Church has been an area called the Tur Abdin, meaning Mountain of the Servants, a high plateau north of ancient Nisibis, where a large number of monasteries were built. At one of them, Deir el-Zaffaran or the Saffron Monastery, built in a beautiful location on the edge of the plateau overlooking the Mesopotamian plain, the Patriarch resided from the fourteenth century to 1920, when he moved to Homs in western Syria. Like the Armenians, the Syrian Church was reduced in number during the First World War, and many people moved south into what is now Syria. From this low point, it has revived under energetic leadership, with a renewed consciousness of the value of Syriac literature and language, and a consequent emphasis on the education of young people. It now has around 1,400,000 members, a significant proportion of whom live in South India.

The Tur Abdin itself, with its many old churches dating from the sixth century or earlier, is in difficulties. It now lies just within the Turkish border, and the Christian population has diminished steadily from 250,000 in 1900, to 20,000 in 1990, to 2,000 in 2000. The most recent decline has been due to the unfortunate position of the Church, which has been trapped in the cross-fire between the Turkish government and local Kurds. The monasteries are surviving – just – and there are signs that hostilities between the two groups may be over, perhaps leading to more peaceful times and even the return of some of the Christian villagers from their places of refuge. Certainly the preservation of this centre of Syriac religion and culture and its monuments of sixth-century Syrian architecture should be of deep concern to the world Christian community.

The Christian population of South India is much larger. The Church is proud to claim that it was founded during the missionary journeys of the apostle Thomas in the first century, a claim which can be neither proved nor disproved. Whatever its early origins, it was a part of the Church of the East which expanded into the region in the early medieval period, and then it had the good fortune to escape the persecutions which destroyed that Church in the rest of Asia. In the sixteenth century, foreign missionaries started to arrive in India. First to come were Portuguese who forced the local Christians to become Catholic. After their power declined it became possible for links with Syria to be re-established and a Syrian Orthodox bishop arrived in 1665. He was from a 'Monophysite' tradition, whereas previously the Indian Church had been 'Nestorian', but these distinctions had been obscured by Catholic teaching and the Indians were glad to welcome anybody from Syria. So Syrian Orthodox influence grew. Then Anglican missionaries arrived. They did not seek to convert Syrian Christians but did encourage a desire to reform some of the traditions along Protestant lines. This resulted in a split in 1889 between those who favoured reform, including independence from the Syrian Patriarch in the Tur Abdin, and more traditional groups who remained loyal to him. This division remains, with the Malankara Orthodox Church (or Indian Orthodox Church), which is led by a Catholicos, who is always called Basilios, and the slightly smaller Syrian Orthodox Church, which recognises the authority of the Patriarch of Antioch in Syria. In addition there are four Catholic and three Protestant Churches of varying sizes which have their roots in the Syrian tradition.

The Coptic Church is the inheritor of an ancient and proud tradition of Christianity which has produced some of the greatest figures in the history of the Church, such as Origen and Athanasius (although of course both of them lived in the period before the Coptic Church became separated from other Orthodox). The name 'Copt' is a form of the word

'Egyptian'. After the Council of Chalcedon in 451 the Egyptian Church immediately rejected its decisions, and this led them into a collision course with the Byzantine Empire, for which the Council of Chalcedon became a touchstone of Orthodoxy. According to some accounts, the Egyptians gave an enthusiastic welcome to the conquering Arab armies, who, they thought, would at least be indifferent to matters of Christian faith and this would be better than the alternate coercion and cajoling of the Byzantines. So the Church became a national Egyptian Church, with its own language of Coptic and a strong monastic tradition. Gradually, however, Muslim influence grew. During the ninth century, Arabic came to replace Coptic and the slowly declining community became a minority of the population. Although the Coptic Church has remained a minority within an Islamic nation, it has displayed a remarkable tenacity. Today it claims the allegiance of about 7 million people – 10 per cent of the population of Egypt and a number who have emigrated to the West. It has considerable economic and political influence in the modern Egyptian state, and boasts among its members the former Secretary-General of the United Nations, Boutros (Peter) Boutros Ghali.

The twentieth century saw a revival in Muslim self-consciousness, especially through the founding of the Muslim Brotherhood in 1928. This has led to a corresponding revival of the Coptic Church as Copts withdrew from general social involvement and instead developed Coptic societies and organisations for mutual support. Two outstanding Patriarchs (called Popes), Cyril VI (1959–71) and Shenouda III (consecrated in 1971), have presided over a dramatic growth in monastic life and of education of the laity. A series of well-authenticated apparitions of the Virgin Mary at the Cairo parish church at Zeitoun has also encouraged the Church. Occasions of killing and other acts of violence against Copts are reported, especially from Upper Egypt around Assyut, and the Church can only hope that the moderation which has generally been a characteristic of Egyptian Islam will continue to prevail over more extreme forms of Islam.

By far the largest and most individual of the Oriental Orthodox Churches is the Ethiopian Orthodox Tawehedo (or 'Undivided', referring to its Monophysite Christology rather than its ecclesiastical unity) Church. With 40 million members it is the second largest Orthodox Church, after Russia, and there is still a strong tradition of church attendance and a large number of clergy, with major churches served by over a hundred priests. The first archbishop was a Syrian, called Frumentius, who was consecrated by Athanasius of Alexandria around 340. The practice of the Church being presided over by a single archbishop appointed from Egypt was maintained until 1951, when the Church became self-governing, and a larger number of bishops were consecrated. In spite of this contact, the Church of Ethiopia was isolated from the rest of Christendom and developed a distinctive style of Church life. It has retained many of the traditions and practices of Old Testament Judaism, observing the dietary regulations of the Book of Leviticus, keeping Saturday as well as Sunday as a Sabbath day of rest, and including among its orders of clergy the *debtera* (a kind of liturgical dancer) derived from the Levites of the Old Testament Temple. The Ark of the Covenant is, according to tradition, kept in the city of Axum, having been brought to Ethiopia by Menelik, the son of King Solomon and the Queen of Sheba, and symbolic replicas of the Ark, called *tabots*, are kept on the altar of every church.

The Christian culture of medieval Ethiopia produced a number of churches carved out of rock, including the famous churches of Lalibela. Much of this medieval Christian culture was destroyed during a prolonged assault by the Muslim emir Ahmed ibn Ibrahim el-Ghazi, usually known as Granj or 'the Left-handed', between 1529 and 1543. Apart from this interlude the Church has been able to maintain its life in peace but in isolation from the rest of the Christian world. After 1973 the Communist government acted against the Church, confiscating its enormous land holdings. This had the unexpected result of strengthening the Church, which was forced to abandon its former privileges and landed wealth and to become more integrated into civic and public life. It has extended its membership to the Caribbean islands, as a Church with a truly African tradition.

In 1994 the diocese of Eritrea was set up as a separate Church by Pope Shenouda of Egypt. This has strained relations between the Coptic and Ethiopian Churches.

EASTERN CATHOLIC CHURCHES

The third of the Patriarchates of Straight Street is that of the Eastern or Greek Catholics. And in addition there are the two further Patriarchs of Antioch who are now resident in the Lebanon – of the Antiochian Syrian Maronite Church and of the Syrian Catholic Church – and the defunct

Patriarch of the Syrian Latin Catholic Church. These four Patriarchs are all under the authority of the Pope of Rome, and are an indication of the extra dimension of Church life which has been introduced by the impact of Roman Catholicism on the Christian East.

The Patriarch of Rome, traditionally known as the Pope, is recognised by Orthodox as well as Catholics as the senior bishop of the Christian world. This is because the Church in Rome had Peter the Apostle as its first bishop, and both Peter and Paul were martyred there. Also Rome is the true capital of the Roman Empire, many centuries older than the parvenu city of Constantinople. It is also sometimes claimed that Rome has an unrivalled record of maintaining the truth of Orthodoxy. This is not strictly true, however. Not only was there the unfortunate lapse when Pope Honorius I (625–38) came out in public support of the Monothelete teaching, which was subsequently decided to be heretical, but also the Popes of the early centuries often favoured Trinitarian deviations such as Monarchianism. Later, of course, the West became separated from the East and the Pope's position as first among equals ceased to be recognised by Christians from the East. The first place of the Bishop of Rome remains as a part of the Christian tradition. It is significant that no other Church has appointed a Bishop of Rome. While it is difficult to envisage a scenario in which the Pope is accepted as Orthodox once again by the Christians of the East, a re-interpretation of the nature of papal authority along conciliar rather than monarchical lines would be of great ecumenical significance and would lead to improvement in relations between East and West.

The Pope's claims combined with the growth of the Roman Catholic Church have led to its expansion in Orthodox lands, and as a result to the establishment of a confusing profusion of Catholic Churches. The basis on which these Churches were set up was the Council of Florence (1438–9). Here a short-lived union between East and West was agreed – and then quickly repudiated by the Orthodox. Its content was relatively simple: acceptance of the authority of Rome, acceptance of specifically Roman doctrines, including the *filioque*; but retention of Eastern liturgy and traditions. This formula might not have had lasting success at Florence, but it proved to be versatile and attractive to many Eastern Christians.

Rome managed to persuade Orthodox Christians to become Catholic in two ways: missionary activity and national boundary changes. The former tended to succeed in the Middle East and the latter was made possible by the expansion of Catholic states into Eastern Europe. As a consequence of this double strategy there are now Catholic Churches in Persia (the Chaldaeans), India (Syro-Malabar and Syro-Malankara), Armenia, Egypt (Coptic), Ethiopia, Syria, the Middle East (Melkites), Ukraine, Ruthenia (the area on the Slovak and Russian border and in south-east Poland), Romania, Greece, Yugoslavia, Bulgaria, Slovakia, Hungary, Russia, Belorussia, Georgia and Albania. These Churches are called Greek Catholic or Eastern Catholic. The title Uniate is also used but has come to have a pejorative sense. They vary enormously in size, ranging from the large Ukrainian Catholic Church with over 4 million members on the one hand, to the tiny group of Russian Catholics, consisting only of a few small communities, or the Yugoslavian Byzantine Catholics on the other. The Yugoslavian Catholics number around 50,000 and originated when a number of Serbs found themselves living in the part of Croatia which was under Hungarian rule and were, in 1611, formed into a diocese under the Pope to enable them to continue to use Byzantine liturgy. This gives an example of the political accidents which have led to the formation of these communities. The total number of Greek Catholics is around 30 million.

All these to a varying degree use Eastern liturgy and customs (such as allowing married priests) but acknowledge the authority of Rome. The Roman Church tends to be more concerned with maintaining unity in the Church than with purity of doctrine. As a result there is a certain vagueness over the doctrinal issues which were the cause of the schism. Even the *filioque* is in practice negotiable, being added to the Creed in Greek Catholic Churches when this is feasible, but omitted if local feeling is hostile to the addition. In some service books it is printed in brackets to indicate its optional character. The Greek Catholics are to be distinguished from Catholics who follow the customs, beliefs and practices of the West. These also exist in all Orthodox countries.

While Orthodox are hostile to Greek Catholics, considering that they have fallen to the seductions of the heretical Roman Church, Catholics consider that they are not true Catholics, since they do not follow Latin traditions. Greek Catholics sometimes see themselves as a bridge between East and West, providing a model on which a future union can be built, but more often they are seen as a barrier, providing further grounds for disagreement and tension between the two great traditions of Christianity.

CONCLUSION

The description so far has been intended to give an idea of where the Orthodox are found, how they got there, and what the differences are between different groups. As well as diversity there is also similarity. If it is right to see the various Eastern Orthodox Churches as different families, yet they are still families with common ancestors. They share much in common: theological method, monastic life, their political experience, how they evangelise, and above all a common liturgy. In describing these themes it is inevitable that much of what follows will refer to the Byzantine Orthodox, a much larger group than other Orthodox, with better articulated traditions. But the points of similarity with and divergence from other Churches will be noted.

3

Liturgy: where heaven and earth meet

CHURCH AS EUCHARIST

A first encounter with the life of the Orthodox Church is likely to
be through worship – and most likely through the celebration of the
Eucharist – referred to as the Liturgy in the Chalcedonian and the
qurbana (or offering) or *qidasse* (or sanctification) in the Syriac tradition. This will probably be a memorable and often a deeply moving
experience, and for many it has been the first step which has led to being
received as a member of the Orthodox Church. The visitor is confronted
by a mysterious and many-sided activity. He finds that the worship is
sung to a chant of unfamiliar and haunting beauty; amidst a congregation who worship with great absorption and devotion, although with
a certain informality as well, coming and going or walking around the
church. The altar cannot be seen as it is concealed behind a solid wooden
screen covered with icons arranged in rows (iconostasis), or perhaps a
curtain, especially in Syrian churches. The walls are also covered with
paintings, called frescoes. The sense of mystery and awe is increased by
the dimly lit interior, glittering with candles, or oil lamps, or perhaps,
less aesthetically, coloured electric light bulbs. The worship has a slow
and measured dramatic quality, in an unfamiliar language, and it may
seem to go on for a very long time. The moments of the service which are
most noticeable are the processions, when the clergy and servers emerge
from behind the iconostasis carrying a gospel book, or the shrouded
elements of bread and wine to be used in the eucharistic offering. The
congregation usually do not receive communion, but if they do it will be

shared equally by all ages, often with more young children than adults receiving. This may be an idealised description and, as in all Church traditions, worship can be performed in a hurried, perfunctory and irreverent way. But whether the liturgy is celebrated with the magnificence and reverence of a large city church, or the simplicity and casualness of a small village, the central truth of the liturgy remains. It is the meeting of God and humanity, and at it the nature of the Church is most clearly seen and experienced.

The Russian theologian, philosopher and poet Alexei Khomiakov (1804–60) described the Church as the reality of the Holy Spirit making us into the Body of Christ. 'The Church is the Truth and it is the inner life of the Christian, since God, Christ, the Church live in him with a life more real than the heart which is beating in his breast or the blood which is flowing in his veins... [it is] the ecumenical life of love and unity.'[1] This states that the nature of the Church is *koinonia* or communion. It exists through the sharing in the life of God, given in Christ and made effective through the working of the Holy Spirit. This claim becomes an event when the liturgy is celebrated, at which the divine life is given to the community of Christian believers. The Church is created, sustained and visibly present at the Eucharist, or Liturgy, or Communion.

Khomiakov's thought is rooted in the patristic tradition. Ignatius, bishop of the great city of Antioch, was sentenced to death in 107 and made his way to Rome for execution. This journey to his death became almost a triumphal procession and, as he travelled, he wrote to the Christian communities he knew. He described, among other things, a vision of the Church, and the place of the bishop, or *episkopos*, in it. Ignatius' bishop is no authoritarian monarch, but the focus of a unity which includes the priests, or *presbyteroi*, and the deacons, or *diakonoi*. He sees these as working together in harmony, and uses the image of a melody made by different strings of a lyre, tuned to harmonise with the bishop.[2] This unity is expressed in the Eucharist, which is celebrated either by the bishop or by somebody authorised by him. The bishop, following an Ignatian ecclesiology, stands in the place of Christ and prays that the Spirit of God will make Christ present in the form of the

---

[1] A. Khomiakov, 'On the Western Confessions of Faith', in A. Schmemann, *Ultimate Questions. An Anthology of Modern Russian Religious Thought* (New York 1965), p. 50.

[2] See Ignatius' *Epistles* to the Smyrnaeans 8 and Ephesians 2.

sacrament of bread and of wine, which are the body and blood of Christ. This action makes the people present into the Body of Christ, and so into the Church. Since this mysterious action is accomplished by the Spirit of Christ who is present, then there can be nothing lacking, or partial. At the Eucharist the Church is made complete and whole.

This has many implications both for theological thinking and for practical life, but here it is of concern because it shows where the unity of the Church lies and how it is that there can be so many national Churches, which are nevertheless conscious of sharing a common life. Following this way of thinking, the basic unit of the Church is the local community meeting in a given place. If the purpose of the Eucharist is to make Christ present, then there can be nothing missing when this happens. The eucharistic community is not part of the Church, but the complete Church to which nothing can be added for it to function as God intends. It follows from this that there is an equality between communities, and so among bishops too. There are no grounds for any one bishop to claim superiority or authority over another. This is expressed by the phrase that ontological identity leads to episcopal equality. The basic unity and identity of each local Church can be expressed by the slogan: one bishop, one Eucharist, one Church.

Two comments should be made. First, this is a corporate rather than an individualistic approach, and has the practical consequence that the liturgy is not normally celebrated more than once in a day in each church. Occasionally in heavily populated urban areas more than one liturgy is served on a given day in the same church, but this would be seen as a sign that a new building is urgently needed. The Eucharist is a single corporate action involving the whole community and through it the church is created and sustained. This is in contrast to Western churches, which start from more individualistic presuppositions and where there can be a variety of acts of worship to meet different needs or preferences of members of the congregation.

Second, the wider organisation of the Church is not discussed by Ignatius. From his starting-point it is definitely a second-order question. If the Church is constituted by the Eucharist, then it will not make much difference what kind of central organisation the Church has. To put it at its simplest, whatever organisation is most convenient for the good ordering of the Church is to be desired. These structures should not, however, be imposed for political or selfish reasons, but there should be good order and peace. Ignatius' image of harmony, with ministry shared and exercised corporately, should apply at both the local and at the national and the universal level. This harmony has proved to be an elusive goal, and it is a constant temptation for the local bishop or the national Patriarch to rule in an authoritarian manner. Though the question of how the whole universal Church is ordered may be less significant theologically, it has much practical importance, and the absence of a clear teaching about what the world-wide Church is and how it is organised has made it hard for Orthodox to resolve organisational and jurisdictional problems.

This 'eucharistic ecclesiology' – so called because it sees the heart and essence of the life of the Church as coming out of the celebration of the Eucharist – has been explored by theologians since Khomiakov. Nikolai Afanas'ev (1893–1966), Alexander Schmemann (1921–83) and John Zizioulas (1931–) have developed an understanding of the Church as communion which has influenced theologians of all Churches, and especially the ecumenical movement. For both Orthodox and others, it gives an understanding of the unity of the Church based on shared faith and life rather than on organisational structures. Orthodox have been able to develop a clear sense of affirming a common Orthodox faith and life, without needing to feel that they are a part of one single Orthodox Church, or, to express it more accurately, to see membership of the Church as based on participating in the life given by God rather than through membership of an organisation.

Thus a modern theologian can write: 'Christianity is a liturgical religion. The Church is first of all a worshipping community. Worship comes first, doctrine and discipline second.'[3] So, when we encounter the worship of the Church – and encounter is the best word to use – we are faced with more than a service with its prayers, hymns and actions. Something of the nature, life and identity of the Church is being presented to us.

The emphasis on the liturgy has had important practical implications for the survival of Orthodox Churches in hostile circumstances. In times of persecution – whether the slow discrimination of the Ottoman or the sudden and vicious pogroms of the Communists – the possibilities for Christian living and witness have been drastically reduced. Evangelism,

---

[3] G. Florovsky, quoted in Bishop Kallistos of Diokleia (K. Ware), 'The witness of the Orthodox Church in the twentieth century', *Sourozh* 80 (May 2000), p. 9.

study, teaching, monastic life have at various times in Orthodox history, and especially in the last century, become all but impossible. Sometimes only the celebration of the liturgy remained, and its success in maintaining the life of the Church through difficult times shows the richness and completeness of its nature. In the Western diaspora, too, Orthodox have had to learn how to exist in isolation from their cultural roots, and here the liturgy has been effective in enabling the continued identity and existence of the Church. So we are considering not a part of the life of the Church, but that life itself in its outward and visible form – expressing the history, theology and spirituality of the Church community.

Patriarch Germanus of Constantinople (*c.*730) once wrote: 'The church is an earthly heaven in which the supercelestial God dwells and walks about.'[4] A church is the meeting of heaven and earth, and within this sacred space all becomes significant. The design, the decoration, the vessels of the Eucharist, all convey something of the coming of heaven into this space on earth.

These theological understandings are incarnated and communicated in a set form of liturgical worship. This has a specific structure and content which has evolved in the course of a long history of development. The sections which follow will not attempt to provide either a history of this evolution of the liturgy, nor a survey of the manner of celebration across the Orthodox world, but to give some explanation of how some of the distinctive elements of Orthodox worship, which we have already noted, originated.

THE LITURGY OF CONSTANTINOPLE

The early history of the worship of the Eastern Churches is hard to decipher but we can be clear that from the fourth to the fourteenth century the liturgy of Constantinople went through a series of developments in response to theological, political and social changes, producing a liturgy of great richness. The liturgy of the capital city gradually came to be used more widely as the ancient patriarchates of Alexandria and Antioch – and even Jerusalem – declined in importance. By 1200 the canonist Theodore Balsamon took the view that all Orthodox should use the rite of Constantinople. There were two very similar forms of the liturgy

---

[4] Patriarch Germanus, *Ecclesiastical History and Mystical Contemplation* 1, in *On the Divine Liturgy*, ed. and trans. P. Meyendorff (Crestwood, NY 1984), p. 57.

used at Constantinople (with the differences occurring in the priest's rather than the congregation's prayers): those of St John Chrysostom and of St Basil. Today, the Liturgy of St John Chrysostom is more frequently used, with that of St Basil, which was once the more common, now used on ten days in the year. The Liturgy of St James, which originated in Jerusalem, is used on St James' Day in Jerusalem and some other places, and the Liturgy of the Presanctified Gifts, which does not include a consecration of bread and wine, is used on certain days in Lent.

St John Chrysostom (*c.*347–407) was born in Antioch in Syria and was made archbishop in Constantinople in 398 (the title Patriarch was not used until later). He was a forthright preacher who was only too ready to denounce the moral failings of the imperial court, and this gained him his nickname Chrysostom or 'golden mouth'. His name refers to his popular standing, and not his reputation with the court, which often found itself the target of his attacks. In due course he was exiled from the capital and he later died as a result of the hardships he endured. With his dying breath he prayed, 'glory to God for all things'. His name has been attached to the usual liturgy of the Chalcedonian Church, and it is probable that some of the prayers in the service were composed by him. In any case the association of the form of service with the fourth-century archbishop makes a claim that the liturgy is old, and reverently preserves a very ancient form of worship. But in fact the liturgy as it is used today is the outcome of a long evolution over more than a thousand years. It did not achieve its final form until the fourteenth century. The liturgies of the West are, somewhat surprisingly, closer in form to the worship of the early Church than those of the East. In spite of claims sometimes made by Orthodox that the liturgy represents a fixed and faithfully preserved patristic tradition, it is in fact the product of rich and creative periods of liturgical development. Within this process several influences can be discerned which have affected the shape and nature of the liturgy.

First, the church itself is a holy place. The various traditions express this in different ways. In Chalcedonian Churches the altar is separated from the nave by the iconostasis, a solid wooden screen covered by icons and with access through three doors. For much of the service the doors are closed and the priest within prays privately while the choir sings in the body of the church. In Syrian Churches the altar is raised to a higher level, with several steps leading to the sanctuary, and a curtain is drawn across to conceal the altar from view. The sense that the worshipper is approaching a defined space where holiness is located is clearly expressed by the architecture.

This development is at least in part a consequence of the establishing of Constantine's Christian Empire. Since the Church had a recognised place in society, its buildings became important. Previously the Christian communities had been clearly defined groups who met to share a ritual meal, which looked forward to the coming feast in the kingdom of God. The focus was on the people and it did not matter much where they met. Within the Byzantine Empire the Church and the state were coterminous. Worship became an action of the whole of society, giving a spiritual dimension and meaning to the social order. Now the Emperor had his part to play in the celebration of the Eucharist alongside the Patriarch. People started to build churches, which was seen as a sign of greatness of soul, and soon basilicas were springing up in all the cities of the Empire. Often they contained the relics of martyrs or holy men. Now holiness resided in the building not in the people, and the liturgy gradually came to be an encounter with the holy, rather than the gathering of an expectant eschatological community.

The low screen which demarcated the boundary between nave and sanctuary grew in size and solidity until it was large enough for a few icons to be hung on it. By the fifteenth century it had become a solid wall on which more and more icons were arranged. It developed a traditional form, with the icons arranged in a consistent pattern according to subject matter. The most elaborate are in Russia, where five rows of icons stretch high above the worshipper. The result of this process of development of the iconostasis was that the holy place or sanctuary became inaccessible. It was as though the door in the screen, above which the icon of Christ stood inviting the worshipper into the holy place, had become closed and the icon had become an object of contemplation above a barrier, looking out at the worshipper, rather than a figure inviting entry. Most of the *anaphora* (or prayer of consecration) and many of the other prayers were said inaudibly by the priest. This went on inside the screen, while outside the singing of the choirs and litanies of the deacon formed a series of acts of worship in which the congregation could participate. And at the same time communion became infrequent. As early as 380 Ambrose, preaching in Milan, urged his hearers not to be like the Greeks who receive communion only once a year, an early sign of a growing trend. This practice has continued, with most Orthodox receiving communion not more than several times a year, although there have been frequent examples of more regular communion, even weekly, being advocated.

This growing sense of the church as a holy place was not only due to the new situation of the Church in the Empire. It seems that the practice of the priest saying parts of the liturgy silently originated in Syria, and shows the sense of reverence and awe characteristic of Semitic cultures, which spread west to Constantinople in the sixth century. But the development of the icon screen, and with it the two levels of worship – 'inside' by the priest and 'outside' by the deacon and choir – took place within a society in which churches were becoming more magnificent and evocative of the holy. This is a style of worship which can include all inhabitants of the Empire but can also retain the distinctiveness, and the exclusiveness, and demanding standards of New Testament Christianity. While in the early Church, the distinction had been between the present age and the eschatological age to come, in the Imperial Byzantine Church this distinction slowly changed and became a separation of the secular from the holy. This was reflected in the evolution of both the liturgy and of church architecture.

A second legacy of imperial court worship are the Entrances. Two moments of the liturgy stand out clearly, as both visually striking and evoking great devotion in the worshippers. The first is when the gospel book is carried out of the north door of the iconostasis, around the church and back in through the central or 'royal' doors. At the second, or Great, Entrance, the vessels containing the holy gifts of bread and wine are similarly carried through the church. These are both parts of the ceremonial which developed within imperial Byzantium and have remained within the liturgy, even though the purpose of the Entrances has changed.

The two Entrances are the remains of the processions which formed part of the liturgical life of the Church in Constantinople. The city of Constantinople has been compared to one huge church – and the processions of the Emperor and his court entourage, and of the Patriarch, along the streets from one church building to another, with stations for prayers and singing, became a part of the worshipping life of the city. The entry into the church was an impressive moment. The people waited outside and then poured in following the bishop, as the Trisagion was sung. 'Holy God, Holy Mighty, Holy Immortal, have mercy on us.' This anthem emerged in the early fifth century as an antiphon to a psalm and developed into a moment of great devotion, later known as the Little Entrance. Today, since the bishop and clergy are already in the church it has evolved into the carrying of the gospel book from the sanctuary into the nave and back again. An even more impressive moment was the later entrance of the Holy Gifts. In the churches of the Empire the elements of bread and wine were prepared in a building called the *skeuophylakion*, or sacristy, at the north-east corner of the church. Originally a simple means of transporting the elements to the altar, the procession came to be seen as the pivotal moment of the liturgy, a kind of funeral cortège in which the dead body of Christ is reverently carried to be placed on the altar. Now called the Great Entrance, it is sung to an anthem expressing the sense of participating in the worship of heaven, called the Cherubic Hymn, and is often the most moving moment of the liturgy. In modern churches the *skeuophylakion* has disappeared; the elements of the bread and wine are prepared on a table inside the sanctuary and carried out of the north door of the iconostasis into the nave and back through the central or 'royal' doors.

Another consequence of the imperial character of the liturgy was the growth of singing. Song and poetry had been one of the vehicles of religious worship, but now the structure of the music of court ritual shaped the worship, with the acclamations addressed in the court to the Emperor being transferred to God, and the melodies being used in liturgical settings. By the fifteenth century the tradition of sung worship was well established, and Symeon of Thessaloniki (1416–29) could write that 'all the Catholic Churches in the whole world have observed it [the Sung Service] from the beginning and have uttered nothing in worship except in song'.[5] The tradition of singing the liturgy has remained, with the result that a 'said' service, as is found in Western worship, is not known in Orthodox liturgy. All Orthodox Churches use some form of chant, usually based on a system of eight musical tones, and, except in Egypt, Ethiopia, and sometimes in Armenia, the singing is unaccompanied by instruments.

Monastic influence

The other main influence on the evolution of the Orthodox liturgical tradition was the monasteries. The iconoclast controversy, to be discussed

---

[5] Symeon is quoted in A. Schmemann, *Introduction to Liturgical Theology* (London 1966), p. 129.

later, resulted in victory for the iconophiles, and, since several important monasteries had been steadfast in their support of the icons, this led to a new ascendancy of monastic spirituality and liturgy. The two leading iconophile apologists were Theodore, abbot of Stoudion, a monastery in Constantinople which had six dependent houses and 1,000 monks, and John of Damascus, from the monastery of Mar Saba in Palestine. As well as these two monasteries, the growing settlement on Mount Athos was also influential, where the two traditions of Stoudion and Mar Saba were blended and then exported to Constantinople and other parts of the Empire. Patriarch Theodore Kokkinos (d. 1389) had been a monk on Athos and wrote down a *typikon*, which described how worship should be conducted. It later spread to Russia and became a respected guide for the conduct of liturgy.

The monastic influence showed itself not so much in the content as in the presentation of the liturgy, and what one might call 'worshipping style'. The smaller monastic-type churches, built for a defined community, replaced the majestic basilicas of an earlier age. Then the churches were decorated with frescoes covering the walls.

Worship also began to follow a continuous rhythm rather than a regular celebration. For the monk, worship is not so much a celebration of the Lord's Day, but rather a constant ascetic effort. So the night office came to be used more widely, and psalms were appointed to be read consecutively so that the whole psalter was used, rather than certain especially appropriate psalms set for a specific occasion. The liturgy started to be celebrated daily rather than only on Sundays. In many monasteries the long series of daily offices (Vespers, Mattins and the shorter services of the various hours of the day) are chanted during the night or early morning, sometimes with the result that the monks spend most of the night in church. Parishes use parts of this monastic worship, according to pastoral need. Services which seem very long are often several services recited consecutively. On major festivals, services in parish churches can easily continue for twelve hours or more, with the choir and clergy singing throughout the night, but the usual Sunday liturgy is much briefer.

Liturgy is seen as being performed most completely and correctly in the larger monasteries, and worship in the parish church is to some extent an adaptation and an abbreviation of monastic worship, especially the daily round of Offices.

The hymns

One reason that services can be long is the number of hymns which are sung, especially at Mattins (in Greek, *orthros*). Hymnody was developed in the Syriac tradition, from where it was passed on to Byzantine Orthodox Churches. The historian Sozomen suggests that the Christian hymn originated with Greek musical and poetic forms. These were used by the rather too conveniently named Harmonius in order to propagate heretical teaching. In response to these, Ephrem the Syrian composed similar hymns in Syriac.[6] But this all seems improbable and it is more likely that the origins of the Syriac hymn are to be found rooted in Semitic culture. Jesus and his disciples sung a hymn after the Last Supper, before they left to go to the garden of Gethsemane, and this is but one example of hymns, psalms and songs in Biblical literature.

Early spiritual songs in Syriac have survived from the first century, but the true flowering of the hymn came with the voluminous writing of Ephrem (*c*.306–73). He came from a Christian family, and was ordained a deacon at Nisibis, where he became a teacher. Later, when Nisibis was captured by the Persians, he migrated a short distance westwards to the great centre of learning, Edessa, where he lived the rest of his life. His high reputation led to reports of a number of visits to other parts of the Christian world, but it seems unlikely that he left Edessa once he had arrived. About four hundred of his hymns have been preserved, although there must have been many more. He also wrote commentaries on Scripture.

Other hymn writers of the fourth century include Aphrahat, the 'Persian sage' who wrote in a style of prose that easily slipped into verse form, Cyrillona, and Marutha of Maipherqat.

The form which Ephrem used was based on the numbers of syllables in a line and used complex metrical patterns, with only very occasional rhyming. We do not know the nature of the music to which they were sung, or how they fitted into the liturgy. Liturgy had not achieved a fixed form at that period, and the poems and hymns would no doubt have been sung during worship, especially at night – as, indeed, is the case today. The hymns consist of stanzas with refrains, which suggests that a cantor would sing the verse and a choir would respond. Some are written for choirs of women. The offices of the Syrian Orthodox Church

---

[6] Sozomen, *Ecclesiastical History* 3.16.

continue to make use of the poems of Ephrem and others, which gives a poetic content to the worship of the Church. The poetry of Ephrem is filled with rich and suggestive imagery stemming from his deep sense of the mystery and wonder of the created order, which he refers to as a source of divine revelation, alongside Scripture. The use of metaphor and imagery has a theological as well as a poetic purpose. He speaks of God as having 'put on names', allowing himself to be clothed in words and so to be described in human language as a result of the Incarnation.

Another influential hymn writer was Romanus, also from Syria, but from the west of the country where Greek was used alongside Syriac. He was born in Emesa (today, Homs), became a deacon in Berytus (Beirut), and came to Constantinople in 510. Here he settled at the Church of the Mother of God in a northern suburb of the city, where he stayed until his death between 555 and 565. A tenth-century source tells the famous story of how he began his compositions. 'The holy Mother of God appeared to him in a dream during the evening of Christ's nativity and gave him a scroll and ordered him to swallow it . . . he awoke from his trance, mounted the ambo and began to chant most melodiously "today the Mother of God gives birth to him that is above all being".'[7] From then on he delivered about one thousand *kontakia*.

Around ninety surviving poems are attributed to him, of which about sixty are accepted as genuine. It is possible that he is the author of the most famous *kontakion* of them all, the Akathist Hymn to the Mother of God, so called because it is sung standing or *akathistos*, which is still sung on the fifth Saturday in Lent.

The *kontakion* is a mixture of a sermon and a hymn. The name comes from the *kontos* or pole around which the scroll was rolled. It consists of a prelude and then between 18 and 24 stanzas, called *ikoi*. Often it is written in the form of an acrostic, following the name of its composer with the 18 stanzas each beginning with a letter of a phrase, such as *tou tapeinou Romanou*, 'of the humble Romanus'. The *kontakion* was probably sung from the pulpit, with a refrain for the choir or congregation. Often a dialogue form is used, with a dramatic encounter between two characters.

From the seventh century a new form developed, called the 'canon'. This was longer and was developed in a monastic setting. It was

---

[7] This story is often quoted, for example in Romanus, *Kontakia. On the Life of Christ*, trans. Archimandrite Ephraim (San Francisco 1995), p. xxvii.

associated especially with the monasteries of St Sabas in Palestine and Stoudion in Constantinople, although not all monasteries approved of the innovations. The originator of this form is said to be Andrew of Crete, another Syrian who became bishop in Crete and who died in 740, whose Great Canon is sung in Lent. The canon consists of nine hymns or odes, which were written to be sung between the nine Biblical canticles sung at Mattins. Since then, the canticles themselves have disappeared but the canon remains.

The hymns of Orthodox worship contain much reflection on Scripture, and usually consist of meditations on the Biblical passages associated with the day. They also contain much doctrinal statement. As a result, the worship of the Eastern Church has a strongly Biblical quality. A worshipper, especially at the Offices of Mattins and Evensong, will be sharing in a corporate meditation on Scripture which provides a corporate study of the Bible. This rich Biblical content of the worship has had the effect of discouraging individual interpretation and hence fragmentation of the Church. And, since it is rooted in the Semitic culture which is related to that of the Bible, it raises a question about whether a poetic interpretation is closer to the mindset of our Lord than the more literalistic interpretations found in some contemporary Western traditions.

The symbolic interpretation of the liturgy

Discussion of the monastic influence and the hymnodic tradition has led beyond the liturgy to other parts of the worshipping life of the Church. But the celebration of the liturgy or Eucharist remains the central act of all Christian worship. The gradual development in the manner of celebrating the liturgy affected the way people understood it, and the way they worshipped. The various changes made the service less a meal in which the community shared, and the receiving of communion became less frequent. The result was that the emphasis moved away from the communicant's partaking of the sacramental gifts and instead gave greater prominence to the meaning of the service as a whole.

The liturgy came increasingly to be interpreted as an action filled with meaning. Each part of the worship was examined and meditated on to reveal the layers of symbolic significance. As early as the fourth century, the writings of Cyril of Jerusalem and John Chrysostom show the beginnings of this new approach. Since the communion of the faithful was less frequent it has to be seen as less important, and instead the whole *anaphora*, or eucharistic prayer, has a salvific quality. It follows that if it is the prayer itself which is effective, then the sacrifice is complete when the prayer of consecration is finished. So this is the moment when the power of the sacrifice of Christ is present, and so intercession is especially effective. A long prayer of intercession was added at this point, interceding for those for whom the sacrifice is offered. This intercession is present throughout the Orthodox world, and is especially emphasised among the Orthodox of South India.

As the whole liturgy came to be seen as a symbolic and dramatic act, people naturally began to ask what it all meant. Thus emerged the symbolic interpretation of the liturgy. The roots of this approach lie in the central fact of Christianity: the Incarnation of Christ. This doctrine states that Jesus Christ is both God and man. Since he is God, Christ reveals the divine nature; but since he is also man, he simultaneously conceals this nature in his human nature. So Christ both reveals and conceals God at the same time. This approach can be extended to other parts of Christian life, including the liturgy, which has the same dual character of concealing and revealing. 'We see one thing and believe another' was a simple comment of St John Chrysostom. The liturgy is thus the saving activity of Christ made present in the community of believers. The words and actions of the Eucharist are symbols of the spiritual realities which lie behind them, and can be appropriated by the believer as they are purified and initiated in order to become participants in the heavenly liturgy.

The symbolic meaning of the Eucharist was explored in a succession of commentaries, written by some of the great figures of patristic theology: Theodore of Mopsuestia, Dionysius the Areopagite, Maximus the Confessor, Germanus Patriarch of Constantinople, Nicholas of Andida, Symeon of Thessaloniki, and Nicholas Cabasilas. There were two methods of interpretation.

The first is that, at the Eucharist, we are led to union with God. This may be called the 'mystagogical' approach, and was set out by Dionysius. For him, the sensible rites are images of the intelligible realities, and can lead the worshipper into this intellectual realm. The fullest exposition was that of Maximus the Confessor. In his *Mystagogia*, he explains that the liturgy is a kind of physical symbol of how the soul ascends to God by grace. The Little Entrance is the Incarnation where Christ comes down to this earth, the bishop going to his throne is the Ascension, the Gospel is the proclamation of the end of the world, the Great Entrance is the Second Coming of Christ to judge the world, the closing of the doors is the separation of the sheep from the goats, and the next moments refer to our union with God, with the communion being man's divinisation in the world to come. The whole action of the Eucharist points us towards the results of Christ's work of salvation in uniting us to God. The text of the *Cherubikon*, the anthem that accompanies the Great Entrance and was introduced into the liturgy in 573–4, says: 'We, who in a mystery, represent the cherubim and sing the thrice-holy hymn to the life-giving Trinity, let us now lay aside every care of this life, for we are about to receive the King of all, invisibly escorted by the angelic hosts. Alleluia.' This summarises the way that Maximus, and those who follow him, understand what is happening in the liturgy.

An alternative understanding came from the more literal approach to the Bible of the Antiochene theologians. 'Do this in remembrance of me' were the words of Christ at the Last Supper, and so the liturgy is how we remember the saving events of Christ's life. In this approach the pivotal moment of the Great Entrance becomes a funeral procession of the dead Christ. 'What follows is in imitation of the burial of Christ when Joseph took the body down from the cross, anointed it and wrapped it in a clean cloth, and with the aid of Nicodemus buried it in a new tomb hewn out of rock. The sanctuary is a likeness of the holy sepulchre and the altar is the resting place where the spotless and all-holy body was laid.'[8] Patriarch Eutychius (552–5, 577–82) tried to tone down the emotional impact of this moment, 'as long as the supplications and the [eucharistic] prayer have not been completed, it is nothing but plain bread'.[9] But subsequent commentators disagreed, and the bread was as though it was the body of Christ from the start of the service. This is shown by the interpretation of the *prothesis*, or introductory prayers, in which the priest ceremonially prepares the bread and the wine in readiness for its transport to the altar at the Great Entrance later in the service. Commentators saw this as a symbolic re-enactment either of the early years of Christ's life before his

[8] Patriarch Germanus, *Ecclesiastical History and Mystical Contemplation* 37, ed. Meyendorff, p. 87.

[9] Eutychius, *On Easter and the Holy Eucharist*, PG 86.2400–1.

baptism, or of his death and burial, because of the sacrificial elements of the prayer, such as cutting into the loaf with a utensil called a 'lance'. In any case, for either interpretation to work, the bread has to be seen as already the body of Christ. From the eleventh century the relating of the *prothesis* to the early years tended to prevail, and this naturally led on to seeing the Little Entrance as the baptism at the Jordan; the Gospel reading as the teaching of Christ; the Great Entrance as the coming of Christ to Jerusalem on a donkey; and the *anaphora* as either the Last Supper (Nicholas of Andida) or the Crucifixion, Resurrection and Ascension (Nicholas Cabasilas).

Symbolism could become complicated and apparently contradictory. So the altar can be the Holy of Holies, the hill of Golgotha, the tomb in which the body is laid, the room of the Last Supper, or the heavenly sanctuary – and the meaning of the liturgy shifts according to which symbol is predominant. But this complexity and variety of symbolic interpretations should be seen as a strength rather than a weakness. The point of a symbolic approach to liturgy is that it does not set out to explain the simple plain significance of the service. Instead it explores and meditates on the words and the actions, and discovers different layers of meaning. This enables the worshipper to find different ways in which he can appropriate and make sense of the rich action of the liturgy. So the two different styles of symbolic interpretation belong together. The liturgy is both a dramatic and symbolic re-living of the events of salvation and also an invitation to the worshipper to share in the life of heaven which the saving events made possible. The commentary of Germanus combines both approaches. For him, union with Christ is achieved through the whole liturgy and not simply through the eating of sacramental bread and drinking of sacramental wine.

WORSHIP IN OTHER CHURCHES

So far the description of Orthodox worship has described the Liturgy of St John Chrysostom. This is the form of service used regularly by many millions of worshippers since it is the usual liturgy of the Chalcedonian Orthodox Churches, and so it is this form of worship which is most likely to encounter the visitor to an Orthodox church. But there are many other forms of worship – a truly bewildering variety. Some of these are of mainly historical interest and are no longer used, but many are in regular use among the Oriental Orthodox.

The Greek historian Socrates Scholasticus, writing about 450, said, 'it is impossible to find anywhere, among all the sects, two churches that agree exactly in their prayer ritual'.[10] The main centres of Christian life developed their own ways of celebrating liturgy, but also permitted considerable flexibility. Something of this early freedom remains within the Eastern Christian world, where many of the Churches still make use of a multiplicity of forms. The liturgical soil of Syria was especially fertile, with Edessa and Nisibis in the east as centres of Syriac culture, and Antioch in the west as a centre of Greek. More than eighty *anaphoras*, or eucharistic prayers, survive from the west Syrian liturgical family alone. Ten contemporary Churches use some form of Syrian liturgy.

There are family resemblances among different liturgies. The widespread use of the Greek language throughout the eastern Mediterranean led to the cross-fertilisation of liturgical texts and their dissemination across a wide area. They were then translated into different languages. So the Liturgy of St Basil appears in Greek – as used in Constantinople – but also in Armenian, Syriac and Coptic. The Armenian liturgy of St James is very close to the Jerusalem Greek version that is still occasionally used in the Chalcedonian Churches.

A limited number of liturgies have survived into the present day. In Egypt, the Coptic Liturgy of St Basil, translated into Arabic, has been used since the fifteenth century, with the Liturgies of St Gregory used on major festivals and of St Clement on one day in Lent. In Syria (where the liturgy is called the *qurbana* or offering), the Liturgy of St James the Apostle, which exists in many variants, is used. In Armenia, the Liturgy of St Gregory the Illuminator is the only form in current use. In Ethiopia (where, as in India, the title *qidasse*, or sanctification, describes the liturgy) the variety that characterised primitive liturgy remains a feature, with fourteen different *anaphoras* still celebrated regularly. By some strange historical circumstance the *anaphora* of the Apostles, the most frequently used, is based on a Western rather than an Eastern form: the Apostolic Tradition of Hippolytus, which was written in Rome and helped to shape Western liturgy in the twelfth century. The East Syrian liturgical tradition survives in the Church of the East, where the Liturgies of the Apostles, St Theodore and Nestorius are used on set days in the year.

---

[10] Socrates, *Ecclesiastical History* 5.22.

Many of the features of Chalcedonian liturgy are shared by other Churches: some form of barrier between the sanctuary and the nave; the importance of processions out of the sanctuary and into the nave; the use of singing or chanting rather than speaking; some kind of daily office including traditional hymns and poems. Whichever Orthodox church a visitor worships in, he will feel that he is in the same liturgical world. But alongside the sense of shared liturgical experience is the variety of ways that this can be expressed and lived in widely differing communities. An account of how the liturgy is celebrated in a Syrian Orthodox village in South India shows both the underlying reality present in liturgical worship and also the adaptability to local circumstances.

Sunday morning in an Indian church is an occasion when the community gathers together. Here there is no iconostasis, but several steps lead up to the altar, which is placed behind a curtain, sometimes richly embroidered. Fans or metal discs hung with bells are used during the *qurbana*, being shaken gently over the head of the priest during the most holy moments. The drawing back of the curtain is used to effect. The first drawing back of the curtain symbolises the Incarnation, and happens at the start of the service. Hymns of the Incarnation follow, and the readings, Creed and Peace (which is seen as very significant, with a frequently used penalty for sin being, in the past, to be excluded from exchanging the Peace). Then comes the *anaphora*, finishing with the *epiclesis*, when the priest waves his hands above the gifts reminding people of the fluttering action of the descending Holy Spirit. Then comes the Great Intercession, and then the veil is drawn across the sanctuary. Within the sanctuary the priest carries out the breaking of the bread, and the curtain is drawn back a second time, to symbolise the rending of the veil of the Temple after the Crucifixion. The eucharistic elements are elevated to singing, ringing of bells, and sometimes the explosions of firecrackers outside. The veil is drawn and, after the priest has received communion, is drawn back a third time to symbolise the Second Coming of Christ. The service finishes with Thanksgiving and Blessing. In the twentieth century the practice has developed of the people receiving communion after the service is over as they leave the church.[11]

---

[11] I am grateful to my greatly respected former colleague the late Bishop Leslie Brown for his descriptions and information about the Syrian Orthodox Church of South India.

THE CHURCH BUILDING

The nature of the liturgy as encounter is expressed not just in the words and actions of the service but in the building and its decoration as well. So, in different ways, the church building is designed to express this truth. One of the great churches of the world is the Haghia Sophia in Constantinople, built by the Emperor Justinian and consecrated in 537. The huge shallow dome crowns the edifice, with light pouring in through the windows, thus expressing the pouring out of divine light from the heavens onto the earth. The contemporary historian Procopius described this dome which

> seems not to be founded on solid masonry but to be suspended from heaven by a golden chain and so covers the space. It abounds exceedingly in gleaming sunlight so that the interior space is not illuminated by the sun from the outside but the radiance is generated from within, so great an abundance of light bathes this shrine all around. The visitor's mind is lifted up to God and floats aloft, thinking that he cannot be far away, but must love to dwell in this place.[12]

Its dedication to the Wisdom of God identified it with Christ, the incarnation of this wisdom, and so it was seen as a body, the temple of his presence, and an animated house. In addition it was a symbol of the Mother of God. The space inside is full of light and was recognised as containing the presence of Christ himself, from which it follows that the structure which circumscribed this Christ-like space could be compared to Mary, who contained the Christ in her womb. The magnificence of the building, with its windows admitting light and its soaring columns supporting the immensely high dome, took people's breath away, and led them to make these associations between the Church and the persons of both Christ and his mother.

The church buildings of the East developed from the Roman basilica, a rectangular building which could be used for a variety of purposes. As this was adapted to the needs of a worshipping congregation, it was built on a west to east axis, with an apse containing the altar to the east, and an aisle built on the north and south sides. From the sixth century, the dome was added, covering parts of the nave, which, as in the Haghia Sophia, became the central architectural feature. Gradually the dome became the focal point, making the church smaller and squarer. This coincided

[12] Procopius of Caesarea, *On the Buildings* 1.1.

with the growth of monasticism, where churches were needed to serve a community of monks rather than being civic buildings located in the city centre, and so churches became more compact. The square domed space then gradually became more complex with the addition of further domes, of aisles, of narthexes, and of several apses at the east. A variety of patterns can be seen in different regions. In Egypt the basilica design remains common. In Russia complex designs with multiple domes, aisles and apses are found. In Ethiopia churches are often round, with the sanctuary as a concentric circular space in the centre, and usually two further circles around it. Here the rounded structure, typical of local building, has resonances with the raised central dome in more traditional Byzantine architecture.

Within this architectural development, two features remain of essential symbolic significance: the dome and the sanctuary. The dome is the vault of heaven, and the sanctuary is the holy place – thus providing a double orientation – up towards heaven and east towards holiness. In the case of churches that are decorated with frescoes and icons on the walls, the traditional design emphasises this. There is of course much local variety, but some general patterns can be discerned. The pictures are arranged hierarchically, with the most significant figures either at the higher levels or towards the east, with the lower orders descending from the height. At both the highest and easternmost points are frescoes which depict the things of heaven: Christ in glory looking down at the worshipper from the centre of the dome, with the Mother of God above the apse that is over the altar. They are often surrounded by angels. Next come the events of the life of Christ and of Mary on the upper parts of the walls. Below them come the saints, the fellow-members of the Church, now glorified but still interceding for the Church on earth. In the sanctuary apse are often frescoes depicting the Eucharist, perhaps Christ giving communion to the apostles, or the saints who composed the liturgy. The worshipper finds himself surrounded by the saints of the Church, who worship with him; he can look at the actions of salvation, also represented of course in the liturgy itself; and raise his eyes to heaven.

This might be expressed in other ways. In Syria the sanctuary is seen as a heaven. It often has a dome above the altar, there is a canopy above the altar, shaped like a church, and curtains are drawn across, which when pulled back show heaven opened to those who worship, 'allowing the heavens to open and the hosts of angels to come forth'.[13] In Ethiopia the church is modelled on the Temple in Jerusalem, with a holy of holies in a central circular room, surrounded by another circular space in which those who are to receive communion stand, and this in turn is surrounded by another circular space in which the *debtera*, or dancers, stand. Most people remain outside church and listen to the worship from there.

Yves Congar commented that, 'Rite' is 'the totality of the forms and signs in which a given community expresses and lives its Christian faith'.[14] The liturgy, art and architecture of the Church combine to express the faith and experience of the Christian community. The liturgy of the Church is more than an act of worship. It invites the believer to receive the salvation brought by Christ and to enter into the kingdom of heaven.

[13] John Chrysostom, *Homily on the First Epistle to the Corinthians* 36.5, PG 61.313.
[14] Yves Congar, *After Nine Hundred Years* (New York 1959), p. 39.

4

Doctrine: believing in the Orthodox Churches

CHURCH TRADITION

The liturgy is the place where salvation is offered and received. This liturgy can only be understood in relation to the tradition of faith which has been handed down from the time of Christ, from the faith given by the apostles and within the Church. The idea of Church tradition is broad and inclusive. It refers to the conviction that the Spirit of God guides the Church in living and articulating the truth about the Christian faith. So the Bible, the liturgy, the canons or rules governing Church life, practices such as fasting and other customs, and most other aspects of Church life which might be imagined, are to be understood as being part of this great Spirit-led process of Church tradition. It is almost true to say that the Holy Spirit, the Christian Church, and the Tradition are phrases which refer to the same reality and, in practice, mean the same. The term Orthodoxy can also be used as a description of this body of truth handed down from generation to generation within the Church. All local Orthodox Churches are conscious of their existing within the one tradition. This sense of all belonging within one harmonious whole must be borne in mind when looking at different components of the tradition.

Tradition, wrote Metropolitan Philaret Drozdov of Moscow (1782–1867), 'does not consist uniquely in visible and verbal transmissions of the teachings, the rules, institutions and rites: it is at the same time an invisible and actual communication of grace and sanctification' – and this, he could have added, is the sole purpose of the Church. So if we discuss the process of believing, and of speaking about the content of faith, it must be recognised that theology is not a separate academic discipline but one way of looking at the one great reality of how God loves and saves his world, conveyed and experienced in the liturgical life of the Church.

In the history of the doctrine of the Church, we can usefully distinguish four distinct phases with different characteristics, even though the divisions between them are not clear-cut. First, there is the period of the Ecumenical Councils or Patristic period, which lasted from 325 to 787, when the basic doctrines of the faith were set out and accepted by the Western as well as the Eastern parts of the Church. Then, in the Byzantine period, from 787 until the fall of Constantinople to the Ottomans in 1453, doctrine took a distinctive Eastern or Orthodox path at the same time as the Western tradition also developed its own character. Then, third, in the Ottoman period which continued until the end of the nineteenth century, the Church sought to preserve what had been given to it by previous generations under difficult and often oppressive political circumstances. Fourth, the modern period has seen a revival of theological reflection in the Orthodox Church, although for many the stifling of theological thought under an oppressive political system continued.

While this classification refers mainly to the experience of the Chalcedonian Orthodox Churches, it also provides a background against which to compare the faith of the Oriental Churches. The Churches of the East separated during the Patristic period as a result of Christological disagreement. All agreed in acclaiming the work of the Council of Nicaea and the first Council of Constantinople. The Church of the East parted company after the Council held in 431 at Ephesus, with the non-Chalcedonian Churches rejecting the definitions of the Council of Chalcedon twenty years later. The Byzantine Church recognises a further three Councils, making a total of seven. The separations, as one might expect, took place gradually over a considerable period of time and as a result of a complex mixture of causes, but the Councils of the Church are seen as moments when truth and error were made clear. The sharp frontiers dividing Orthodoxy, right belief, from heresy, or deviation from the path of truth, were marked out by the bishops of the Church meeting together in council.

While the Councils did not limit their discussions to matters of doctrine but decided on disciplinary and organisational matters as well, the main business and the reason for their being summoned was to resolve matters of dispute over the content of faith.

THE PATRISTIC PERIOD: ECUMENICAL COUNCILS

After the Emperor Constantine had established his new city of Constantinople on the Bosphorus, and five years before its solemn dedication, he summoned the bishops of the Church to meet together at Nicaea (modern Iznik), fifty miles south-east of the capital. His purpose was to resolve a simmering dispute which had broken out in Alexandria in the previous century over the status and nature of the Word or Son of God. Arius, a presbyter in Alexandria, had, out of a concern to safeguard the total transcendence of God, held that the Son had to be included within the order of creation, however exalted a part of it. This had divided the Church, and the calling of a Council was the method chosen by the Emperor to resolve the controversy. It was the first of seven such Councils, all but one of which met either in or near Constantinople (the other took place in Ephesus on the south-west coast of Asia Minor, as a result of the political manoeuvring of the Emperor's elder sister Pulcheria, who wanted a location where there was more likely to be sympathy for her favoured cause).

The Council of Nicaea was the beginning of a huge work of articulation of doctrine that was to involve all orders of society, both in the capital and in the provinces, from the Emperor to the crowds who thronged into the hippodrome, and which would be extended over a period of more than four centuries. The subjects under discussion were the central Christian doctrines of the Trinity and the Incarnation. One of the most quoted sentences from the Fathers is the succinct statement of Athanasius of Alexandria: 'God became man that man might become God.' The prolonged debates could be seen as an exploration and explanation of the first half of this formula, just three words in English, 'God became man.'

The list of the Councils, the items of doctrine they were mainly concerned with and the main personalities involved, is as follows:

> Nicaea (325). The Son is 'of the same nature' (Greek: *homoousios*) as the Father. This Council rejected the teaching of Arius, who held that the Son was created by the Father. Athanasius, then a young deacon but later the bishop of Alexandria, was among those who argued for the *homoousion*, as it has become known, and defended it against later

imperial and episcopal attack, being exiled five times before his death in 373.

Constantinople (381). The Holy Spirit is also fully God. A continuation and conclusion of the work of Nicaea, and associated with the Cappadocian Fathers, especially Gregory of Nazianzus, known simply as the Theologian, and the most often quoted of all Church Fathers in the Eastern tradition. Here the bishops also confirmed the text of the Nicene (more correctly Niceno-Constantinopolitan) Creed, used as a basis of faith by both Eastern and Western churches.

Ephesus (431). Jesus Christ is to be identified with the Son of God, and so Mary should be called *Theotokos* (a Greek word commonly translated as Mother of God, but more accurately Bearer of God). Nestorius, Patriarch of Constantinople, had emphasised the human person of Christ in a way that seemed to separate the divine nature, calling Mary *Christotokos*, or the Bearer of Christ. Cyril of Alexandria emerged as the great advocate of the unity of the person of Christ and of the use of the title *theotokos*. The Nestorians, to evolve eventually into the Church of the East, were condemned.

Chalcedon (451). Jesus Christ has a divine and a human nature, but he is one person, or *hypostasis* (a Greek term meaning a concretely existing being). An attempt at precise and careful definition, influenced by the Latin and Roman approach of Pope Leo I, of how the divine and human interacted in the person of Christ, was given. The Churches which were to become the Oriental Orthodox did not accept this and ultimately seceded.

(Second Council of) Constantinople (553), also known as the Council of the Three Chapters. Since Chalcedon had not brought agreement, this Council provided a clarification by stating that to ascribe two natures to Christ in no way implied two persons. It recognised the authority of Cyril of Alexandria and specifically condemned the writings (or Chapters) of three theologians who upheld the two natures of Christ: Theodore of Mopsuestia, Theodoret of Cyrrhus, and Ibas of Edessa. It hoped that this would satisfy the Oriental Orthodox, but this hope was not fulfilled.

(Third Council of) Constantinople (681) saw a further clarification of the Chalcedonian definition stating that there were two wills and two 'energies' or operations in Christ (in other words, that he could act both as God and as man), in response to those who were trying to find a way of reconciling the Oriental Orthodox through the formula of one will or energy.

(Second Council of) Nicaea (787) supported the use of icons as proper images of divine things and not as idols or mere pictures. The great defenders of icons were John of Damascus and Theodore of Stoudion.

Although the Councils took place within the eastern part of the Christian Empire and although the controversies which were the occasion of their meeting were primarily of concern to the Churches of the East, they have been recognised as Ecumenical or universal. Their decisions have been accepted by other Churches. The Roman Catholic Church also accepts a further fourteen Councils as Ecumenical, including the Second Council of Lyons and the Council of Florence, both of which tried to resolve issues of controversy between East and West, and the First and Second Vatican Councils of the last two centuries. The Seven Councils have a unique standing in the Orthodox Churches, and there is really no other authoritative source of doctrinal decision. So the way that the Councils worked provides a model for decision-making and conflict-resolution in the church.

The Councils were primarily gatherings of bishops, although others attended. In theory all bishops could attend, but in practice varying numbers came. It was important that the bishop of Rome, the Pope, shared in the decisions, but, with the exception of the Second Council of Constantinople, when Pope Vigilius (537–55) was forcibly detained in the capital in order to be present, he was represented by envoys, called legates. But the bishops were present as representatives of the whole Church, and it was with the whole Church that the responsibility for the work of the Councils rested.

They were called Ecumenical because they had a universal dimension, and this meant that they functioned as part of the ordering of the Christian Empire, or, in Greek, *oikoumene*. Thus they had a political as well as a religious dimension. The Emperors were conscious of the heavy responsibilities which they bore in governing the whole Christian world. Many were deeply pious, such as Anastasius I (491–518), who put a chair in the cathedral and used to invite selected groups to attend his lectures on aspects of the faith – something which irritated Patriarch Euphemius, who asked the next Emperor, Zeno, for permission to remove the offending chair; or Nicephorus II Phocas (963–9), who had planned to become a monk in his youth and remained an enthusiastic – if critical – patron of monasteries. It was the Emperor's task to convene the Council, and to preside, either personally or through a deputy. The only exception to this practice was the Second Council of Nicaea, which was summoned by the Empress Irene, since her son, Constantine VI, was only 17 at the time. On this occasion the Patriarch Tarasius presided, while Irene and Constantine sat and watched. The Councils both responded to and initiated political policy. Some were called when a political opportunity arose, such as the Third Council of Constantinople, which was summoned only after the eastern provinces of the Empire, the stronghold of Monophysitism, had been lost to the Arabs. This loss made the Christological compromises known as Monotheletism and Monoenergism – which had been evolved as an attempt to satisfy Monophysite groups in the east – no longer relevant to the needs of the Church and the Empire, since those to whom they were intended to appeal were no longer within the Empire. So a Council was called to anathematise them. The political dimension of the Councils is shown by the status of the disciplinary canons passed at the Councils, which had, from 530 onwards, the force of imperial law.

Since they were political they were also popular. If we can refer to some modern societies as 'politicised', then we could refer to Byzantine society as 'theologised'. Arriving in the capital from his small-town world in Cappadocia (today central Turkey), Gregory of Nyssa was struck by the lively interest in theological debate. He tells how bakers and bath-house attendants would engage the passer-by in discussion of points of Trinitarian theology – to the possible frustration of those trying to conduct daily business.[1] Teachers would often frame their teaching in popular form. The arch-heretic Arius, for example, composed a series of popular songs called the *Thalia* designed to be sung in the seamen's bars of Alexandria. This interest in theological debate led to active involvement by all sections of society. Bishops arriving at the Councils would often bring a band of supporters with them, who could, on occasions, have a decisive influence on proceedings. At a Council at Ephesus held in 449, an assortment of soldiers, monks and an Egyptian militia burst in at a key moment of the debate which, not surprisingly, led to a vote in favour of the Alexandrian Patriarch and inflicted injuries on Flavian, the Patriarch of Constantinople, leading to his death a few days later. This Council has not been regarded as Ecumenical, and was called the Latrocinium or 'Hooliganism Council' by Pope Leo of Rome. Private militias became a part of the entourage of the bishops of major sees. At Alexandria, the *parabalani*, or guild of hospital porters, developed

---

[1] The account of Gregory of Nyssa coming to Constantinople is in *On the Deity of the Son and the Spirit*, PG 46.557.

into the armed guard of the Patriarch; and at Antioch the *leticiarii*, or pall-bearers, carried out a similar role.

Not all Councils turned out to be Ecumenical. In order to become accepted as universal a Council had to be 'received' or recognised as truthful by the conscience of the Church. This was no formality, as is shown especially by the need to convene no less than four Councils over a period of over two hundred years before it was possible to consider the tricky subject of Christology to be adequately defined.

Reflecting on the nature of the Church some thirteen centuries later, A. Khomiakov used the Russian word *sobornost*. This word is untranslatable, combining ideas of catholicity and conciliarity. He used it to refer to the presence of the Spirit of God within the harmonious functioning of the community. True authority lies in the whole body of the Church bound together in love, rather than in the hierarchy of the bishops or the teaching of Scripture. The Conciliar process is an expression of this view of authority.

The Councils represent the politicisation of doctrine. In the old pre-Empire days Churches were local and did not have the same integral and inescapable relationship to the society as a whole. So while there were debates – often bitter – the definitions of orthodoxy and heresy only later acquired a greater precision and led to irreconcilable division in the Church. At the Councils the concept of heresy was sharpened. The word heresy is derived from the Greek *hairesis* or choice, so it implies not so much total error as selecting an element of the truth and emphasising it to the exclusion of others parts. The opposite of heretical is catholic, which refers to the wholeness of revealed truth. We may say that there is a political as well as a doctrinal dimension. In a later age and a different intellectual climate, things can look different. Sergei Bulgakov, the Russian theologian, once remarked that the ecumenical movement is the discovery that heretics are in fact orthodox.

The days of the Ecumenical Councils are over. There is no longer an *oikoumene* or universal Christian Empire, so there can no longer be an Ecumenical Council. Councils of bishops have continued to meet regularly at a local level, and in the last century the Ecumenical Patriarchate has taken the initiative in summoning a series of Councils to prepare for a Holy and Great Council which will bring together bishops from all Chalcedonian Orthodox Churches. It is not clear when this will meet; it will not have the standing of an Ecumenical Council, and it will deal with organisational, disciplinary and ecclesiological matters.

THE CHRISTOLOGICAL CONTROVERSIES

The crisis which engulfed the Empire, which occupied most of the energy of the bishops at the Councils, and which turned out to be beyond the ability of the Emperors to resolve, was over who, or what, Christ was: Christology. This was the direct concern of Councils Three to Six, and was at the root of Council Seven too. Since it led to the division of the Church, we should consider some of the issues at stake. The debate was, in part, over the use of words to describe and define the mysterious and inexpressible nature of Christ. There is both unity in Christ, since he is obviously one person, but there is also duality, since the events of his life showed that he had both human and divine characteristics. There are a variety of possible terms used, from three different languages, to communicate this mysterious congruence of unity and duality. Not only was there considerable flexibility in the meaning of the key terms and so confusion about what each writer was actually affirming, but also the meanings of terms in the three languages of Greek, Latin and Syriac did not exactly correspond. It can be said, at the risk of over-simplification, that the idea of the nature of an object, or essence, was conveyed by *ousia* or *physis* (Greek), *essentia* (Latin) or *qyane* (Syriac); the concrete form in which the nature subsists was the *hypostasis* (Greek), *substantia* (Latin), and *qnume* (Syriac); and the person who is the subject of the experiences was the *prosopon* (Greek), *persona* (Latin) or *parsufa* (Syriac). An important part of the debate between different groups concerned which words to use in what way to express the delicate nuances of meanings and to express the scriptural accounts of our salvation.

The Nestorian view was expressed in its classic form by Babai the Great, who lived in the seventh century, and was head of the Church of the East during an interregnum, although he declined the offer of this position on a permanent basis. He insisted that an *ousia* has to exist in an *hypostasis*, and that it makes no sense to think of human nature as an abstract quality without a concrete existence. So therefore in Christ there must be both two *ousiai* and two *hypsostases*, but there is one person – since person is the quality of *hypostasis* that expresses its distinctive character. This account makes good sense in the context of the Syrian Antiochene tradition of Biblical exposition, which began from meditating on the words and actions of Christ in the New Testament, some of which were clearly divine in character and some equally clearly human, and then went on to deduce the unity as an inevitable consequence.

The Monophysites had a different view. According to one of their great theologians, Philoxenus of Mabbug (*c.*440–523), the *ousia* denotes what, in the Trinity, is held in common by the three persons, but *hypostasis* what is distinctive. So, he can go on to say, the divine nature or essence of the Son or Word remains in heaven but the being which is the Son or *hypostasis* descends to the earth, and so 'the Word [i.e. the *hypostasis*] became flesh [i.e. human nature] and dwelt among us' (John 1.14). The classic summary of this reaching is the phrase used by Cyril of Alexandria: 'one incarnate nature of God the Word'. Cyril thought that this had been said by the impeccably authoritative Athanasius, but it was in fact written by Apollinarius, who was widely held to be a heretic.[2] The *hypostasis* of the Word assumes human nature, but since there is no human nature that is separate from the Word of God, there is therefore no separate human *ousia* or *hypostasis*, but only one nature and one *hypostasis*. A Monophysite view can recognise that Christ came into existence 'out of' two natures but not that he was 'in two natures'. He is 'one composite nature'.

The Chalcedonian expression of this conundrum is that there are two natures, but one person. They also considered that there is in Christ no human *hypostasis*, and this expresses the difficult concept that Christ is, according to this view, not a human individual but has a human nature. Christ is everything we can imagine as belonging to human nature – body, feelings, will, intelligence, instinct – but these universal characteristics do not exist in a single human being or *hypostasis* but only in Christ, the Son of God. Far from making Christ more distant from us, this in fact makes him more like us, since this means that it is *our* human nature that we can recognise in the Son of God, not the nature of somebody else. We see in Christ our human nature as God intended it from the beginning, and not the fallen human nature that is our present experience.

Nestorianism disappeared out of sight – at least out of the sight of the Emperor. Its ideas were adopted by the Persian Church, to become

---

[2] The phrase is used by Apollinarius in *Ep. Jov.* 1, PG 28.28a, and in several places in Cyril of Alexandria such as 'Contra Nestorium proem', in *Acta Conciliorum Oecumenicorum* 1.1.16, p. 331.

the Church of the East, at the Synod of Seleucia in 486, and while the movement remained very much alive, it ceased to be an issue in the Byzantine Empire. The word Monophysitism is used to embrace a variety of viewpoints. While some individuals were condemned, especially a certain Archimandrite Eutyches for whom the human nature of Christ was not the same as our human nature, mainline Monophysitism remained as an acceptable version of Christian teaching. The leader of the Monophysite party at Chalcedon was the Patriarch Dioscorus of Alexandria, who was condemned for his high-handed actions when he had, two years earlier, led the group who deposed and man-handled Patriarch Flavian of Constantinople at the Latrocinium Council, but he was not accused of heresy. Later, John of Damascus was to describe Monophysites as schismatics rather than heretics. Continual efforts were made by successive Emperors to achieve reconciliation but without success, and the solution of the problem of the schism was left to the Arabs, who conquered large parts of the East and, by doing so, forcibly removed the Monophysites from the Empire. Again a political solution solved a theological problem.

Further refinements of the Monophysite view of Christ were developed in theories called Monotheletism and Monoenergism – both concerned with the unity in Christ and where it is to be located. For the Monotheletes, it is in the will, and so Christ with his two natures operated with a unified divine will. Maximus the Confessor developed a more sophisticated argument showing that Christ, if he had a human nature, must have had a human will, and he formulated the notion of a 'gnomic' will, or the will by which we make decisions, which is distinct from the natural human will. Christ had one unified 'gnomic' will, since his decisions were made in conformity to his divine will, but the human will remained. For the Monoenergists the unity lay in the acting or energy of Christ – bearing in mind that *energeia* is not just doing things but is that part of the nature which expresses itself in its relations with what is outside itself. Again this was not seen as doing justice to the duality essential for a true salvation.

These later stages of the Christological debate took place when the Byzantine Empire was under attack from both east and west. To the west, the Avars were advancing through the Balkans, and to the east first the Persians and then the Arabs threatened the Asian provinces. In this critical situation, imperial policy redoubled its efforts to reconcile the

Monophysite groups in the eastern parts of the Empire, and the Emperor Heraclius (610–41), with the support of the Patriarchs Sergius (610–38) and Pyrrhus (638–41 and 654), made these suggestions that Christ could be seen as having a single energy or activity, Monoenergism, or, later, as having a single will in Christ, or Monotheletism. This was set out in the *Ecthesis* or Exposition of Faith, which was publicly issued in the Great Church of Haghia Sophia in 638. Maximus became involved, first through a public disputation with the now-deposed Patriarch Pyrrhus in Carthage, then at the Lateran Council in Rome of 649, and then through his arrest by the Emperor Constans in 654, followed by a trial, torture and exile to the Caucasus in 662, where he died in the same year. His sufferings on behalf of the Chalcedonian faith, against the imperial Monothelete teaching, led him to a martyr's crown, and the enhancement of his reputation.

THE EARLY FATHERS AND THEIR TEACHING

All Orthodox Churches revere their saints, who are not figures in the past but remain as present guides. Their lives are read in churches, their icons look down on the worshippers, and often their relics continue to give protection. So it would be a distortion of the truth not to recognise that the Conciliar process was guided and the doctrines formulated by a succession of teachers who are remembered with love by the Church.

Origen of Alexandria (*c*.185–*c*.250) falls outside our period, and has a reputation blemished through his being judged a heretic. In spite of this condemnation he is generally recognised as the greatest scholar of the early Church, who also established a method of scholarship to be followed by later Fathers. He was a Biblical scholar, who produced the *Hexapla*, a huge work giving two Hebrew and four Greek versions of the Bible in parallel columns, and also wrote a large number of commentaries on Scripture. In addition, he was also an ascetic, writing on prayer and on martyrdom, and, in his zeal, probably castrated himself to be more acceptable as an inhabitant of the Kingdom of Heaven. He was also a philosopher, and presented the faith in the categories and language of Plato and his followers. This agenda, once set, remained throughout the Patristic period. The style and form of the thinking of the Fathers owes much to Origen. He was also a lively and speculative thinker, ready to advance opinions on disputed topics. This was an aspect of his work which was not well received, and in 553 at (or possibly just after) the Second Council of Constantinople, he was condemned as a heretic for some of his more daring speculations.

Gregory of Nazianzus (*c*.329–90) is the most quoted author in the East after the Bible. He is called simply Gregory the Theologian, a title also given to John the Evangelist and Symeon the New Theologian (949–1022). He was briefly Patriarch of Constantinople, and attended the First Council of Constantinople, but he was first and foremost a monk. He loved silence and would often spend Lent without speaking. One of the three Cappadocian theologians – along with Basil and Gregory of Nyssa – his theological thinking set out much that was to be of fundamental importance later. There are two great themes running through his writing: God as light, and deification. The notion of light is present in the other 'Theologian', John the Evangelist, and was also to be a feature of the 'New Theologian' Symeon. God is light – and so reaches out towards us and makes the incomprehensible God knowable, but through participation and experience rather than academic enquiry. So deification – or the sharing in the life of God and in that sense becoming God – becomes the cornerstone of theology. It is based on the Incarnation of Christ not on the Cross. Since God became man, there is the corresponding movement that man becomes God – a union is established. It is an idea to be found in the thinking of Plato and the philosophers, but there it refers to something rather different, to an intellectual process whereby the mind frees itself from the darkness of the body and returns to the Mind from which it originated. For Gregory and the Christian tradition, the whole human person, body and soul, is united with God. 'That which is not assumed is not healed', wrote Gregory in another of those short definitions, pointing to the need both for Christ to take on all human nature, but also to show that all human nature can as a result find its place with God. Knowledge of God is Union with God, and it is achieved through membership of the Church, receiving the sacraments, following an ascetic life, doing good works. Theology becomes not an academic discipline but a way of describing membership of the Church.

During the Christological controversies of the fifth to the seventh centuries the undisputed authority was Cyril of Alexandria (412–44). He occupied the hugely wealthy and powerful see of Alexandria, and his blend of uncompromising theological writing and political influence made him some enemies. In a notorious passage Theodoret of Cyrrhus expressed anxiety that after his death, the inmates of hell might return the departed Cyril to earth, and requested the undertakers to choose an especially heavy stone for the grave.[3] This suggests the passionate and uncompromising nature of the Christological debates which made it so difficult to negotiate solutions to these problems. The basis of Cyril's Christology is the affirmation that Christ must be fully God in order to bring us salvation. Salvation is seen not in legal terms as a declaration that sin is forgiven, but in personal and relational terms in giving us unity with God and so has a transformative effect. The Biblical text that expresses this most clearly is 'the Word became flesh' (John 1.14). Cyril's opponent was Nestorius, Patriarch of Constantinople from 428 to 431, who was deposed at the Council of Ephesus (431). Cyril's writings vary in tone from the strongly polemical and uncompromising Twelve Chapters attached to one of his letters to Nestorius, to the eirenic letter called *laetentur coeli*, or 'let the heavens rejoice', written two years later to John of Antioch when both sides were seeking peace. So Cyril's towering authority could be invoked both by extreme Monophysite groups, using early and polemical material, and also by those who adhered to Chalcedon but interpreted it in the light of Cyril's writing – the viewpoint of the Fifth Ecumenical Council, using the more moderate sections of Cyril's writing. Later Monophysite writers – Dioscorus of Alexandria, Severus of Antioch and Philoxenus of Mabbug – are the guiding authorities of the non-Chalcedonian Churches but anathematised as heretics by the Chalcedonians to this day. The problem of rehabilitating those previously vilified remains a serious obstacle in the path of reunion between the two families of Churches.

An important writer is pseudo-Dionysius. He presents himself as the Dionysius the Areopagite who was converted by St Paul in Athens (Acts 17.34), using a literary device that was quite common – not, one supposes, intended to deceive, but rather to suggest that the views expressed could be rightly attributed to the associates of the apostles. His origins are shadowy, but it is agreed that he probably wrote in Syria in the early sixth century, and may have come from a Monophysite background. He is quoted by later writers, Eastern and Western, including both Gregory Palamas and Barlaam of Calabria, both of whom based their arguments on Dionysius but interpreted him in contradictory ways. He is associated especially with apophatic, or negative, theology. This approach is

---

[3] Theodoret, *Ep. 180*, in PG 83.1489c–1491a.

based on the truth that God is unknowable, and so is unlike anything that we can think of. It is a fruitful way of thinking – refreshingly austere and stretching the limits of thought. The successive suggestion of things God might be compared to are rejected in turn, until we realise that we cannot even speak of God as, say, good or even an existing being – since he is not in himself good as we use the word, or existing in the sense that we exist. This is intended to lift up our minds closer and closer towards God, towards a union given beyond knowledge, without words, and in darkness. In fact this apophatic theology occupies only a small part of his writing, and needs to be read in the context of the longer treatises on the *Names of God* and on the *Ecclesiastical and Celestial Hierarchies*, which present a more unified and consistent doctrinal vision. He sets out a hierarchical approach to the Christian faith that results from the overflowing fullness of God which reaches out towards us and gradually draws us back into unity with him.

Some would claim that the greatest Orthodox theologian is Maximus the Confessor. The Empress Anna Comnena thought that his 'writing was highly speculative and intellectual and makes the reader's head swim'. But Irene said, 'I myself do not approach such books without a tremble. Yet I cannot tear myself away from them. Wait a little and after a close look at other books, believe me, you will taste the sweetness of these.'[4] His thought has become better appreciated in recent years through the publication of a number of studies by contemporary theologians, and by the increasing availability of translations. He is not an easy writer to approach. He does not set out his theological thought in systematic treatises, as did John of Damascus or later Western theologians, but in collections of aphorisms, many collected into groups of a hundred, or a 'century', which was seen as having a quality of completeness or perfection; or of commentaries on the Fathers; or of a series of answers to questions directed to him. The clue to the appreciation of Maximus' work is to grasp that he is primarily a monk and a teacher of monks. His work has been described by Georges Florovsky as 'not so much a system of theology as a system of asceticism'. Like Gregory he interprets prayer as based on love rather than knowledge, seeing the root problem of the human condition as resulting from disordered love – described as *philautia* or 'self -love'. So he provides a sensitive and comprehensive account of

[4] Anna Comnena, *Alexiad* 5.9.

the nature of the will, or rather different expressions of the will, and how it can co-operate with the divine will, as happened in the person of Christ. He shows how man is created of the same stuff as the rest of creation and therefore can be described as a microcosm or small world, reproducing the alienation of the fallen world on a smaller scale, and so having the capacity to bring a new unity through ascetic struggle.

The writings produced by these authors are varied and include commentaries on Scripture, sermons, letters, and polemical treatises attacking a supposedly heretical viewpoint. None produced anything like a systematic theology, expounding the full content of the faith. None, that is, until John of Damascus (*c.* 665–749). John spent much of his adult life at the monastery of St Sabas near Bethlehem, and wrote a number of works including a three-volume *Fount of Knowledge*, which contains, in the second part, an extensive attack on Islam, and a third part which is a systematic account of the teaching of the Fathers, *On the Orthodox Faith*. It contains much quotation from earlier Fathers, especially Maximus the Confessor, and is sometimes seen as a summary and conclusion to the theological work of the Fathers, with John as the last theologian of the Patristic period. But few today would wish to draw so firm a conclusion to the work of the Fathers. The open spirit of enquiry, the interpretation of the faith in the language of contemporary society, the insistence on the central importance of salvation and as a result teaching about the ascetic and moral life – all the qualities that made the time of the Church Fathers so vibrant and creative – have lived on in the great theologians of the Church.

THE BYZANTINE PERIOD

As a result of the work of the Fathers of the seven Ecumenical Councils, the fundamental doctrines of the Trinity and the Incarnation were set in place. The cornerstone of Trinitarian theology was the statement of the Council of Nicaea that the Son was of the same substance or *homoousios* with the Father – an insight shared by all the Churches. Then the decisive Christological statement was the Definition of Chalcedon that Christ is One Person but in Two Natures – a statement that led to the separation within the Eastern Churches. In the next stage of doctrinal history the focus shifted, in a direction which can be seen as relating to the second part of Athanasius' dictum. God became man – 'in order than man might become God'.

The last of the seven Ecumenical Councils took place at the mid-point of a long-drawn-out controversy about whether or not icons were a legitimate expression of the truth of the Incarnation. While there is no necessary connection between the Christological discussions and the question of icons, it so happened that the icon question did follow on as the next step in the great process of dogmatic definition. It brought together religious art and the doctrine of the Incarnation to produce the distinctive form of Byzantine religious art, the icon (although Orthodox would deny that the icon can properly be described as art in the sense in which the word is used in the West, since its roots are in the corporate experience of the Church rather than in individual and creative expression). The icon is not discussed here and is the subject of its own chapter. The iconoclast controversy was brought to an end in 843 with a day still celebrated each Lent by the Byzantine Orthodox: the Triumph of Orthodoxy. With it the shape of the Orthodox understanding of salvation, an understanding shared by Western churches, was in place.

The next stage from the Triumph of Orthodoxy in 843 to the fall of Constantinople in 1453 can be referred to as the Byzantine period. West and East had diverged to such an extent that different questions preoccupied the two halves of the Church. The debates carried out in Constantinople have a local character, and did not extend their influence outside the area of Byzantine influence. Among the writers from this period who express the developing tradition are Symeon the New Theologian and Gregory Palamas.

Symeon (949–1022) was a senior civil servant who became a monk at the age of 28 at the monastery of Stoudion, then was expelled from it after only a year for not co-operating with the common rule and for being too attached to his spiritual father, Symeon the Pious. He moved to the monastery of St Mamas outside the city, became its superior at the age of 31, and spent the next twenty-five years teaching and guiding his monks. But then he was in trouble with the authorities again, apparently for his continued reverence of his spiritual father, and in 1009 was sent into exile where he spent the rest of his life.

His writings – which include a set of sermons delivered to his monks and a number of hymns and poems – develop familiar patristic themes of God as light, and the reality of the encounter with him which leads to transformation and union with God, known as *theosis* or deification. He is frank and open about his own experiences, telling both of his visions of light and his periods of darkness, with a degree of honesty and self-revelation not found in other Fathers of the Eastern Church. This emphasis on personal experience is also shown in his belief in the capacity of each individual to encounter the reality of God, through the Church, by sharing in the sacraments and the life of the community. His own Christian life had been shaped through the guidance of his spiritual father, and, as a result, Symeon was determined to venerate him by setting up his icon and celebrating an annual memorial. This form of guidance was open to be given by any of the baptised with the spirit-bestowed gifts, and, in one passage (admittedly of dubious authorship) he suggests that lay people can give absolution after confession.

Conflict with authority was a continuing theme of Symeon's life, and his teaching was individual and rebellious. Behind his problems with the authorities lay a challenge to the previously accepted authority structure of the Church. He was a wealthy, successful and influential figure who left the court and moved to a monastery, setting up a popular alternative to the court and patriarchate. This moved theology and doctrine into a new arena, affirming a popular and potentially anti-intellectual style which was present as a kind of sub-text throughout the centralised imperial Byzantine approach to Church life. So his main contribution to theology and monasticism is to provide the basis for the spread of a spontaneous and local form of monastic life.

It was some time before his importance was recognised. After his death his works were seldom read, and on the occasions when they were copied, they were often abridged to leave out the more controversial passages (such as allowing lay people to offer forgiveness). They were preserved on Mount Athos, and he later received the title of the 'New Theologian' to place him in the succession of the two great poets of light – St John the Evangelist and St Gregory of Nazianzus, each called simply 'the Theologian'.

The implications of this experiential and personal approach to the relationship with God were brought out during the debate between Gregory Palamas (1296–1359) and the Greek–Italian Barlaam of Calabria. Gregory was a monk on Mount Athos who was involved with the Hesychast approach to the monastic life. The Hesychasts, from the Greek *hesychia* or quietness, based their life on a disciplined approach to prayer and the ascetic life, including the use of physical techniques, which were designed to bring the worshipper into union with God. This showed itself, among other ways, in the kind of vision of light which Symeon had written of and which they maintained was a vision of God himself.

Barlaam held that God was unknowable, that the Bible gave only an indirect knowledge, and that the Hesychast approach was completely misguided in understanding God to be visible to the eyes of the worshipper as light, and so understanding God to be material.

Gregory based his response to Barlaam and his thinking on the basic tenets of Christianity: that the whole person, body as well as soul, receives salvation through the Incarnation, and that through the sacraments this whole person is united with God. As a result God can become part of our experience – which includes the physical as well as the intellectual. To enable him to explain this, he draws on a distinction between the essence and the energies of God. The 'essence' of God is God as he is in himself, and this is – as Barlaam rightly pointed out – unknown and unknowable; but God also makes himself known, in creation, in the Incarnation and in all his dealings with us, and these are also God – but God's 'energies', or God as he is in his relationship with us. The vision of divine light, which the Hesychast can behold in prayer, can be described as a joining together of divine and human energy, in which we see God as light – or, we can say, God is in us seeing himself as light. This is expressed in his book *Triads in Defence of the Hesychasts*.

Two Councils were held in Constantinople in 1341 and 1351 which supported Gregory's teaching and have the status in the East of Ecumenical Councils.

The Hesychast controversy took place as the Byzantine Empire was in decline. The Crusaders had occupied the city in the previous century and the territory under the control of the Empire was shrinking rapidly as the Turkish armies advanced. But the cultural and intellectual vitality of the Byzantines continued, with other places, such as Mount Athos in Greece and Mount Paroria in Bulgaria, developing as centres of religious life. The ascetic and Hesychast traditions were thus preserved, awaiting rediscovery in later centuries by those sincerely seeking to follow in the ways of the Fathers.

THE OTTOMAN PERIOD

The fall of Constantinople in 1453 was the final end of the millennium of history in which the Byzantine Empire had dominated the eastern

Mediterranean. The four centuries or so of Turkish rule began, called by the Greeks *Turkokratia* and by the Serbs 'the centuries of slavery'. In fact, of course, the Orthodox Churches had been progressively overcome by a growing Muslim ascendancy over a period of several centuries, with the eastern provinces being conquered by the Arabs in the seventh century, the central part of Asia Minor falling to the Turks in the eleventh and twelfth centuries, and the advance of the Ottomans continuing steadily until, finally, the great city fell. The Russian Church, although outside the range of the Ottoman expansion, also suffered its own form of oppression under the secular absolutism of Peter the Great and his successors. Thus, the use here of the idea a Turkish period of theological development refers to a variety of different political experiences, which had in common that a non-Orthodox government ruled over an Orthodox Church, with marked consequences in the field of theology.

Theological creativity was maintained for a while. Under the Arabs, the Church had carried on a vigorous intellectual life, at least at first. John of Damascus (*c.*665–749) wrote hymns, a summary of doctrine and his treatises in defence of icons from within the territory ruled by Arabs, at the monastery of Mar Saba, near Bethlehem. In the following century, Theodore of Abu-Qurrah (*c.*750–*c.*825) is one among several theologians who wrote in Arabic and Syriac, commending icons and the Christology of the Ecumenical Councils, and engaging in debate with Muslim scholars. He was also a monk of Mar Saba before becoming bishop of the Harran in Mesopotamia. But, as Islamic influence grew, so Christian theological creativity declined. In Egypt, Christian writing was based on the monasteries, and tended to emphasise spiritual topics. Even the great Alexandrian theologians, Athanasius and Cyril, were preserved in Egypt only in the form of homilies and excerpts from their polemical writings. The survival of Christian theological writing after the Islamic conquests should be seen as an indication of the slowness of the advance of Muslim cultural infiltration. As this process continued, so educational and other institutions of the Church declined and with them the vitality of the theological tradition of Orthodoxy.

But why should this have been the case? Oppression was not so vicious that thinking, praying, writing and debating were prohibited. The answer lies in part in the Byzantine integration of theological scholarship into the life and culture of the Empire. After Byzantine civilisation was overcome by Ottoman ascendancy, all aspects of Christian life went into decline – among them theology. But a further reason for the decline of theology in the East, it could be argued, is that the theological task which the Fathers undertook had been completed. The doctrines of the Trinity and the Incarnation had been defined, and the nature of the Christian ascent to God had been explored. Where would the theological task of definition have gone next? The West was taking a different path, and was debating the nature of salvation, of justification, of faith and works. But these would have been of little relevance in an Eastern context where salvation was seen in terms of incarnation and deification. Maybe Byzantine theology had completed its work, and provided the Church with the self-understanding that it needed to maintain its life.

After the fall of Constantinople, Greek scholarship moved westwards into Italy. By the sixteenth century there were professorial chairs of Greek studies in Venice, Padua, Florence and Bologna. In 1570 the Greek College of St Athanasius was founded in Rome by Pope Gregory XIII. He intended this establishment for Greek boys who were deprived of education, but it quickly developed into a seminary for Greek-speaking Catholic priests. Some Orthodox attended, and these either converted to Catholicism, and became influenced by Western ways of thinking, or became confirmed in a traditional anti-Western form of Orthodoxy. The college produced both Rome's greatest friends and also her greatest enemies. Within the Ottoman Empire itself, educational opportunities were limited. The Patriarchal Academy in Constantinople continued, and had moments of revival, for example under Patriarch Jeremias II (1572–9, 1580–4, 1587–95), who broadened the range of studies, but generally educational initiatives were short-lived. An Academy was founded on Mount Athos in 1749 and its numbers rapidly expanded from twenty to two hundred students. Unfortunately the monks approved of neither the first principal, Eugenios Voulgaris, who they felt was tainted by Western Enlightenment ideas, nor of the second, Athanasius of Paros, who erred in the opposite direction by supporting the rigorist Kollyvades movement, described in a later chapter. The Academy lasted just twelve years and closed in 1761.

The lack of facilities led to a general decline in education among the clergy. When, after the end of Turkish rule in Greece, the Church was re-established in 1850, it was estimated that ten out of the thousand priests were able to sign their own name. This extraordinary figure is an indication of a generally low level of education. In these circumstances it is hardly surprising that the theological output of the Church declined.

At the same time as Byzantine Christian scholarship was in decline, Western scholarship was on the ascendant. This resulted in Western influences on Eastern theologians. If Orthodox students had to go to the West to study, they were inevitably going to have their way of thinking shaped by Western categories. The Turkish period was called, by Georges Florovsky, the Western captivity of the Church, or the *pseudomorphosis*. Western influence is generally seen as destructive, introducing non-Orthodox ways of thinking into the Church.

There were two possible forms of Western influence: Catholic and Protestant. Among the attractions of Catholicism were its educational resources and its sophisticated method of doing theology. It was, however, often seen as a predator seeking to convert Orthodox to Catholicism, and so Protestants were useful allies in the struggle to resist this encroachment. Different attitudes to Western theology are shown by three Orthodox Confessions of Faith, all produced in the seventeenth century.

Cyril Lucaris (1572–1638) was known as the 'Calvinist Patriarch' and has become a controversial figure. Regarded by many as the most able occupant of the Patriarchal throne in the Turkish period, his theological views have become notorious for combining Orthodox and Reformed influences. Cyril went to Poland in 1596, after the Union of Brest, to strengthen the Orthodox against the new Greek Catholic Church, and there he learnt to hate and distrust Roman Catholicism, writing in 1615 that:

> we for our sins no longer have a Christian king; and Christ is our only helper in whom we live and breathe. Yet the wretched Jesuits would deprive us of Christ himself, making another to be the head and foundation of the Church. With this in mind they have begun to attack even Constantinople itself and our people are so ignorant that they make no objection.[5]

In his struggle against Catholics, he found support and help from Lutheran and Calvinist divines. He worked alongside them and became

[5] See T. P. Themelis in *Nea Sion* 8 (1909), pp. 30–3.

influenced by their approaches to the faith, which he found an effective counter-argument to Catholicism. Some time between 1615 and 1618 he became more attracted by the rigorous Biblicism of Calvinism, preferring to rely on Scripture rather than human tradition, remarking once that he could no longer endure to hear people say that the comments of human tradition are of equal weight with the Scriptures. In 1601 he was elected Patriarch of Alexandria, and then in 1620 was transferred to the see of Constantinople. In 1627 he set up a printing press, and in 1629 he published his great work, the *Confession of Faith*. It upholds several points of Calvinist teaching, including predestination and justification by faith. He was a man of great learning and energy, and it is a sign of the tragedy of the Orthodox Church under the Ottomans that his career ended in ignominy. He was deposed and re-instated six times before being assassinated by Turkish janissaries and his body thrown in the sea. The key to understanding the career of Cyril is to see it in the context of the times – with politics and faith inter-related, a confident Counter-Reformation Catholic mission, and a highly insecure grasp of the Patriarchal throne.

A response to Cyril, and an alternative approach to that of the Protestant sympathisers in Orthodox theology, came from Peter Moghila (1596–1647). He was appointed Metropolitan of Kiev in 1633, with the support of Cyril Lucaris, and, like Cyril, struggled against the Greek Catholic Church, but, unlike Cyril, preferred to enlist the support of Roman Catholic ideas and language. His response to Cyril's *Confession of Faith*, called an *Orthodox Confession*, was published in 1640, and included many Catholic teachings. It was hastily revised by a Greek, Meletios Syrigos, who expurgated it, removing some of the most Roman passages, such as that affirming that the consecration of the Eucharist was achieved by the words of institution and the doctrine of purgatory. In this form it was approved by the Council of Jassy (today Iasi in Romania) (1642), but even in this revised form contains strong Catholic influence.

Another document provoked by Cyril's *Confession* was yet another *Confession*, this one by Dositheus, Patriarch of Jerusalem. Dositheus was born in the Peloponnese in 1641 and was consecrated as Patriarch of Jerusalem at the age of 28, remaining in this position until his death in 1707. While still only 31 he convened the Council of Jerusalem (actually held in the Church of the Nativity at Bethlehem). His *Confession of Faith* is contained within the Acts of the Council, and is based on the writings of Dionysios IV of Constantinople, among others. In spite of some Catholic influences it is more clearly Orthodox in its teachings. He wrote other works, including a massive *History of the Jerusalem Patriarchs*, in 1,247 pages in the 1715 edition, and also founded a printing press at Jassy in Moldavia to enable the circulation of Orthodox literature.

THE ATTRACTION OF CONSERVATISM

During the Ottoman period, people felt that the first priority was to maintain the tradition, handed down from the times of the apostles. The conditions of oppression led to the conservatism that many associate with the Orthodox Churches. There had been lively debate during the Byzantine Empire with the rigorist and conservative monastic party often challenging the more pragmatic and compromising policies of the Emperor and Patriarch. This tradition had been maintained since the fall of the Empire, with conservative and traditional movements dividing the Church. Conservatism has always been a tendency in the Church, and the sense of being under attack from hostile governments, aggressive evangelism from Western Churches and compromising Orthodox Church leaders ensured that conservative forms of Church life continued. Among these are the Old Believers of seventeenth-century Russia and Old Calendarists of twentieth-century Greece and elsewhere, who should be seen as extreme examples of the conservatism that is deeply rooted in the Church.

The occasion of the Russian schism was the reform movement of Patriarch Nikon of Moscow (1605–81). He planned to bring the Russian forms of liturgical worship into line with Greek practices, and also to introduce some Greek practices – including making the sign of the cross with three fingers (symbolising the Trinity) instead of the older Russian practice of using two fingers (for the two natures of Christ). It was not just that Nikon liked things Greek, but now that service books printed in Venice were arriving it became clear that there were variations between the manuscripts used in Russia and the printed texts that were becoming generally used. In addition, Russia was becoming conscious of its responsibilities as the senior bishopric free from the Turkish yoke, as the Churches in the Ottoman Empire turned to Moscow for financial and practical help. Nikon wanted to bring the practice of the Church in

Russia closer to that of the ancient Patriarchates to assist it in extending its influence southward towards Constantinople. How could he celebrate the liturgy together with the Patriarch of Constantinople, Nikon wondered, if they were using different service books and doing different things at different times? The Old Believers shared the same view of Russia's God-given mission but drew the opposite conclusion – that the superiority of its traditions should be recognised. The Old Believers refused to compromise by adopting Nikon's Greek alterations – and were persecuted. A leader was the Archpriest Avvakum (Habbakuk), a popular priest in the capital and in the court. In his *Autobiography*, he has left a vivid record of his sufferings in exile, and his imprisonment, of which twelve of the twenty-two years were spent in an underground hut.[6] Finally he was burnt alive.

The Old Believers survived bouts of persecution, and gained new adherents in reaction to Westernising policies of the Tsars after 1700. They remained a substantial community up until 1917, consisting, according to some estimates, of 10 per cent of the population of Russia, but were seriously weakened during the Communist persecution. They have preserved old styles of icon painting, church chant, crosses, and sometimes dress. Some of the more conservative groups avoid potatoes, as an import of godless Russian society.

As self-contained communities isolated from the central institutions of Russian society, the Old Believers have often developed qualities of self-reliance and commercial enterprise. They have sub-divided into smaller groups, some accepting priests who have converted from the Orthodox Church (the *popovtsy*), and some refusing to do so (the *bezpopovtsy* – those without priests). Many of the latter group were based in the west of Russia, and, somewhat surprisingly, found that they had much in common with Protestant Churches. In 1846 one *popovtsy* group was able to set up its own hierarchy of clergy through a deposed Orthodox bishop, Amvrosy of Bosnia, who joined the group. Known as the Old Believer Church of the Belokrinitsa Hierarchy, after the monastery where the clergy were first ordained, it was recognised by the Moscow Patriarchate in 1971. Often Old Believers are called the Old Ritualists, to show that the schism concerned matters of worship rather than belief – but

---

[6] Avvakum's *Autobiography* is conveniently printed in G. P. Fedotor, *A Treasury of Russian Spirituality* (New York 1965), pp. 137–81.

the title Old Believers makes the point that worship and ritual cannot be separated from faith and dogma, and this is exactly what the Old Believers claimed.

The Old Calendarists are a more modern phenomenon. In 1582 Pope Gregory XIII of Rome had reformed the old Julian calendar. This became used in the West but not in the East, where Patriarch Jeremias II anathematised those who used the new calendar. In 1923 Patriarch Meletios of Constantinople summoned a conference to adopt the Gregorian calendar, but with some modifications. This received a rather patchy acceptance, with Bulgaria not adopting the new calendar until 1968 and some Churches (including Jerusalem, Russia and Serbia) still using the old Julian calendar. (The Oriental Orthodox Churches were not involved in this change of course and use the old calendar.) Opposition to the changes quickly emerged. In Greece numerous laity, amounting to over a million, formed an Old Calendarist movement and were joined in 1935 by three bishops, including Metropolitan Chrysostom of Florina, a popular preacher. Several groups have since emerged, controlling parishes and monasteries, and forming hierarchies of bishops. The Old Calendarists have united and divided with confusing rapidity, with, at present, five different Old Calendarist archbishops of Athens. There is also a strong Old Calendarist group in Romania, where the calendar changes included the celebration of Easter on the Western date. Various Russian, Greek, Romanian and Bulgarian Churches combined in 1994. Old Calendarists vary in their attitude to New Calendarists, some hoping to encourage all Orthodox to reject these novel innovations, and others seeing themselves as the only true Orthodox.

While these changes can seem trivial to an outsider, it must be remembered that Orthodoxy is formed from a unified and holistic tradition. It is not a selection of beliefs and practices which can be added to or subtracted from, but rather it is the meeting of God and man that is expressed and incarnated in the community of the Church. This gives to the Church a wholeness and a harmony, in which the whole tradition of the Church hangs together. While the Empire was in existence, the Byzantine Church was creative and innovative, but after the Turkish conquest, conservatism became an attractive way of expressing a firm commitment to Orthodoxy, both within the Ottoman Empire and beyond it. This tendency has remained – perhaps a lasting legacy of Islamic overlords to the Eastern Christian world.

THE MODERN REVIVAL OF ORTHODOX THEOLOGY

The Orthodox theological tradition emerged from its 'Western captivity' in the nineteenth century in Russia. Two modern doctrinal movements had their roots in the Russia of the Tsars. One did untold and unimaginable damage to the Church, and the other helped to initiate a remarkable theological revival that has given to the modern world an authentic Orthodox style of theologising which has had as much, if not more, influence on Western thinkers as on Eastern. One was atheist and had as its aim the replacement of Christianity with a socialist paradise achieved here on this earth, while the other that emerged from it reaffirmed the Christian gospel in a way which proved to combine modern and traditional elements. It is in the rise of Marxist thought that the revival of modern Orthodox theology can be discerned. Both Marxist atheism and Russian Orthodox theological thinking have had influence – although clearly of differing styles and orders of magnitude – on the religious life of the world.

Since Russian Communism has materialism and atheism as non-negotiable presuppositions, it is easy to overlook its deeply religious character. Russian Communism emerged from Christian roots. This is clear in the life of one of the early leaders, Nikolai Chernyshevskii (1822–89). He was the son of a country priest who was expected to follow in his father's calling, and so he was educated in the Church schools. While there he discovered Western thinkers, such as Feuerbach and Fourier, and, under their influence, he became socialist in his political thinking and atheist in his faith. He became a journalist and wrote extensively, becoming popular among students, before being exiled to Siberia in 1863. The hero of his novel *What is to be done?* is a young revolutionary who is totally committed to the welfare of the common people. He devotes his life to the service of the poor, sleeping on a hard board studded with nails as part of his training. The book is strangely reminiscent of a traditional saint's life, except that God has disappeared and the heaven that is promised is to be achieved on this earth through human struggle.

He was not alone in this truly religious zeal. Those who shared these convictions formed an identifiable grouping which had a harmony and a purpose hard for a Western observer to appreciate, forming an identifiable class of the intelligentsia. One of their number, Sergei Bulgakov, compared them to a religious order. In place of the Western,

Enlightenment qualities of liberalism, individualism, and a scientific search for truth, there was the unquestioning faith of the Russian peasant, the millenarian belief in a kingdom of justice and the nostalgic longing for the old days before the absolutism of Peter the Great. It was a heady combination, which led directly to the ruthless opportunism of the Bolsheviks.

The new faith of nineteenth-century Russia affirmed a paradise awaiting humanity once it was freed from oppression and alienation. But it was a paradise that belonged firmly on this earth, and God was absent from it. Nicolas Zernov referred to Marxism–Leninism as a 'Judaeo Christian apocalyptic sect born among a people familiar with the Bible'.[7]

If Marxism had its roots in Christianity, then much modern Orthodox theology has its historical roots in Marxism. Four leading Marxists became Christians in the years leading up to the Revolution: Piotr Struve (1870–1944), Sergei Bulgakov (1871–1944), Nikolai Berdyaev (1874–1948) and Simeon Frank (1877–1950). This new movement was heralded by the publication of the collection of essays called *Vekhi*, or 'Signposts', which was published in 1909 and went through five editions in six months. One of its contributors summarised its aim: 'It asserted the necessity of a religious foundation for any consistent philosophy of life, criticising the revolutionary and maximalist tendencies of the radical-minded Russian intelligentsia.'[8] In it the same writer wrote: 'The problem of happiness is seen by the Marxists as a problem of social organisation.' Bulgakov pleaded for 'an intelligentsia reconciled to the Church which could combine Christianity with a dedication to work for the cultural and economic uplifting of the nation'.

Places

From 1917 onwards, Christians were among those exiled from Russia. The curious oversight of the Communist authorities in allowing some of the outstanding theological minds of the Church to leave the country led to the remarkable renaissance in Orthodox life and theology nurtured by a rootless community of exiles. Russian émigrés fled to Belgrade, Prague – but above all to Paris. Here in 'Russian Paris' an

---

[7] See N. Zernov, *The Russian Religious Renaissance of the Twentieth Century* (London 1963), p. 328.

[8] S. Frank, *Reminiscences of P. B. Struve* (New York 1956), p. 81, cited in Zernov, *The Russian Religious Renaissance*, p. 111.

extraordinary community of tens of thousands of refugees established itself, dreaming of the return home but also carrying on a vibrant intellectual and religious life. The centre for theological study was the Orthodox Theological Institute of St Sergius at 93 rue de Crimée. The first dean, appointed in 1925, was Sergei Bulgakov. Its distinguished list of teachers includes Georges Florovsky, who will be discussed shortly; and Nikolai Afanas'ev, associated with a key theme of Orthodox theology, the Church.

At this stage St Sergius' was the only Russian theological academy, since the Communists had quickly acted to close theological institutions within Russia. This situation continued until 1944 when, during the Stalinist thaw, academies were opened at Moscow, Leningrad and Odessa. Several threads of theological tradition came together in St Sergius'. There was, first, careful study of the Church Fathers. This continued the work of the nineteenth-century Russian academies, which had divided the patristic corpus between them and had set out on a huge corporate task of providing translations and study of the Fathers. Second, there was liturgy, with magnificent worship in the neighbouring Cathedral of St Alexander Nevsky, celebrated with the care and passion of a community torn from its roots but able to preserve the fullness of its worshipping life. Then, third, was the speculative, philosophical style of thinking that had been popular in Russia and could flourish in Paris, free from ecclesiastical control. Fourth, perhaps it should be added, was openness to the West, with a consciousness of the welcome received, and the need to join forces with other Christians to resist the terrifying darkness of atheism combining with the adventurous and speculative spirit brought with them from nineteenth-century Russia. It is not surprising that these led to a wellspring of creativity at St Sergius'.

Before identifying some of the characteristics of this theology, it should be recognised that St Sergius' was not the only theological centre. At its foundation there was already a faculty of theology at the University of Athens, which had been founded in 1837, using Western models of education. This was joined by another University at Thessaloniki, founded in 1925, but without a faculty of theology until 1942. Generally, the international character of the sea-port of Thessaloniki has contributed to a more open style of theology than at Athens. There had been a centre of study, under the Ecumenical Patriarchate, at Halki since 1844, although this was closed by the Turkish government in 1971 and suggestions that it might be re-opened have not yet borne fruit. Three seminaries were founded in quick succession in the USA. The first was Holy Cross, which was established in 1937 by the Greek archdiocese, and is now located in Brookline, Massachusetts; its teaching has an ecumenical dimension since it is part of the Boston Consortium of Theological Schools. St Vladimir's and St Tikhon's were both set up in 1938 by the Russian Metropolia. Of these, the teaching, writing and publishing work of St Vladimir's have assisted in the development of twentieth-century Orthodox theology. Many of the best known teachers at St Vladimir's, including John Meyendorff and Alexander Schmemann, had studied in Paris. The St Vladimir's tradition has not been limited to Russia. It has published works of leading Greek theologians: John Zizioulas, Christos Yannaras, Panagiotis Trembelas, George Mantzaridis, and Fr Vasileios of Iviron.

So, from the modest beginnings in the foundation of an academy dedicated to St Sergius of Radonezh and a Western-style university at Athens, there has been a steady growth in a style of Orthodox theology that is both traditional and contemporary, rooted in the East and also open to the West. The achievement of a relatively small number of theologians with relatively modest financial resources has been of considerable importance to world Christianity.

Some modern theologians and their work

The early years of the life of St Sergius' was dominated by a debate between two different approaches to the theological tradition. This debate influenced the future direction of Orthodox theology. The two main protagonists were the two great leaders of the Russian theological revival: Sergei Bulgakov and Georges Florovsky.

Sergei Bulgakov was the Dean of the Institute, a speculative writer and a creative and visionary theologian who was daring and controversial in his thinking. The part of his thinking which provoked controversy concerned the idea of Divine Wisdom or sophiology.

In the New Testament, Christ is, in one verse, identified with the figure of wisdom – 'wisdom is justified by her works' (Luke 7.35). This identification was made also in the dedication of the cathedral of Haghia Sophia in Constantinople to Christ. In contrast, however, Russian cathedrals dedicated to Haghia Sophia (among them those of Kiev and Novgorod) were associated with the Mother of God, thus introducing an element of femininity into the idea of Wisdom. There are, in Russian culture, further feminine influences on the figure of Wisdom, which was as a result associated with ideas as diverse as Mother Russia, the Holy Spirit, the Church and the Mother of God, and were reflected in Russian iconography. The figure of Wisdom appeared in the writing of Vladimir Soloviev (1853–1900) and Pavel Florensky (1882–c.1937), but above all in that of Sergei Bulgakov. In Bulgakov's thought, the idea of Wisdom has a similar function to that of the divine energies in the thought of Gregory Palamas. It provides a way of speaking of God's immanence in the world while not compromising the total transcendence of the being of God – and Bulgakov once referred to the teaching of Palamas as an incomplete sophiology. Bulgakov had a deep concern for the created order, and saw it as transfused by God's presence. 'The world is not only a world in itself, it is also the world in God, and God abides not only in heaven but also on earth with man.'[9] So, he went on, God's relationship with the world – and us – is enclosed within God himself, so that we can speak of a divine presence in the world which responds to the divine presence in God. God's love is not only an active going forth, but also a receiving and responding as well – a 'loving of love'. Sophia is the mysterious and unknown element in God who is the responding to love, alongside but distinct from the outpouring of love. It is something of the divine which is breathed into us and which makes us capable of loving in return. So Sophia can show herself under several guises, as the Mother of God at the Annunciation, as the Church, as the origin from which creation emerges and as the end towards which it tends. So far so good – this is similar to the language of Gregory Palamas about the divine energies. But Bulgakov goes further, speaking of Wisdom having a personality and a face. She is a subject – a *hypostasis* – indeed a fourth *hypostasis*, and Bulgakov, in his early work, did use this language. It was at this point that the notion was seen as spilling over into error – not conforming to the teaching of the Church.

Georges Florovsky (1893–1979), like many others, disagreed strongly with this thinking. While he did not leave St Sergius' as a direct result of this debate, he moved to Yugoslavia during the Second World War and, afterwards, decided not to live in Paris again. Instead he went to America,

[9] S. Bulgakov, *The Wisdom of God* (London 1937), p. 34.

where he became Dean of St Vladimir's Seminary from 1949 to 1955, before leaving for Holy Cross Seminary, then Harvard and Princeton Universities. He is seen by many as the most influential figure in Orthodox theology in the twentieth century. His books are rooted in the teaching of the Fathers, whom he saw as providing a continuing and authentic witness within the Church, a witness that is contemporary rather than purely historical. He used the phrase, 'forward to the Fathers'. He also wrote about Russian traditions of theology and philosophy, in his *Ways of Russian Theology* (1937), which enunciated his alternative understanding to that of Bulgakov. He rooted his work in an understanding of the Church as a charismatic community, in which the fullness of salvation is given and appropriated. From this perspective he made an active contribution to the ecumenical movement. His importance lies in his work on the patristic tradition within a framework that was uncompromisingly Orthodox yet accessible to Western students.

Florovsky's work on the Fathers of the Church was followed by a succession of studies and researches on various theologians of the early centuries of the Church whose thought had been overlooked. An innovative and vibrant series of studies flowed from the new Orthodox theologians: John Meyendorff on Gregory Palamas, Vladimir Lossky on Dionysius the Areopagite, Basil Krivocheine on Symeon the New Theologian, and a succession of works on Maximus the Confessor. Figures who had been virtually forgotten became prime sources for the theology of the twentieth century.

Amongst these books, one of the best known is the hugely influential *Mystical Theology of the Eastern Church*, written by Vladimir Lossky (1903–58), who was part of the Paris circle but, since he remained within the jurisdiction of the Patriarchate of Moscow while most other émigrés left, was not a teacher at St Sergius'. His book is a systematic summary of patristic thought, re-affirming the apophatic or negative theology of Dionysius, and the Hesychast spirituality of Gregory Palamas. Lossky wrote it as an Orthodox riposte to modern Catholic theology based on Thomas Aquinas, while staying for long periods in a Benedictine monastery. Even this work which was so influential in reaffirming the Orthodox theological tradition came from the surroundings of a Western religious community. Here, too, the interaction of West and East was producing a style of writing and thinking that was no longer a captivity to the West, but a new exposition of the patristic tradition stated from within a Western environment and in collaboration with Western writers.

All these have been conscious of the opportunity and difficulty of presenting and articulating Orthodox theology in this Western context. The background of Western thinking – existential philosophy, Biblical criticism, liturgical renewal – was a strong influence on the work of these institutions, sometimes as inspiration and encouragement, sometimes as a stimulus for debate and disagreement, yet always present. Yet this was no 'Western captivity'. The quality of creative research and the clear reliance on the teaching of the Church Fathers ensured that the theological work of the twentieth century reflected the distinctive traditions of the Orthodox Church and made its own contribution to the task of theological reflection – which transcended denominational boundaries. Scholars from a Western background have shared in the task of rediscovery of some of the great writers of the Byzantine period. Fifty years ago, Maximus the Confessor was little read in East or West, but as a result of a wide interest including important studies by Lars Thunberg, a Swedish Lutheran, and Hans Urs von Balthasar, a Roman Catholic, his thinking has become familiar and has influenced modern theology.

Modern Orthodox theologians have not continued the repetition of Western theology and have remained critical of, for example, much Western liberal scholarship. But many of those working in the West have been convinced that the task of Orthodox theology is to present the teachings of the Fathers, and to interpret these in the context of the present times. Their prime audience is the members of the Orthodox Churches, but they have also contributed to Western theology, in, for example, the ecumenical movement.

The vigour of the Orthodox theologians writing in the West should not lead us to ignore the traditions of historic Orthodox nations. These provide somewhat different styles of writing and different ways of understanding and doing theology. They have emerged from a more Eastern environment, and are less easily available to a Western reader. Among them are Dumitru Staniloae, from Romania (1903–93); Justin Popović, from Serbia (1894–1979); and Matta el-Meskin, or Matthew the Poor, from Egypt (1919–).

Staniloae was born in Transylvania, the province of Romania with a rich mixture of Orthodox, Roman Catholic, Greek Catholic and Reformed communities. He was conscious of the position of Romania as a meeting point and melting pot of Christian culture, bridging the Greek and Slav cultures within Orthodoxy, and East and West within Christianity. He spent most of his life teaching first at the Theological Institute at Sibiu (1939–47) and then at Bucharest (1947–73), except for a period of imprisonment for his faith between 1958 and 1964. He was dismissive about this, calling it an 'experience like any other, except somewhat difficult for my family', but admitted that it was in prison that he was able to practise the almost continuous recitation of the Jesus Prayer. He produced two massive works. The first was a translation of the *Philokalia* into Romanian, adding to the Greek original large sections of the writings of Maximus the Confessor, Symeon the New Theologian and Gregory Palamas, as well as lengthy footnotes of his own. The Romanian edition consists of 4,650 pages in ten volumes. His second huge work is a three-volume *Dogmatic Theology*, which he called 'a concrete theology, a theology of experience'.[10] Quoting extensively from Eastern, and some Western, sources, especially St Maximus, it discusses the nature of our relationship with God, presenting a synthesis of patristic and contemporary themes in a way that is both authentically traditional yet startlingly contemporary.

Justin Popović was born in Serbia. As a student, he developed a deep love of Russian Christianity and an equally deep distrust of the West. With his studies in St Petersburg cut short by the Revolution, he was sent to Oxford. His thesis on the religion of Dostoevskii was failed because he refused to modify his criticism of Western religion. He continued his passionate and fearless criticism of all he saw as opposed to Orthodoxy, which included the Communist government of Yugoslavia, and as a result he spent the last years of his life under a form of house arrest at the monastery of Ćelije, south of Belgrade. He too wrote a dogmatic theology, in two volumes, the *Orthodox Philosophy of Truth* (1934–5), and a massive twelve-volume *Lives of the Saints* for each day of the year, collecting texts from many sources and languages. His writing is poetic and lyrical, inventing a style both sensitive and passionate. Implacably hostile to the West and to ecumenism, he was a man of great hospitality and gentleness, which I benefited from during a memorable weekend spent in his company in 1974. He was a spiritual father to several young monks who have now become leaders of the Church.

---

[10] One volume has appeared in English: *The Experience of God* (Brookline 1994).

Like the theologians working in the West, his writing was rooted in the traditions of the Church, the lives of the saints and the ascetic disciplines of the monastery, but the setting of his life was in a more traditional Orthodox environment. His approach is close to that of the writing which has emerged from the Russian Orthodox Church Abroad, the conservative tendency of Russian Church life. It has produced a large volume of ascetical works, lives of the new martyrs under Communism, and anti-Western polemic, which has circulated widely inside Russia.

If a main characteristic of the Western school of Orthodox theology is the recovery of the Fathers, then the main characteristic of these two writers is the inseparability of theology and spirituality. Both the life and the writing of these two hugely influential figures are living testimony to the location of theology. It belongs not in the university but in the monastery and – in the twentieth century, we must say – the prison. The knowledge of God is the experience of God, approached by prayer, asceticism and liturgy. Justin Popović began his life as a teacher, but his main contribution was as a spiritual father, writer of saints' lives and as a witness against the government.

The final writer to be considered here comes from a Middle Eastern, Oriental Orthodox background. Father Matta el-Meskin, or Matthew the Poor, is from Egypt, a Coptic (and so a non-Chalcedonian) Orthodox. He was a pharmacist in Alexandria and in 1948 became a monk. He left his monastery in the 1960s to live as a hermit in the desert following the traditions of the desert Fathers. Then in 1969 he was asked to move to the ancient and decayed monastery of St Macarius in the wadi el-Natrun. It is now a thriving community, and has been the focus for a revival of monastic life in Egypt. He has written extensively: a major work entitled *Orthodox Prayer Life* (1952), commentaries on several books of Scripture, works on monastic history, and numerous essays, articles and sermons. The themes of his work include a clear insistence on the Incarnation of Christ as bringing together heaven and earth, and God and man. From this he writes, with the clarity and realism of the desert, of communion between God and humanity, the Eucharist, prayer and asceticism – all ways in which the Incarnation is worked out in human lives. Especially remarkable is the blend of influences in his use of Scripture. Protestant missions were active in Egypt, and at one stage missionaries from the English Church Missionary Society managed the Coptic Orthodox Theological School. This led to a much greater emphasis on the Scriptures within Egyptian Christianity. However, rejecting both Protestant fundamentalism and liberal criticism, Fr Matta is able to read the Bible with the corporate and repetitive attention of the monk, as well as using the resources of the old Alexandrian traditions of spiritual and allegorical interpretation. Also, of course, the Islamic reverence of the text of the Holy Book has entered deeply into Egyptian society. Here is a creative blending of diverse elements of the Christian tradition leading to a revival in Coptic theological writing.

It would be convenient to add here a representative of the remarkable theological tradition of Ethiopia, but this is not a Church that encourages creative and original individuals, certainly not individuals whose writings might be translated. The tradition can easily be overlooked. Visitors to Ethiopian churches and monasteries are often met by clergy, sometimes begging for their church, poorly dressed, and clearly used to a simple lifestyle. It is easy to dismiss them as uneducated and unsophisticated, and so it comes as something of a surprise to discover that many of them have spent many years in disciplined study, according to a clearly defined syllabus, which – if completed – would require over forty years of study. The clergy of the Church are, in fact, intensely well educated but within a tradition completely foreign to Western models. The programme includes languages (mainly Amharic and Ge'ez, or classical Ethiopic), the liturgy (or *qidasse*), church music (called *deggwa*), liturgical dance (*aquaquam*), poetry (*qene*), and commentary on Scripture. The student travels from teacher to teacher, begging for his food, and serving at the monastery where the subjects are taught. The culture is oral, and even young boys can recite large parts of the Bible by heart. The traditional patristic interpretations of Scripture are memorised by students, and lively debates especially about Christology take place between the different schools of interpretation. Theological traditions are associated with the major regional centres of Church life and arouse passionate debate. The topic of the anointing of Christ at the Baptism and how this can be integrated into a single-nature Christology has been the subject around which much discussion has developed.

Whereas in the West, individual creativity and an independent mind are encouraged and nurtured, such qualities are frowned on in a traditional society such as Ethiopia. Instead, the purpose of the education system is to ensure that the student is enrolled and fully integrated into the society of which he is a part. The heritage, which includes religious, poetic and musical elements, becomes a part of the student's consciousness and he becomes a part of it. While few Eastern Churches encourage a theological tradition quite so complex and sophisticated, the corporate or communal aspect of theological learning remains significant. The importance of the corporate can be seen in the Syriac tradition with its emphasis on learning the language and the hymns of the great Syriac poets, especially St Ephrem. It is present – perhaps in an attenuated form – in the seminaries of Russia and other Eastern countries where teaching is oral and students are expected to memorise and repeat lessons read out by teachers. While recognising the importance and creativity of the theological thinking and writing produced within the Orthodox Churches in the twentieth century, the place of the traditional, oral, memorised culture needs to be valued and affirmed.

5

Icons: revelation in image

'What is a house without icons? A shelter for animals.' These words of
a villager from Euboea in Greece express something of the grace which
reaches out through the icon and show how the presence of the icons
surrounding the worshipper both in church and at home are a part of
Christian living that is indispensable. Icons have an almost universal
appeal. The immobile, luminous, hieratic and stylised way of depicting holy men and women has become known beyond the cultures that
produced them. An icon condenses all that many people find attractive
about Orthodox worship: the colour, the beauty, the simplicity. Some
Orthodox deplore this popularity of icons which, they feel, tears the
icon out of its theological and liturgical setting, and so removes its character as an icon. Others are less fastidious, and mass-produced prints of
Western religious art are popular and revered as icons in all Orthodox
countries. In the non-Chalcedonian Orthodox Churches, icons have a
much less important position and are little used.

Amidst this variety of understandings, the icon retains its place as an
essential part of at least the Chalcedonian Orthodox tradition. It is more
than a painting. What this 'more' is will be the subject of this chapter.

The revelation of God's salvation is communicated within the tradition of the Church, and this is contained within the text of the Bible,
recognised by the Church as the Word of God. The Church came to a
fairly rapid agreement as to the identity and content of this part of the
tradition, and which writings should be included in the text of the Bible.

Within this consensus of agreement, there were some variations in the canon of Scripture across the Christian world. The text of the Bible used in the East was that of Alexandria, which includes the Apocryphal books. There is some disagreement over the status of 4 Maccabees, included in an appendix in the Greek Bible, and 4 Esdras, found in Russian Bibles. The book of Revelation has an ambivalent position, being included in the Bible but not read in church. The Ethiopic Bible contains several more books not found in the Scriptures of other Churches. These local differences do not affect the clear understanding by all that the words of Scripture have a revelatory character, and that those reading the words of the Bible have access to the thoughts and purposes of God. The books of the Bible are in a class of their own, different from other books.

But the tradition can be passed on through other methods. Words alone do not have this privileged character of conveying God's message. The content of the Christian tradition is that Christ brought salvation to the world, and it is this salvation that is the subject of the teaching of the Church. In the view of the Fathers of the Orthodox Church, the scope of the tradition should not be too closely confined – and should be broad enough to include all that the apostles handed down both by word of mouth or in written texts. It is certainly conveyed through Scripture, but is not restricted to Scripture. Among other possible means of communicating the revelation of God are pictures, visual images. Can the images or pictures that are seen by the eyes depict the things of God, as the words of Scripture tell of the thoughts of God? The development of iconography should be understood in this context and as an attempt to answer this question. Icons can be seen as the pictorial equivalent to the Bible. So it is clearly the case that iconography has little to do with art, and everything to do with theology. The word 'icon' is a transliteration of the Greek *eikon* or 'image', and the iconographer is literally the *writer*, rather than painter, of images.

It is clear that visual images came to be accepted quite quickly into the Church. They are found in many places and situations, and are rooted in a number of different sources. There are traditions that locate the beginning of iconography in the New Testament. An early account tells of King Abgar of Edessa, who asked Christ to come to heal him of his leprosy. Instead Jesus sent a cloth on which his features were marked. This cloth was kept in a succession of places until it disappeared from the records in the eleventh century, and is the origin of a type of icon called *acheiropoetos* or 'not made with hands'.[1] Another tradition recounts that three icons of Mary were painted by St Luke, of which two are traditional types of icon, the *hodigitria* and the *eleousa*. A large number of these icons attributed to the Evangelist are to be found in many countries – in Kosovo, in Syria, in Cyprus, and elsewhere. Eusebius of Caesarea, writing in the fourth century, reports seeing a statue of Jesus and paintings of Christ and the apostles.[2] The wide distribution of an early iconic style of painting is indicated by the discovery of the synagogue of Dura Europos, on the eastern Syrian frontier, and now preserved in the National Museum in Damascus. Although Jewish, the frescoes, dating from the third century, closely resemble later Christian frescoes and icons, and are even inscribed with the subject's name. Another influence on Christian painting were the images of the Roman Emperor, who was seen as a deity, and whose pictures influenced the portrayal of Christ, the true emperor. Among the earliest icons which have been preserved are those in the monastery of St Catherine on Mount Sinai. Some of these were painted in the sixth century, indicating that the practice of painting icons was well established by then.

THE ICONOCLAST CONTROVERSY

In the eighth century a movement developed which tried to remove icons from the churches. It was initiated by two successive Emperors who came from the northern part of Syria, in the east of the Empire: Leo III (717–41) and Constantine V (741–75). Iconoclasm, or the breaking of icons, led to a crisis that disrupted the Byzantine Empire for more than a century.

The roots of the iconoclast movement have been hotly debated. It has been suggested that iconoclasm reflects the outlook of a Semitic rather than Greek culture. It combined, first, a religious longing for a pure spirituality that ruled out material images, with, second, the teaching of Monophysite groups (or some of them) with their emphasis on the one nature of the Word of God, and not the human Jesus, as the subject of Christ's experience, and also with, third, the influence of Judaism and Islam with their clear prohibitions of images. No doubt these were all significant influences on the complex culture of iconoclasm, but the strongest argument of the iconoclasts was that God disapproved of icons.

---

[1] Evagrius, *Ecclesiastical History* 4.27.   [2] Eusebius, *Ecclesiastical History* 7.18.

The movement started in response to the shocking and rapid military conquests of the Arabs – who were clearly non-iconic in their uncompromisingly spiritual faith – and surely, it was argued, their success should be interpreted as a sign of divine favour, and hence of divine disfavour towards the icons. And then, when the island of Thera in the Aegean Sea (also known as Santorini) blew up in a huge volcanic eruption, this was interpreted as a further sign of divine wrath. It was clear that something had to be done to remove the icons from the Empire. The first icon to be formally removed was the mosaic icon of Christ above the *Chalke*, or brazen door, of the imperial palace in Constantinople, and other removals of icons followed. To confirm the rightness of the policy, the iconoclast Emperors Leo III and Constantine V turned out to be quite successful, achieving some military advances and bringing a measure of stability to the Empire.

Iconoclast teaching was set out at a Council in 754. The Emperor Constantine V addressed a treatise called the *Queries* to the Council, and this was the basis for the *Horos* or Definition. Constantine argued that if the icon is to be a true image, it must, first, have the same nature as the prototype. Then its holy status has to be confirmed through it being blessed by a priest. On this basis the only true icon or image of Christ is his body and blood in the Eucharist. In addition the church building, in which Christ is made present, and the cross, the sign of our salvation, can be considered as true icons. Pictures could, according to some iconoclast theories, be hung in churches, but they have an educative function only, and so should be positioned high on the walls to avoid any risk of veneration.

Within popular devotion, the icon was more than a picture and more than an educational tool. The *Life of St Mary of Egypt* tells how Mary, who had lived as a prostitute, visits the church of the Resurrection, or Holy Sepulchre, in Jerusalem. She wants to go in to worship at the place of Christ's crucifixion but feels a force like a hand pressing her back and preventing her from entering. In her desperation she turns to the icon of the Mother of God set up by the door and she promises that she will repent and change her way of life. She looks into the face of the figure on the icon, and then is able to enter the church.[3]

---

[3] *The Life of Mary of Egypt* 15–17, translated in B. Ward, *Harlots of the Desert* (London 1987), pp. 46–8.

This popular story shows the atmosphere of devotion within which the great defenders of the icons wrote. The icons are not only improving pictures, but are ways in which the bringers of salvation – Christ, the Mother of God and the saints – are present to us. So John of Damascus writes: 'I have seen the human image of God, and my soul is saved.'[4] At issue is the presence of Christ in the church, and so the salvation of the believer. This concern lies behind the important decision of the Council in Trullo (or Quinisext Council – so called because it was held in a chamber or *in trullo*, or because it completed the work of the fifth and sixth Councils of 554 and 681) of 692, that Christ should not be depicted in symbolic form, for example as a shepherd or a vine. 'We decree that henceforth Christ our God be represented in his human form and not in the ancient form of a lamb.'

The most influential defenders of icons, sometimes known as iconophiles or iconodules, are St John of Damascus and St Theodore of Stoudion. John (*c*.665–749) was born in Damascus and had been in the service of the Arab caliph. He lived in the monastery of St Sabas, east of Jerusalem, and so outside the Byzantine Empire and beyond the reach of iconoclastic imperial regulations. He developed a theological defence of icons in the form of three apologies. Theodore (759–826) was an abbot and reformer of monastic life who presided over his monastic community for eighteen years.

The arguments can be briefly summarised.

First, while it cannot be denied that the Old Testament forbids the making of idols, this refers to the period before the Incarnation and cannot properly be applied to the new dispensation when God appeared in human form, and in any case, as well as prohibiting images, Moses also gave directions for the building of the Temple which included a number of images, including cherubim. The Biblical prohibition of idols refers to objects falsely taking the place of God, not to proper representations of Christ.

Second, God is, it is clear, uncircumscribed and infinite, but in becoming human he assumed human qualities. Among these is the quality of being circumscribed and also of being describable. The painting of icons is a consequence of the Incarnation. John of Damascus wrote: 'In former times God, being without form or body, could in no way be represented,

---

4 John of Damascus, *Apology* 1.22 trans. Anderson, p. 30.

but today, since God has appeared in the flesh and lived among men, I can represent what is visible in God. I do not worship matter, but I worship the Creator of matter who became matter for my sake and who through matter accomplished my salvation.'[5]

Thirdly, worship is offered to the subject depicted on the icon and not to the icon itself. This is the important part of the argument and the part which can seem unfamiliar today, since it is an idea rooted in Platonic ways of thinking, in which spiritual realities are made known within some kind of material form. So if the icon of Christ is given the name of Christ and recognised as being Christ, then it represents Christ and has the *hypostasis* or identity of Christ, although it does not have the essence or nature of Christ. Therefore clearly it is proper to venerate the icon, since we are venerating the figure represented on it. As a refinement of this, John of Damascus – and later and more systematically Theodore – distinguished two levels of worship: *latreia* or adoration, which is properly directed to God alone; and *proskynesis* or veneration, which can be offered to the icon (and, in secular usage, had referred to veneration directed to the Emperor).

The battle over icons continued intermittently from 726 to 843, with two distinct phases. In the first period, the Emperors Leo III and Constantine V carried out a spasmodic removal of icons from churches and public places, and persecuted those who refused to comply. This ended in 780 when the Empress Irene, the mother of the new ten-year old Emperor Constantine VI, became regent and convened a Council at Nicaea in 787, which supported the use of icons and became recognised as the Seventh Ecumenical Council. Then there was a second phase of iconoclasm under the Emperors Leo V (813–20) and Theophilus (829–42). After Theophilus' death it was another woman, his wife the Empress Theodora, who became regent on behalf of Theophilus' two-year old son Michael III, who finally ended the controversy on 11 March 843, the first Sunday in Lent, when Orthodoxy was restored. It is not clear exactly what happened on this occasion. It involved a Church Council of modest proportions and a new Patriarch called Methodios. Later it was celebrated by the reading of a document stating the true faith called the *Synodikon*. This event is referred to as the Triumph of Orthodoxy and remains an important celebration in the life of the

---

[5] John of Damascus, *Apology* 1.16 trans. Anderson, p. 23.

Orthodox Church today, with the *Synodikon* recited on the First Sunday in Lent. From that date, the arguments of the iconophiles came to be accepted by the Church, and icons have had a growing part to play in the life of the Chalcedonian Orthodox Churches.

THE NATURE OF AN ICON

It was clearly understood that the icon belonged within a theological tradition and was a part of the revelation of God's salvation. It gains this character by being a faithful reflection of the prototype. An icon painter was not free to construct a scene image using his imagination, nor could a human model be used. Instead he had to follow the tradition handed down as to how each person or event should be depicted. The importance of this tradition is that it makes clear that the icon is a true representation of the person concerned, and shows what the subject actually looked like. Somebody looking at an icon of, say, St Peter sees the features and the appearance that St Peter had in his lifetime.

In later centuries the tradition came to be written, and volumes of directions and descriptions of icons became popular. These ensured that the traditional features of the saint and the composition of the scene were not adulterated by individual preference and imagination.

While it matters that the tradition of the icon originates in the event, it is not intended to be a photograph. It is the deified nature of the person that is depicted, and so it is a theological creation. The style of the painting conveys this. Since divine light is the presence of God, the icon is built up of a series of many layers of paint, beginning with the darker and finishing with the lightest colours. This shows the light gradually shining out of the person, giving a luminous effect. The lips are closed, because the icon reflects the silence of God rather than the words of humanity. It is two-dimensional and flat, with the background of the building or the landscape presented in a stylised form behind the figure. And it is often pointed out that the lines of perspective are strangely reversed so as to give the effect of drawing the viewer into the icon. The figure itself looks out at the viewer, addressing him and inviting him to look and see face to face. The eyes will be large, the lips narrow, the features refined, the mouth unsmiling.

The painting must be done carefully. The Russian Council of One Hundred Chapters (1551) decreed that the painter must be 'meek, mild, pious and not given to idle talk or laughter, not quarrelsome or envious, not a thief or murderer'. He will prepare to paint with prayer and also pray during the process of painting. The materials used are natural, with boards of well-matured, non-resinous wood and several layers of chalk-based ground called gesso, with paint made from egg, water, vinegar, and natural pigments. Afterwards the icon is covered with a varnish made from linseed oil. There are many layers and stages, and the completion of an icon requires at least a year. The last part of the painting is the addition of the name of the saint or title of the subject.

Once finished the icon is taken to the church and blessed by a priest. It can then be placed on the wall of a church, or in the corner of a home; and be drawn into the liturgical life of the church, making God present, and working the salvation and deification of the worshipper. Through the icon, the person portrayed becomes present to the worshipper, who will become acquainted with the saints and be able to spend long hours at his ease before the visible images of invisible presences.

The clear directions might imply that icons have a static lifeless quality to them, but the viewer finds a variety, sensitivity and creativity in icon painting. The tradition has grown and developed in the life of the Church.

Two well-known icons are the Vladimir Mother of God and the Old Testament Trinity painted by Andrei Rublev. Now both are in a secular art gallery – the Tretiakov Gallery in Moscow, which houses a large collection of works of Russian art. They are well known from reproductions, but the originals have an unexpected beauty and power when viewed face to face, even though they are no longer in a church setting. Often people are to be seen praying in front of them. They illustrate some of the history of icon painting.

The Vladimir Mother of God is an example of one of the main types of icon of Mary, the *eleousa*, or in Slavonic the *umilenie*, or in English the loving kindness. It depicts the Mother of God holding the Christ child, who has his arms around her neck. She inclines her head towards him, expressing a tenderness that is not only directed to her child, but extends to the worshipper as well. It was painted in Constantinople in about 1130 and was sent later sent to Kiev in the Ukraine, from where it went to Vladimir in 1155, and then to the Kremlin in Moscow in 1315. After the Communist Revolution it was placed in the art gallery. In 1993 it was taken out of the gallery and used by the Patriarch Alexis II to bless the city of Moscow during a time of crisis. Its long history and its perambulations show how an icon is more than a painting but becomes the protecting presence of the Mother of God. By a strange irony the final stage of its life has been significant in that the covering of precious metal over the icon allowing only the face and hands to be seen (known as *oklad*) has been removed and it has come to be valued as a supreme work of art, assisting in commending the icon to non-Orthodox Christians (for better or worse).

The other icon is the Old Testament Trinity of Andrei Rublev (*c.*1370– 1430). Andrei is one of the few icon painters to be known by name. He was a pupil of Theophan the Greek and worked with him. It was forbidden – in the Chalcedonian but not other traditions – to depict God himself, since he is unknowable. So the three angels who visited Abraham were seen as a proper depiction that indicated the godhead (Genesis 18.1–8). Andrei Rublev's version was painted around 1425 for the iconostasis of the church of the Holy Trinity at St Sergius' Monastery, and retains the traditional content but uses a simplicity and movement lacking in earlier examples. Each angel represents one of the Trinity, although there has been some debate about which angel corresponds to which person of the Trinity, and the circular form of the arrangement and meeting of the direction of the eyes shows both the unity of the Trinity and the relationships of the persons.

From 1700, Western forms of representational art influenced icon painting in, for example, the work of the Russian, Simon Ushakov. In the twentieth century, painters began to study again the work of Byzantine iconographers and to return to traditional models. Among the influential figures of the Russian diaspora are Gregory Krug and Leonid Uspensky; in Greece, Photis Kontoglou; in Russia, Fr Zinon; and in Serbia, Pavle Aksentejević.

Outside the Byzantine Orthodox Church icons are much less prominent, so much so that the question of the survival of iconoclasm presents itself. In Syria, for example, the attention of the worshipper is drawn to a Bible placed on a stand in the centre of the church and which is reverenced by those entering and leaving the church. The sanctuary is often raised on a low platform and is demarcated from the nave by a curtain. There may well be pictures around the walls, and these are sometimes surrounded by coloured or flashing lights, and will present a mixture of traditional iconographic scenes, with both Syrian and Western saints (St Francis of Assisi is a popular subject). Churches in Egypt, Ethiopia and South India present a similar appearance. It would seem that the reticence and suspicion of images, which lay behind the iconoclast controversy, remains within these Churches, which have lived for so long within, or close to, Muslim communities. Pictures have been borrowed from elsewhere – either Orthodox or from Catholic sources – and have given rise to a lively and vibrant Church art, but this cannot be considered as constituting an iconographic tradition. The use of icons is similar to that within a moderate iconoclasm, with pictures accepted for didactic reasons so long as they are not venerated.

6

Monasticism: shaping of saints

A difficulty in discussing the Christianity of the East is that words do not quite mean what you want them to mean. This is because the available vocabulary has become so overlaid with connotations and nuances from a Western environment that it does not refer easily to the different context of Eastern society and faith. The word 'theology', which has been used for want of any better word, is a case in point. In the East the theologian is committed to the experience of God not to the discussion of God. The saying that summarises most succinctly this quality of theology is the often repeated sentence of Evagrius of Pontus: 'A theologian is a man who prays truly, a man who prays truly is a theologian.'[1] The place where theology – meaning 'God-words' – is carried out is therefore the monastery and not the university.

Monasticism is an institution that contributes to the life of the Orthodox Churches in many ways. Without monasteries it is hard to see how the life of the Church could be maintained. Although there have been times when monasticism has all but disappeared, such as in the Russian and Armenian Churches under the Soviet regime, it has been rapidly restored as soon as conditions permitted. The briefest of visits to one of the historic Orthodox societies will quickly show how important the monastery is to the faith of the people. It is a versatile and comprehensive institution, fulfilling many functions within the Church. First,

---

[1] This text is in Evagrius, *153 Chapters on Prayer*, included in the *Philokalia*, ed. G. Palmer, vol. 1 (London 1979), p. 62.

the monasteries are places of liturgical celebration, where the full round of liturgical worship will be observed in a way that is not possible in a parish church. The influence that was exercised by the monasteries on the Church's worship during the Byzantine Empire is still effective today. Not all monasteries have the resources for full and exact liturgical worship, and few communities are able to spend as many hours in church as the larger communities on Mount Athos, but people continue to look to the monastery as a place of spiritual strength, encouragement and example of liturgical vitality. Then, secondly, the monasteries are centres for education and study, providing teaching for all age-groups, from basic instruction in reading for young boys to seminary training for future monks and clergy. This also, thirdly, gives them a role in providing the future leaders of the Church, especially since only monks can be consecrated as bishops. (According to Orthodox tradition, clergy are divided into two types: married clergy and monks. The decision is made at ordination, and since a monk cannot marry, this has the consequence that marriage has to precede ordination.) Fourthly, they are centres of hospitality and pilgrimage, often with relics, miracle-working icons or a holy spring as a focus for this. Not least, they can be places of economic activity, providing employment for local people on monastic lands or a market for the exchange of goods.

Each monastery has a life and character of its own, and there is enormous variety. There are secluded and remote monasteries, with a strong contemplative tradition, such as those on Mount Athos; urban monasteries, which can be centres for the administration of the Church; and small village monasteries with one or two monks providing a centre for local Church life. Generally there are more nuns than monks, although nuns tend to lead a more secluded life. There are no monastic orders like those in the West, although large monastic houses can influence others by providing an example to be followed or even the written *typikon* or rule for other neighbouring monasteries. Generally, a vibrant and growing monastic life suggests that the Church is also in a healthy state.

THE BEGINNINGS

The honour of being the first monk is usually assigned to Antony of Egypt (*c*.250–356), although earlier examples of this style of living can be found. As a young man in Egypt, Antony was struck by two passages of Scripture which he listened to in church: 'If you wish to be perfect, go sell your possessions, and give the money to the poor ... then come, follow me' and 'do not worry about tomorrow' (Matthew 19.21 and 6.34).[2] He decided to carry out these precepts as literally and fully as he could, and so, at the age of 20, he went out into the desert and lived alone, devoting himself to ascetic struggle. First he moved to a hut on the edge of the town, then to a deserted fort deeper in the desert, and finally to a still more remote spot. He lived like this for eighty-five years, dying at the advanced age of 105. This outwardly undramatic life story, told by no less a biographer than Athanasius of Alexandria, was laced with some spicy detail about demons appearing in a variety of forms, and with a long improving sermon, and, with these additions, turned out to be the most read book in the Christian world after the Bible. Many people followed Antony's example, causing the desert to become like a city, as the saint's biographer put it. An essential part of Antony's style of life was solitude, and he found himself penetrating ever deeper into the desert in an unsuccessful effort to escape the crowds wanting to visit him, or to join him.

The second great monastic pioneer was Pachomius. In his case it was not the words of Scripture that attracted him but the Christian way of life. As a soldier in the Roman army he was amazed at the love and practical charity which a local Christian community showed to him. So much so that he was converted to this impressive faith and founded a community at a village called Tabennisi in the Nile delta to live out the gospel. He was joined by others, and eventually founded ten more communities, including two for women. He wrote a set of instructions for living this kind of life, which were developed by his successor Theodore into a more structured rule.

There has been much discussion about the historical roots of Christian monasticism. The blend of self-discipline and celibacy, separation from the secular world and the search after truth can be identified in different religions and philosophical schools, but the monastic movement emerged as an identifiable institution in the century following the lives of the two early monastic saints, Antony and Pachomius. It happened as the Roman Empire was adopting Christianity as its approved religious faith in the course of the fourth century, just at the time when we have

---

[2] Athanasius, *The Life of Antony* 2–3, trans. Gregg, p. 31.

observed that the distinctive forms of Eastern Orthodox Christianity were taking shape.

It has been suggested that the monk was the successor to the martyr.[3] According to this theory, the Christian communities had grown used to the idea that a faithful following of Christ would lead them – as it had Jesus himself – to an innocent death at the hands of the state authorities. Under Roman Emperors such as Aurelian, Diocletian and others, there was sporadic but violent persecution, which provided a kind of ever-present background threat that shaped the way the early Church understood its discipleship. Once the persecutions of the Roman government ceased, there was a disorientating hole in the centre of Christian devotion. So the monastery became the place of a kind of living martyrdom, where everything was sacrificed for God. This was often described as a 'white martyrdom', with white as the colour of virginity and celibacy, rather than 'red martyrdom', with red as the colour of blood. (This colour symbolism was extended in the Irish Celtic tradition to include the 'green martyrdom' of the wandering rootless life.)

But the rise of the monasteries needs to be seen in a wider perspective – as a response to respectability and universality, rather than simply to the end of persecution. In the years after Constantine, the Church became established, and was expected to be inclusive of all the inhabitants of the Empire. As a result, the Church found that it had lost its character as a distinct community, gathered out of the pagan society. It now saw its vocation as being the 'soul' of the body of the Empire, providing a spiritual dimension to a universal world society. Within this Empire, monasteries formed distinct and separated communities, keeping alive the idea of a band of disciples bound by ties of brotherly love and a keeping to God's ways. They had a 'maximalist' approach to Christian living within a Church which was adapting to become a part of imperial society.

Both Antony and Pachomius were moved simply by the hearing and experiencing of the gospel. Their way of life was a response to this call. Later, in the West, Benedict would write his Rule of Life as a simple way for beginners. They did not see themselves as doing anything extraordinary, but simply living in obedience to the gospel. The purpose of the monasteries was to enable people to follow Christ sincerely.

---

[3] This is set out in E.E. Malone, 'The monk and the martyr', *Studia Anselmiana* 38 (1956), pp. 201–25.

Looking back from the vantage-point of many centuries of history in which monastic communities have become a regularised and disciplined institution within the Church, and also have evolved a rather specialised and distinctive style of living, it is easy to forget that there was nothing very unusual about the early monasteries. The monks lived either alone or in groups; they ate a diet of bread or vegetables which was much the same food as any peasant farmer would enjoy; their clothing was a simple robe as worn by the poor; the work was either in the fields or in workshops following simple crafts such as basket-making or rope-making. Products were taken to the local market. The monastic vocabulary reflects its location in the ordinariness of contemporary society. The word cell, for example, is the Greek *kellion*, which describes a small house in which the labourer both slept and worked, a common sight in any Greek or Middle Eastern city. And a lavra, or *laura*, the name used for a community of hermits, was an alleyway or path in which rows of *kellia* were grouped, equivalent to the Syriac *souka*, or suq, which is a familiar sight for visitors to Middle Eastern towns. A Greek farmer recently visiting Mount Athos is reported to have noted with surprise that the monk's life was just like his own – except that the monk prayed in the church for several hours before setting out to the fields.

THE MONASTERY IN SOCIETY

As enclaves of total Christian living, monasteries were integrated into the life of society and functioned within it. Communities provided care for the poor, hospitality for travellers, and work for the unemployed. It is noticeable that at times of economic uncertainty vocations to the monastic life increased. The beginnings of monasticism took place at a time of social dislocation in the Empire, when, in the east, tax burdens were increasing and putting extreme pressure on small farmers and, in the west, the arrival of barbarian tribes was eroding the territory of the Empire. The monastery, with its religiously based community and the benefactions it began to receive from the imperial government or wealthy individuals, was an attractive option to those who were struggling to make ends meet. Evidence from the early saints' lives show a flexible approach to membership, with monks going out of the monastery when there was work in the fields around and returning after the harvest, or with labourers choosing to live attached to the monastery which provided them with a livelihood.

Monasteries have continued to function effectively as part of the wider society around. Take, as one of many examples, the desert monasteries of modern Egypt, where the monastic tradition has been renewed over the last thirty years. A visitor to the large monasteries of the wadi el-Natrun, of Macarius or Anba Bishoy, finds not only a thriving community of monks but something more like a town in the desert, with workmen and other staff, centres of care for the disadvantaged, workshops for local crafts, and a thriving agricultural settlement, pioneering techniques of desert agriculture. The skills developed by the monks are being exported to new towns being set up in arid regions.

The government of the Empire was well aware that monasteries were useful. As well as being agents of social care and providers of employment, they also played a strategic role in the defence of the Empire. Since monks liked living in remote and hostile environments, they proved to be helpful in securing and extending national frontiers, as they established themselves in marginal areas, which provided both a line of defence against invading tribesmen and the beginnings of new settlements that could extend the territory of the state. As a result, many monasteries in eastern frontier regions of the Byzantine Empire in the fifth and sixth centuries were given military support by the Emperor as part of the campaign against Persian and then Arab invaders. And later, in medieval Russia, the monks were the advance guard of the expanding new kingdom. Defence and support were provided not only by the physical presence but more especially by the prayers of the monks. In conferring benefits on the Great Lavra of Mount Athos in 978, the Emperor Basil II wrote: 'What foundations are to a house and oars are to a boat, the prayers of the saints are to the Empire. Who can doubt that what the sword, the bow and military strength could not achieve, prayer alone has brought to pass easily and splendidly.'[4]

So far, the remarks made apply more to the larger communal monastery, which provided a clear focus for the life of the wider community. But the hermit, leading a more solitary ascetic life, had a place in the local community too. In a fascinating article, Peter Brown compares the holy men of fourth- and fifth-century Syria to the figure of the rural

---

[4] See K. Ware, 'St Athanasios the Athonite, traditionalist or innovator?', in A. Bryer and M. Cunningham (eds), *Mount Athos and Byzantine Monasticism* (Aldershot 1996), pp. 3–16 at p. 7.

patron, who had been a leader of the community providing assistance to the villagers in a variety of ways.[5] He shows how the holy man, living a solitary and ascetic life in the neighbourhood of the village, became the broker of a form of power that enabled the community to function. He adjudicated in legal disputes, arranging tax remissions with local government officials, as well as working healings and exorcisms. The blend of being an unusual figure coming from outside the community, living a detached life, and having access to a form of power and authority allowed the holy man to become a blend of village doctor, judge and representative to the government.

The place of the holy man in Russian society shows how this social role continued to develop and evolve. The best loved of Russian saints is Seraphim of Sarov (1759–1833). After entering the monastery of Sarov as a novice in 1778, he experienced a longing to live a solitary life as a hermit, and soon after 1794 he was granted his desire. Then came twenty-one years spent living alone in extreme asceticism, apart from a few short intervals when he left his seclusion for medical treatment or other reasons. Once he prayed for a thousand days standing or kneeling on a rock. In 1825 he left his solitude and began to receive visitors and to give advice. Huge crowds came to him, sometimes, we are told, as many as five thousand in a single day. He had the gift of discerning their situation and need, and of giving the right advice to them, as well as gifts of healing and exorcism. He once said: 'achieve stillness and thousands around you will find salvation', a clear statement that the most solitary life is lived among and for others.

The monastic life grew up within society, and was a part of it. It proved to have chameleon-like qualities, adapting to take on many different forms – often apparently contradictory. So monasteries both upheld the government of the day and also challenged it; monks withdrew from society and sought out remote and inaccessible places, and also thrived in large towns; monks were glad to be simple and uneducated, but monasteries also provided centres for study and scholarship. Monks and the monasteries in which they live belong at the heart of the life of the Church and of society.

---

[5] P. Brown 'The rise and function of the holy man in Late Antiquity', *Journal of Roman Studies* 61 (1971), pp. 80–101.

SOLITUDE AND COMMUNITY

Within monasticism there are two distinct forms of life. They are shown by a comparison of the lives of Antony and Pachomius, and could be understood as representing the two great commandments of Christ: first, to love God with all the heart, soul, mind and strength; and, second, to love one's neighbour as oneself. The first is the eremetical or hermit life (from the Greek *eremos* or wilderness), and the second is coenobitic or communal life (from the Greek *koinos bios*, or common life). For the hermit, to follow Christ meant to leave the world and to live in solitude, following the example of Elijah or John the Baptist, or other desert dwellers – although this was not necessarily a turning away from the neighbour, since prayer for the neighbour is a form of love for the neighbour. For the monk in a coenobium, or communal monastery, the Christian life was based on love and love could only function within a community. For Basil of Caesarea the community was a holy place, where the Christian life was fulfilled. He warned the brothers not to try to make progress too quickly and to outstrip the others. If you live alone, whose feet can you wash and how can you learn patience if there is nobody to irritate you?[6] The solitary and communal ways of life were both recognised to be authentic, and although at first sight communal and solitary lives might seem incompatible, the Church succeeded in nurturing both within the one institution.

The solitary life was always valued, and even had a certain priority. The name 'monk' is the Greek *monachos* or solitary. An even more suggestive mixing of ideas is conveyed by the Syriac *ihidaya*. This has the basic meaning of 'single' but in various senses: single as unmarried, or single as single-minded and resolute, or, in a theological context, single as only-begotten, so referring to Christ. The use of this word suggests that the monk's way of following the Only-begotten is to be single-minded in living the celibate life. Another phrase from the Christian Syriac vocabulary was applied to the precursors of the more formal monastic communities. They were called the *bnay qyama* – or sons and daughters of the covenant – and were groups of men and women who had made a *qyama* or covenant at baptism and were living together in informal ascetic groups. So again we are shown that the monastic life is simply an attempt to live the Christian life to the full.

---

[6] Basil, *Moralia* 30–4.

The two ways – of solitude and community – have remained within monasticism. Sometimes a third style of life, the laurite, is mentioned, but this is really a blend of the other two. The laurite life was common in Palestine, where hermits lived together in colonies, in caves in the side of a ravine, or in huts around shared community buildings. They met on Saturdays and Sundays for a common meal and for worship, but the rest of the week they stayed alone in their cells. More often a monastery would offer opportunities for both the solitary and the community option to its members by setting up a number of hermit cells attached to the coenobium. So when St Athanasios (of Athos, not Alexandria) founded the Great Lavra on Mount Athos in 963–4 (not a real lavra in the technical Palestinian sense), he allowed a number of hermits to live in the hills around. In Egypt the solitary tradition has always been strong. Around the monasteries of the wadi el-Natrun, an old monastic settlement dating from the fourth century, the walled monasteries are surrounded by flat desert sand in which many hermitages are scattered at various distances, with the tracks of vehicles taking food and other supplies to the hermits inhabiting them clearly visible.

An uncharacteristic clash between the two forms of life developed in Russia in the fifteenth century in the dispute between the Possessors and the Non-Possessors. Nil of Sora (1433–1508) was a disciple of Sergius of Radonezh who travelled from Russia to Mount Athos, where he learned Greek, studied the writings of the Fathers, and then returned home. On his return he found himself one of the best educated members of the Church and settled in the north-west of the country by the river Sora. He taught a strict ascetic life-style, combined with a gentle and compassionate approach to others, especially towards any who had fallen into sin or error. His teaching is given in an unoriginal but very attractive set of writings which form a kind of rule, but one that encourages each individual to develop his own way of living. He requested that, after his death, his body should be 'cast into the desert to be eaten by beasts and birds, for it has sinned much before God and is not worthy of a funeral'.[7]

An alternative approach was taken by another disciple of St Sergius, Joseph of Volotsk, also named after his monastery of Volokolamsk,

---

[7] The Testament of Nil is conveniently translated in G.P. Fedotov, *A Treasury of Russian Spirituality* (London 1950), p. 133.

which lies to the west of Moscow. Joseph presided over large communal monasteries, although the word 'presided' is something of an understatement for his leadership style. All aspects of life were regimented and prescribed. He permitted no women or beardless youths to enter inside the monastery walls. He supported the strict punishment of heretics and offenders, promoting a Russian version of the Spanish Inquisition. While this approach can seem less attractive than that of Nil, Joseph's monasteries became centres of charitable work, supporting hospitals and orphanages. He ordered huge stockpiles of food to be held so that nobody would be turned away hungry. His life tells how the last piece of food was distributed, and the monks protested vigorously. 'Pray', he commanded, and soon carts of grain arrived at the monastery gates.[8] At a Council in Moscow in 1503, Nil attacked the monasteries that owned lands, wanting them to return to the simple life of poverty, but the lifestyle of Joseph gained the support of the state. The northern hermits who followed Nil were later persecuted. Some would see the inability to harmonise these two traditional strands of monastic life as a cause of some of the later difficulties of the Russian Church in the schism with the Old Believers and later its domination by the Tsar.

THE EXTENSION OF MONASTIC LIFE

It used to be thought that monastic life spread from Egypt to other parts of the Empire, but it seems as though the life blossomed in many different areas spontaneously at around the same time. Chariton, who founded three monasteries near Jerusalem, and Julian Saba in Syria were more or less contemporary with the two Egyptian pioneers. Both Syria and Palestine became major centres of monastic life.

The Palestinian desert is a relatively narrow stretch of arid land offering a varied terrain ranging from agricultural land to grazing country, to arid desert. It proved popular as a final destination for travellers who came to Jerusalem as pilgrims. A multi-ethnic group of monks settled around Jerusalem, Bethlehem and Jericho. Among the leaders were Euthymius, an Armenian, and Sabas, a Cappadocian. The monasteries were Greek-speaking and had an international flavour. They were loyal to Chalcedon, and prevented a local Syriac Monophysite community

---

[8] For this event, see G.P. Fedotov, *The Russian Religious Mind*, vol. 2 (Cambridge, MA 1966), p. 267.

developing, as happened in other parts of the eastern end of the Empire. Their nearness to the city of Jerusalem ensured that they were in touch with ecclesiastical life in Jerusalem and in Constantinople. The vigour of the monasteries survived the Arab invasions, and for a while expansion continued. The monastery of Mar Saba south-east of Bethlehem became a centre of Christian Arab learning, and leading writers such as John of Damascus, Theodore of Abu-Qurrah and Andrew of Crete were monks there. Its liturgical practice influenced all Chalcedonian Orthodox worship. It still stands, overlooking an impressive section of the gorge of the brook Kidron, and now contains a dozen or so monks.

Syria had a reputation for wild and strange ascetic achievements. Theodoret of Cyrrhus (c.393–c.458) wrote a series of brief lives of some of the holy men he had known, called the *Historia Philothea*, a source for early Syrian ascetic life. Later, large communal monasteries were founded which became centres of scholarship after the Arab conquests, such as Qenneshre on the river Euphrates south of Samosata. Further east, the mountainous plateau not far from the Christian centres of Nisibis and Edessa was known as the Tur Abdin or Mountain of the Servants. It combined wild and rugged hilltops with pasture and agricultural land, and proved suited to those seeking an ascetic life. Many monasteries were founded, which had a large impact on the development of the Syrian Church. Abraham of Kashkar, the ruins of whose monastery – known as Mor Abraham – can still be seen on Mount Izla, initiated a reform of monastic life that spread through the Church of the East. The monasteries of Mor Gabriel, at Qartmin, and Deir el-Zaffaran, at Mardin, along with others, became centres for the Syrian Orthodox Church. The Syrian non-Chalcedonian Church was progressively excluded from the cities, which were controlled by Byzantines and then Persians and Arabs, and so retreated to the hills, building up a rural base in the monasteries from which the villages could be evangelised and ministered to.

In Constantinople a famous early community was that of the *Akoimetoi*, or Sleepless Ones, which became a fervent supporter of the Council of Chalcedon, as well as developing a gruelling – and unusual – liturgical routine. As late as the seventeenth century we hear of them celebrating hourly liturgical worship. Under the Byzantine Empire, monasteries spread fast. By the end of the sixth century there were sixty-eight monasteries in Constantinople. Further growth took place under Theodore (759–826), who moved into the abandoned Stoudion monastery and built up a community of around six hundred monks, influencing a cultural revival and encouraging further monastic foundations.

In all parts of the Eastern Christian world, monasticism spread. Each area still reveres its monastic saints who encouraged the rapid growth of communities. In Egypt a successor of Pachomius, Shenute or Shenouda of Atripe, attracted all elements of society, but especially any who were rejected and cast out, to his communities. He was the first to set out a written form of the monastic profession, which was the beginning of the monastic vows. In the far north of Russia, Sergius of Radonezh founded the Holy Trinity monastery, now a large centre not far from Moscow, and encouraged a spate of monastic foundations in the cold northern forests of Russia, extending even to the Solovki islands of the White Sea. At the other end of the Orthodox lands in Ethiopia, Tekla Haymonot, a name meaning 'the tree of faith', extended the territory of the medieval Ethiopian kings through his foundations at Debre Libanos and elsewhere. The list could be extended indefinitely.

A special place belongs to Mount Athos, a thickly wooded peninsula ending in a high rocky peak protruding into the Aegean Sea east of Thessaloniki. Ascetics were often attracted to mountains, and in many regions a hilly area was a centre for the monastic life. Mount Olympus, on the edge of Bithynia, was the home of fifty monasteries by the eighth century, and a centre of the inconophile party. Paroria in northern Bulgaria became known for the asceticism of its monasteries from the eleventh to the fourteenth century, from where Hesychast traditions spread across the Balkans and into Russia. But the most famous of all the monastic mountains is Mount Athos, which has remained as the main centre for Orthodox monasticism into the modern age. Hermits had settled there for many years before the first big coenobia were founded in the tenth century. They were attracted by the isolated position, the thick woods to the north and the caves on the rocky slopes to the south of the mountain. The peninsula became a monastic republic with monks from many countries, including briefly a community of Latin-speaking Benedictines. No women are allowed on the mountain. It has become an international centre, with Serb, Bulgarian, Romanian and Russian as well as Greek monasteries. It gained huge benefactions from the imperial government and from wealthy Byzantines but lost these under the Ottomans, who otherwise left the monasteries relatively undisturbed. There are many communities, ranging from the large coenobia to isolated hermitages perched on steep cliffs. All fall under the jurisdiction of one of the twenty ruling monasteries that send representatives to the governing council of the mountain. The fortunes of the mountain have fluctuated. Under the Ottomans the idiorrhythmic way of life, in which each monk lives as he wishes in his own apartment, became popular and helped to attract especially wealthy monks. This helped the communities to adapt to the conditions of the time. By 1833 numbers had sunk to under a thousand, but with the arrival of Russian monks, among others, this grew by the end of the century to 7,432, with more Russians than Greeks. This was followed by decline and then revival. The mountain of Athos is one of the truly international treasures of the Chalcedonian Churches, and its vitality is sometimes seen as an indicator of the health of the Church as a whole.

Monastic life spread west as well as east. John Cassian (360–432) was a determined traveller. He lived in monasteries in Bethlehem and Egypt, then became a deacon in Constantinople, went on a diplomatic mission to Rome, and then continued his travels even further west to found a monastery at Marseilles. He wrote several books which conveyed Egyptian ascetic ideals to a Western audience. Among those he influenced was Benedict (480–547), who lived as a hermit and then as the leader of a community. Benedict attracted many disciples and formed them into twelve monasteries, each with an abbot and twelve monks. His *Rule* contained guidance in living the ascetic life. He arranged for Cassian's writings to be read in the evenings, which perhaps suggests that he considered these to contain more advanced material to which his monks progressed after they had mastered his simple way. Benedict's Rule became the model for all monastic life in the West. In the West, the name 'monk' is usually reserved for those who follow some form of the Benedictine Rule.

As in the East, ascetic life in the West had a dynamic missionary impulse. Around the time of Benedict, monasteries were growing in the west of Europe – in Ireland, Scotland and northern England. The monks of this region were travellers, and took their ascetic version of Christianity to other parts of England and to north Germany, and even as far as what is now Switzerland. Since carvings of St Antony of Egypt can be found on carved crosses in Ireland, it is clear that there was communication between different parts of the Christian world, and an exchange of ideas and practice. The monastic life exercised its attraction in all parts of

Christendom, although in the West it was to develop in distinctive ways with the evolution of the different orders of monks, friars and active religious orders. The existence of monastic communities in the British Isles and their links with Egypt has encouraged modern Orthodox in these regions to see their Church as reviving – after a long gap of many centuries – a tradition of Christianity that was thriving in Britain before the arrival of St Augustine of Canterbury's mission from Rome in 596.

STYLITES AND FOOLS

The monasteries were a part of the communities that they served, enabling people to live a Christian life, in a full, committed but unspectacular and inconspicuous way. But as well as this wholesome normality, there is a continuing tendency to encourage monks and nuns to experiment and discover bizarre forms of ascetic behaviour. These should be seen as an aspect of the hermit life, an extension of the drive which pushed the monks out of the settled urban communities into the desert.

The desert has been recognised as the proper home of the monk. It has exercised a magnetic pull, beckoning the ascetic who found it a place both attractive and frightening. It is the place of beauty and purity. Origen said of John the Baptist, 'he left to go into the desert where the air is purer, the sky is more open and God is closer'.[9] It was also experienced as a place of religious purity, as the Israelites remembered as they looked back longingly from their settled life in Israel to the time when the Children of Israel were in the wilderness with Moses. But it was also a place of struggle. Conditions were harsh, with extremes of heat and cold, and the difficulty of finding food and water. It was challenging psychologically, too, facing the monk with his weaknesses, fantasies and fears – and these often appeared as devils testing the monk.

The geographical desert could take many forms. In Egypt it was the arid wastes that began over the hill from the Nile river basin and stretched for miles; in Syria it was the mountains, which were wilder than the fertile plain below; in Palestine it was the marginal grazing lands between the Judaean hills and the Dead Sea. In Russia it was the *pustyn*, or desert, of the virgin forests of the north.

[9] Origen, *Homilies on Luke 11*.

The desert was the place for the hardened ascetics. Syria, especially, had a reputation for extreme feats of endurance. A large monument north of Aleppo in Syria commemorates the most famous of them all. Qal'at Sima'an is a complex of four large basilicas built in the form of a cross meeting at a central place where, today, a boulder is set on the base of a pillar. This boulder is the site of the column on which St Symeon Stylites (*c*.390–459) spent thirty-six years of his life. He had been a monk for twenty years, living a life of growing asceticism. His life on his pillar was an extension of this. Originally the column was quite low, but he gradually built it higher and higher until it was over 15 metres. Huge crowds came to consult him, and he became a widely known attraction for travellers and pilgrims. He had many imitators. As late as 1848 a recluse living on the top of a pillar was encountered by a visitor to Djqondidi in Georgia in the Caucasus.

Another form of sanctity were the 'fools for Christ', in Greek *salos* and in Russian *yurodivii*. The fool pretended to be mad, challenging and opposing the conventions of normal living. He, or she, scandalised people, but performed exorcisms, healing and conversions. Symeon Salos (d.590) arrived in the city of Emesa, tied a dead dog to his belt and rushed around the streets. He lived in the open air, ate sausages on Good Friday, disrupted church services by throwing nuts at the worshippers, and went into the women's section of the local bath-house. Only a few realised that this was his chosen ascetic path, and that he healed many and brought others to faith in Christ through his teaching and prayers. There was a continuing tradition of fools for Christ in Russia. Basil the Blessed, or Blazhennii (d.1552), walked naked through the streets of Moscow, threw stones at the houses of the respectable and wept over those of sinners. He encountered Ivan the Terrible as the Tsar was destroying the city of Novgorod, and offered him blood and raw meat, showing him in a vision the souls of those Ivan had butchered being welcomed into paradise. The colourful cathedral in Red Square in Moscow is dedicated to St Basil the Blessed. Fools became common in Russia, developing, like Basil, into critics of the misdeeds of kings.

It would be right to consider Mother Maria Skobtsova from the twentieth century as an example of a modern fool for Christ. Born Elizaveta, she arrived as an émigré in Paris in 1923, with her (second) husband and three children. Some years later the couple became estranged, and in 1932 she made monastic vows, living in a house in the Rue Lourmel in Paris with her son. She shocked people by often missing the church services, by smoking – even in public, and by spending time alongside the destitute, sometimes sleeping among them under the bridges of the river Seine. Along with others she founded Orthodox Action to provide care for all kinds of persons in need. After the arrival of the Nazis she extended her care to Jews, whom she protected and helped to escape. Her arrest followed in February 1943 and she spent the next two years in Ravensbruck concentration camp, where she died on 31 March 1945, voluntarily taking the place of another prisoner chosen for the gas-chambers. It was the day before Easter and the day before the Red Cross arrived to begin the release of prisoners. Fellow-prisoners later wrote: 'All that was left of her was skin and bone, her eyes were festering, and she exuded that nightmarish sweet smell of those infected with dysentery... She radiated the peace of God and communicated it to us.'[10]

The clue to understanding these unusual forms of discipleship – and indeed the solitary way of life generally – is to remember that the love of Christ does not naturally fit into sensible worldly patterns of living. It cannot be contained in any vessel and cannot be made sense of. It overflows from any human and rational limits and appears in unexpected and bizarre forms.

TEACHERS AND GUIDES

The monasteries have produced many writers who have become guides to the ascetic life. The distinction between theological and spiritual writing is not clear-cut. Since theology is understood as a way of referring to the encounter with God, then the practical works that encourage the monk in doing this are just as much theological works as the most philosophical works of Christology or Trinitarian theology. The Fathers of the Church such as Athanasius or Gregory of Nyssa or Evagrius of Pontus wrote extensively and are respected as ascetical teachers as well as dogmatic theologians. Several writers have gained a special respect within the monastic tradition, and have become recognised as authoritative guides to the practice of prayer.

One of the most widely read teachers of the spiritual life was Evagrius (c.345–99). A native of Pontus, he was influenced by the great Gregory of

---

[10] S. Hackel, *A Pearl of Great Price* (London 1982), pp. 144, 148.

Nazianzus and accompanied him to the capital when he became bishop of Constantinople in 380. An unfortunate love-affair caused him to leave and go to Jerusalem. From there he went to the new ascetic settlements of Egypt, where he stayed from *c.*383 until his death.

In Evagrius' system of thought, God originally created pure intellects, but these fell away from him, and as they fell they became clothed in various kinds of bodies: angelic forms for those who fell least, human bodies for those who fell further, and demonic shapes for those who fell further still. The purpose of the Christian life is to regain the unity of the mind with God, which is achieved as we gradually free ourselves from the prison of the body and allow our intellects to return to their origin – and herein lies our salvation. In describing this process Evagrius sets out some of the approaches that have become classic ideas of Christian spirituality.

First, he says, there are three stages or processes in the spiritual life, often called the three ways, a schema which later writers were to repeat again and again. They are, first, *praktike*, or the ascetic life of cultivation of virtue; second, *physike*, or the knowledge of created beings; and thirdly, *theologike*, or knowledge of God. The spiritual life develops in stages which, for Evagrius, have an intellectual orientation; this is especially marked in the second stage, which is characterised by a true knowledge of the nature of things. The mind then moves beyond this state of resting in a grasp of the true reality of the created order, to encounter God himself.

Second, he had an acute understanding of human behaviour. He described how disordered thoughts (*logismoi*) are of eight kinds: gluttony, fornication, love of money, depression, anger, accidie (a kind of reluctance to do what needs to be done), vainglory and pride. These eight thoughts or passions were adapted in the West, and reduced by the removal of the rather monastic vice of accidie, to become the familiar Seven Deadly Sins. Evagrius teaches that thoughts, once welcomed, become more firmly rooted until they become passions, or disordered affections and sicknesses of the soul. The purpose of the first stage of the ascetic life is to struggle against these until the soul acquires the state of *apatheia*, or passionlessness. This state became the goal of much monastic endeavour, and is sometimes criticised as being a negative state of absence of any feeling. Surely, it is objected, we should try to cultivate positive feelings of pure love rather than a state of uninvolved apathy.

But Evagrius' *apatheia* should be seen as transcending rather than re-moving human passion, equivalent, on some views, to the sinlessness of Christ. For Evagrius, it was essential to become free of bodily passions, so that the intellect can move on to the true knowledge of spiritual beings and thence to reunion with God who is pure knowledge.

Evagrius was a controversial figure in his own lifetime. He gathered a group of more intellectual monks around him, who were misunderstood and rejected by the simpler Egyptian monks. The controversy that he evoked continued after his death, and he was declared a heretic by, or possibly after, the Second Council of Constantinople in 553. His works mostly survived in Syriac translations or in books believed to be by somebody else, Neilos. His approach was later re-worked by Maximus the Confessor, who replaced Evagrius' emphasis on knowledge with that of love exercised through the will, and the three ways became purgative, illuminative and unitive.

The next set of writings to be considered to have had a lasting in-fluence also date from the second half of the fourth century: a set of fifty homilies and some other writings attributed to a certain Macarius. For five hundred years, until an Athonite monk, Neophytos Kavsoka-livites, challenged the assumption in the early eighteenth century, it was believed that these writings were the work of the great monk of the Egyptian desert, Macarius the Egyptian (*c.*345–410), so the author of these writings has sometimes been called the pseudo-Macarius. In fact, internal evidence makes it clear that they were written in eastern Syria or Mesopotamia by a monk who has remained anonymous but who was a powerful preacher with a gift for vivid imagery and clear statement of the principles of the spiritual life. He has a unified holistic understanding of human nature, drawn from his Semitic background. In a Biblical way of thinking, he sees the heart as the thinking, feeling, willing centre of the human personality, and emphasises the need for inner purification as well as external works. The heart, along with everything else in the world, is taken over by sin and its effects. Baptism does not remove sin but introduces a new principle, an 'image of perfection'. Our life is a struggle – to practise virtue, to learn to love, to pray – and slowly good-ness is nurtured and matures. Perfection is given by God as we struggle, and it may be possible in this life or may be given in the next. This theme of good and evil co-existing in the human heart and the need for con-tinual vigilance and struggle provides a simple account of the spiritual life, and one well suited to a monastic society; then the promise of light filling the heart provides a goal to attract the ascetic.

While he does not emphasise the distinction between the mind and the body, which is a presupposition of Evagrius, and before him Origen, nor does he use the imagery of divine darkness, associated with the writing of Dionysius the Areopagite, who was active at around the same place and around the same time (also found in Gregory of Nyssa, with whom there are close parallels), the ascetic programme taught by Macarius values the same virtues of vigilance, humility and persistence in prayer.

There has been debate about how far Macarius was a Messalian, a sect which emphasised continual prayer at the expense of sacraments and the ecclesiastical hierarchy, from the Syriac *messalleyane* or 'those who pray' (in Greek *euchites*). Some manuscripts attribute his writings to a certain Symeon of Mesopotamia, who seems to have been a Messalian although nothing is known of him, and there are similarities between the Macarian body of writings and the Messalian teachings. Further, some parts of the Macarian corpus (but not the homilies) were condemned as Messalian at the Council of Ephesus (431). All this goes to show that the Macarian writings emerged from the same culture and society which gave rise to extreme and heterodox movements; and that boundaries between orthodoxy and heresy were not clear-cut. The Macarian homilies went on to influence Eastern spirituality – especially St Symeon the New Theologian and Gregory Palamas – and also Western spirituality, and are often quoted by, for example, John Wesley.

Isaac of Syria was born on the shores of the Persian Gulf, in what is today Qatar. Some time between 660 and 680 he was consecrated bishop of Nineveh, in the Church of the East, but resigned after only a few months, for reasons we do not know. Then he lived in various Persian monasteries. His writings were translated into Greek at the monastery of Mar Saba near Jerusalem in the eighth or ninth century, and then into other languages. His writings consist of two collections of material. The first has been often published, but the second was lost until a manuscript was recently discovered in the Bodleian Library in Oxford by Sebastian Brock – an exciting discovery of an important work previously thought to have been lost.

Isaac's writing contains many themes familiar to Syriac literature. He teaches that tears and mourning will be a constant part of ascetic life – a monk was often called in Syriac *abila* or mourner. He also describes a state different from and above that of prayer which he calls wonder, the equivalent to the Greek *ekstasis* or ecstasy. But most characteristic is his consistent emphasis on the Christian life as love. This leads him to develop a distinctive understanding of the nature of hell. He considers that even hell is the product of divine love, and is a preparation for the future rather than a punishment for the past. The idea that there is a divine retribution is, for him, blasphemous, and he believes that both heaven and hell are instituted by God's grace to bring all creation to perfection. So all will be saved.

This is in contradiction with traditional Christian teaching, within which the pains of hell are a divine punishment for sin. Some have maintained that Isaac's uncompromising insistence on the power of God's love, to the exclusion of all that opposes it, emerges from his own experience of God in prayer, and was seen as heretical and led to the rapid ending of his tenure of the bishopric of Nineveh. Others suggest that it was a usual feature of the teaching of the Church of the East. It has not detracted from – and indeed has contributed to – his popularity as a spiritual writer.

So these three great figures in the history of spirituality all have a suspicion of heresy attached to them: an Origenist, a Messalian, and a Nestorian with universalist leanings. This suggests that asceticism was an easily adapted way of life which was shared across the ancient world, and was wider than any doctrinal approach or framework. It is doctrinally neutral, and the root insights of self-denial, fasting, hard work and prayer have a wide, and perhaps universal, appeal.

JOHN OF THE LADDER AND THE ORAL TRADITION

These three sets of writings provide consistent theories of the spiritual life. Another tradition teaches a more hand-to-mouth, experimental style of living. Groups of ascetics gathered around a holy man, and tried to follow his example. These informal communities were shaped by personal example and instruction. Here teaching was not passed on by books but by word of mouth. Monks sought out those more experienced and asked for a 'word', which would be a simple and practical piece of guidance. This short instruction would then be lived out by the disciple. Thus developed the 'apophthegmatic' literature or sayings of the fathers. These are collections of sayings and anecdotes arranged either in alphabetical form attached to the names of the monks to whom they were attributed or by theme. At first sight they are random and miscellaneous, but patterns emerge and the main teachings soon become apparent. The personal style of teaching has become deeply rooted in the Eastern Church, when the words and example of a practised ascetic are seen as authoritative, and a disciple relies on the personal direction. The disciple places his trust in his teacher, reveals his inner thoughts and feelings to him, and obeys him implicitly. Here, in the desert, is the beginning of the practice of spiritual fatherhood, which was to be developed by Symeon the New Theologian, and the *startsy* of the Russian *pustyn*.

One of the classic texts of Eastern monasticism belongs in this tradition of apophthegmatic literature. Although the first freshness of early monasticism had passed by the time the *Ladder of Divine Ascent* was written, the immediate personal style of teaching remained. The sayings of the fathers were remembered, written, reflected on and added to, to provide a growing corpus of wisdom. Lying between the deserts of Egypt and Palestine is the mountainous region of the Sinai, its associations with Moses combining with its rocky mountains to make it an attractive home for monks. Little is known of the life of the abbot of St Catherine's Monastery, John Climacus or John of the Ladder (*c*.579–649), apart from his authorship of the *Ladder*. The book is divided into thirty sections or 'steps', each devoted to a virtue or vice of the spiritual life. Although presented as a progressive system, it is really a collection of sayings, often unsystematic and random, although presented with acute psychological analysis. The attraction of this style of writing, which can be used by each according to his own needs, is shown by its popularity. In many monasteries it is read in its entirety each Lent.

Thus the main features of Eastern spirituality appear at an early date. Already by the end of the fourth century the way of monastic life was established, and a developed literature in place. Later writers drew freely on these and other sources. The speculative philosophical elements of Evagrius were ignored and later anathematised, but the next generation of writers proved to be adept at selecting the passages of Evagrius' writings they found helpful and discarding the rest. So collections of advice and encouragement were produced. These are often based on certain virtues to be cultivated and vices to be removed. The monk becomes a person who has a certain way of being before God. He will be a person of obedience and humility (emphasised by monastic authors), tears and mourning (especially among the Syrians), fasting and hard work (from the Egyptian sayings tradition), compunction and vigilance (more general attributes which came to be emphasised by later writers), and prayer and silence (increasingly emphasised).

HESYCHASM

Hesychasm describes the tradition of prayer which makes inner stillness its aim. The word Hesychasm is derived from the Greek *hesychia*, or silence, or quiet. The word can be used in several contexts. It can describe the way of life based on silence, which can be seen as something external, such as the life of the hermit rather than the monk in a coenobitic monastery. Or it can refer to a more inner silence, and the discipline of trying to achieve an inner stillness and silence of the kind that Evagrius wrote about. Or it can also be the technique which developed so as to achieve this silence: the Jesus Prayer.

The Jesus Prayer consists of a simple phrase, often 'Lord Jesus Christ, Son of the living God, have mercy on me.' This phrase is repeated either for a set period of time or a set number of times, or it can be used at frequent intervals through the day, while carrying out any kind of activity such as the traditional monastic form of employment, the making of baskets or rope for the monks. It is simple, versatile and centred on the person of Jesus. It is also compact, with its expression of the longing for the mercy of God, and its statement of the doctrines of both the Trinity and Incarnation set out in just a few words. In a short formula, then, it summarises the attitude the Christian should have towards God. The simplicity of the Prayer combines suitability for a wide range of people with the possibility of continuing into the deeper regions of the silence of the heart to discover the simple knowledge of God. Used in this way it can be integrated with the act of breathing or the beating of the heart; and some of the medieval texts recommend certain physical positions. Because it has this capacity to lead into a deeper prayer, writers always emphasise that anybody trying to use the Prayer regularly should have an experienced spiritual father, or guide, to turn to for advice. It can be contrasted with the more mental or imaginative forms of meditation in which the person is encouraged to imagine and think about events from Christ's life or sayings from the gospel. Sometimes the Prayer has been compared to the meditation techniques of Eastern religions, and it is possible that there was some interaction between Hesychasts and Sufis, but this cannot be proved.

It is not hard to understand how the use of this style of praying developed in the monastic life of the desert. Monks worked and also spent long hours in solitude. They needed a way of praying that was demanding but did not require reading or the use of books. The repetition of a simple prayer was an obvious way of proceeding, and we can assume that this form of prayer was used from the very beginnings of the monastic movement. The use of verses from the Psalms was also common.

Diadochus of Photike, who lived in Greece in the earlier part of the fifth century, drew on elements in both Evagrius and Macarius to suggest a double strategy for achieving stillness: for the purification of the will, the monk should use active hard work; and for the purification of the memory, 'we should give it nothing but the prayer of Lord Jesus . . . Let the intellect continually concentrate on this phrase within its inner shrine with such intensity that it is not turned away to any mental images.'[11] Development of the use and teaching about the Prayer is found in the writings of three monks from Mount Sinai – St John of the Ladder, St Hesychius (eighth–ninth century) and St Philotheus (ninth–tenth century) – and it seems that the monasteries of Sinai transmitted the prayer of Jesus to later generations, although it had originated elsewhere.

Its distribution was local. It does not occur in, for example, the writings of Maximus the Confessor or Symeon the New Theologian. Not until the fourteenth century did the Jesus Prayer begin to spread beyond a few isolated monastic centres. Gregory of Sinai (d.1346) discovered the Prayer in Crete, and then came to Athos. Apparently he had to search hard before he found a monk able to instruct him in inner prayer. In 1335 he settled in Paroria on the borders of Bulgaria, and from there his disciples developed the use of the Jesus Prayer and Hesychast spirituality in Bulgaria, Serbia and Russia. It was not present in Syrian or Egyptian traditions. Indeed it is reported that the Jesus Prayer was not known in Egypt until the translation of *The Way of the Pilgrim* in the 1950s and it is seen there as a foreign innovation.

The practice of the Jesus Prayer is becoming more widespread. Still by no means universally known in the East, it is extending into Western forms of Christianity. It is becoming a way in which the contemplative strand of Orthodoxy is influencing the whole Church.

---

[11] Diadochus, *On Spiritual Knowledge and Discrimination*, 59, in the *Philokalia*, vol. 1, p. 270.

THE PATRISTIC REVIVAL

Under the Turks, monastic life was generally in a poor state. Among those responsible for its revival was Paisii Velichkovskii (1722–94). At the age of 13 Paisii went to study in Kiev. Here he found himself frustrated by the Latin classical influence on the theology taught and, after three years, left to become a monk. This decision began a life-long struggle to be able to live in silence according to the traditions of Hesychast prayer, although this was little understood at the time. He looked for an elder to guide him, but without success. He moved from one monastery to another, in the Ukraine, in the Vlach area of what is now Romania, and then on to Mount Athos. In 1747, at the tender age of 25, he gave up the search to find his spiritual father and started to live alone. Others gradually joined him, and in 1758 he was persuaded to accept ordination as a priest and to become the confessor of his growing monastery. He then founded the monastic community of the prophet Elias, which, in the next century, was to become a major centre of Russian monastic life on the Holy Mountain.

It was while he was on the mountain that he began the task which was to absorb him for the rest of his life: the correction and translation of patristic texts. This was a huge task, since many mistakes had crept in through successive copying and since so few manuscripts were available for cross-checking. As a result it was often hard to work out what the text meant. Few others shared his interest, being more preoccupied with coping with Turkish control and becoming caught up in the beginnings of the interest in Greek nationalism. In any case, few of them could understand the style of Greek in which the Fathers wrote. Paisii described his effort to improve his version of St Isaac the Syrian, who wrote, of course, in Syriac, but was read in defective Greek versions. For 'six weeks day and night I corrected my book of St Isaac the Syrian from another copy of it, believing the assertion of one person that the copy corresponded in all respects to the Greek text, but this labour of mine was in vain, for in time I came to understand that I had ruined my better copy from a worse one.'[12] However, he persevered and slowly built up his collection of books, and learned to correct and to translate them.

In 1763 Paisii returned to his former home in Vlachia, taking many of his monks with him, and settled first in Drogomirna, until twelve years

---

[12] See S. Chetverikov, *Starets Paisii Velichkovskii* (Belmont 1980), p. 122.

later the area was conquered by the armies of the Austro-Hungarian Empire and the community decided to retire to Orthodox Moldavia. There he lived in the monastery of Sekoul and then the larger community of Niamets until his death in 1794.

A similar revival movement had developed among the Greek monks on Mount Athos. This group was known as the Kollyvades, from the *kollyva* or sweetened boiled wheat used at memorial services for the dead. The group was given this name because of their resistance to a new practice which was developing of holding memorial services for the dead – for which money was often paid – on Sundays as well as the more traditional Saturdays. Their resistance brought the monks into conflict with the majority, who succeeded in expelling them from Mount Athos, a fortunate outcome since, as a result, the Kollyvades travelled through Greece spreading their ideas. As well as taking a firm stand in the debate from which they derived their name, they were enthusiastic educators, translated patristic texts on prayer, and encouraged the faithful to receive communion each time they attended the liturgy. They included Athanasios of Paros (1723–1813), who was the second – and last – head of the theological school on Athos; Makarios of Corinth (1731–1805), who was briefly archbishop of Corinth but then went to Mount Athos; Nikodemos the Hagiorite (1749–1809), who also translated Western spiritual texts; and Cosmas Aitolos (1714–79), who founded 200 elementary schools and ten higher schools in different parts of Greece. Makarios and Nikodemos collected, edited and introduced a series of patristic texts, especially those concerned with the practice of prayer, which they published under the title of the *Philokalia* ('love of the beautiful'). The texts concerned came from the fourth to the fifteenth centuries and consisted of selections from the Fathers on the ascetical way of prayer. It is a large collection and includes many of the classic texts on the Jesus Prayer. There are long sections by Maximus the Confessor, Symeon the New Theologian, Gregory of Sinai and Gregory Palamas, with other writings as well. It was published in Venice in 1782. Paisii produced a Slavonic version in 1793, a year before his death. The book has become an invaluable collection, widely used throughout the Orthodox Church. It is a large book, containing a huge amount of material, and is not easy to use without guidance, but it has enabled the recovery of the patristic theological tradition, and its availability and use is sometimes seen as an indication of the health of the Church.

In Russia, word of Paisii's Slavonic translation of the *Philokalia* was spreading, and reached the leading churchman in Russia, Metropolitan Gabriel Petrov of Novgorod and St Petersburg. In 1791 he sent a copy to Moscow, which was carefully checked by a panel of experts before being published in 1793. This was followed by a Russian translation by Bishop Theophan the Recluse in the following century. The book had an incalculable influence and was read throughout Russia. One of the most attractive accounts of its use is to be found in the anonymous *Tales of a Pilgrim*, which describes the experiences of a simple peasant who wanders through the countryside seeking true prayer and finally achieves this through the careful practice of the Jesus Prayer as described in the *Philokalia*.

Paisii's teachings were also spread through personal contact and instruction. The process of dissemination was providentially assisted by the secularisation of Russian monasteries under the Empress Catherine II (1762–96). Both the number and size of monasteries was restricted, with the result that many monks left Russia and entered monasteries abroad. By 1778 there were over 1,000 monks in Paisii's monasteries in Moldavia, most of whom were Russian. Later these monks returned to Russia, taking with them the disciplines of Hesychastic prayer and *starchestvo* or spiritual fatherhood. Many of Paisii's disciples became influential. For example, the *staretz* Cleopas had been on Mount Athos and at Dragomirna with Paisii, and returned to Russia, where he became abbot of the Ostrov Vedensky Monastery and introduced an Athonite style of monastic life. Another of his disciples, Macarius (d. 1811), became abbot of the Pesnoshky monastery, and from there the monastery of Optina was reformed. Thus a direct line of influence can be traced from Paisii to the celebrated Optina *pustyn* monastery. This pattern of descent was repeated many times, spreading a Hesychast style of monastic life through Russia.

Paisii's influence led to a resurgence of the practice of *starchestvo*. While the roots of spiritual fatherhood lie in the desert monasteries and it has been a continual part of the monastic tradition, it now became popular throughout Russia. The practice could refer to a formal relationship between a disciple and the elder, but also to the practice of travelling to seek the advice of a celebrated monk or ascetic. The subjection of the Church to state control made the freedom and holiness of the monk an attractive alternative form of authority and guidance.

In one of the monasteries founded as part of this movement, Optina, a succession of celebrated – and fashionable – elders gained a reputation for the asceticism of their lives and also for the individual guidance they gave. Huge numbers came to see the elder, and ask his advice on a wide variety of topics. The *startsy* seem to have been given charismatic gifts of healing, discernment and clairvoyance, providing random but clear and authoritative guidance to people they had never met before. The most famous of the Optina *startsy* were Leonid Nagolkin (1768–1841), Makarii Ivanov (1788–1860) and Amvrosii Grenkov (1812–91). Among the visitors was Fedor Dostoevskii the novelist, and the character in his novel *The Brothers Karamazov*, the elder Zossima, was based on one of the Optina *startsy*, Amvrosii. Dostoevskii was deeply committed to the Orthodox Church, but many have pointed out that there are several aspects of Zossima's teaching, such as his veneration of the earth, which are contrary to the clear Orthodox principles of the Optina elders. Valaam monastery north of St Petersburg was also a centre to which many people were drawn for advice.

The Bolshevik Revolution led to a new kind of sanctity in Russia, that of the martyr. But examples of the Hesychast tradition have remained. Silouan of Mount Athos was a monk at the monastery of St Panteleimon. His teachings have become well known in the West through his disciple Sophrony, who moved to England and established an unusual monastery at Tolleshunt Knights in Essex. Here the Jesus Prayer forms the basis of the prayer of the monastery, being recited corporately in the evening and morning on days when it is not a festival.

The Greek Kollyvades also encouraged the revival of the spiritual father, called in Greek the *gerontas*. An example of this tradition continuing is Fr Amphilochios of Patmos, who died in 1970. When farmers came to him for confession, he would often ask them to plant a tree as a penance, showing the love of the natural world, present in the ascetic tradition, which has been pointed out by recent writers on ecology.

Another famous *staretz* of modern times was the elder Cleopas of Sihastria (1912–98). He entered a monastery in 1927, at the age of 15, and took monastic vows nine years later. He was a *staretz* in the classical tradition, giving guidance to large numbers of people. During the period of Communist rule in Romania he was persecuted, and in 1953 he left the monastery and built himself an underground cell in the forest, where he lived for ten years, living off what he could find and from food brought from time to time by the few people who knew of his whereabouts. He later emerged from his retreat and lived in various monastic communities. He described his vocation as a *staretz* in words which summarise the Orthodox understanding of the role of the monk: 'The spiritual father is the soul of the monastery and the village. He should be a light which illumines the world by his life and by his words.' Fr Amphilochios, Cleopas and many others are a sign of the vitality and continuity of the Hesychast tradition.

7

Popular piety: people, places, pilgrimage

'Holy fasts are tokens of the transfiguration of the body; the holy relics which we kiss are gleams of the Resurrection; the holy sacraments are the sources of deification.'[1] In this sentence, the Russian writer Pavel Florenskii presents a vision of the world in which physical objects can become filled with holiness, or, to use a more poetic metaphor, chinks through which the light of God can shine into a dark world. It hints at a world of spiritual experience that is wider and more extensive than the formal structures and disciplines of the Church.

The historian Peter Brown has suggested, in several books and articles, that there is a tension between two forms of spiritual power, and even between two locations where this power is to be found. This suggestion concerns the Byzantine Empire but is relevant to the religious life of every age.[2] The power of God is usually expected to be found in the Church, which meant – in the case of the Byzantine Church – centralised in the capital, under the control of the Emperor and his bishops, and made present in the liturgical celebrations in the churches. But there was, and is, another kind of power found in different places. It is dispersed around the countryside, focussed in holy and ascetic men and women, and in the shrines that commemorate them after their death. Here villagers can

---

[1] From P. Florenskii, *The Pillar and the Ground of Truth*, cited in A. Schmemann, *Ultimate Questions* (New York 1965), p. 156.

[2] This is set out in P. Brown, 'A Dark Age crisis: aspects of the iconoclast controversy', *English Historical Review* 346 (1973), pp. 1–34.

go to find healing and practical help in the difficulties and uncertainties of rural life.

The question of where spiritual power is to be found is not academic purely. It concerns the day-to-day survival of the village dwellers. In times of distress, sickness, infertility, economic hardship, pressure from overbearing officials – where do you go? To the bishop in the city or to the ascetic in the hills? To the church in the town or to the holy well and the chapel with the bones of the martyr? The two levels of religion are not necessarily in conflict (although Peter Brown considers that at some periods, such as the iconoclast controversy, they were; and he suggests that the iconoclastic policy was directed against the form of spiritual power which was dispersed in a variety of places and objects, including icons), and they have both contributed to the practice of the Christian faith in the East.

Popular faith is based around holy places. Festivals are important in all Orthodox countries, and examples could be cited from all over the Eastern Christian world. As the day of the saint to whom a monastery is dedicated approaches, many thousands of people will come, sometimes from large distances. They will arrive the day before, spend the night around the church (singing songs, listening to impromptu sermons, and talking, while a long liturgy is carrying on inside), then after the liturgy the next day they will have a meal provided by the hosts, and then return home. If the monastery or church boasts a miracle-working icon or a healing spring, this will add to the attractiveness of the site. What seems to be significant is simply the action of coming to the place, and being there at the holy time. It is important that the liturgy and other services are being conducted, but most people will not feel the need to enter the church, and are happy to remain outside. The worship at such a festival clearly demonstrates the dual nature of official and popular religion. The bishop serves the liturgy inside and the local people sit outside. It is a pattern that is repeated throughout the Orthodox world, and points to the existence of a kind of ancient popular spirituality, practised alongside the liturgical piety of the bishop's church.

In the spirituality of place, pilgrimage is an essential form of devotion. Jerusalem is, of course, the holy place *par excellence*, and many pilgrims, from all ages, have left accounts of their experiences, from Egeria in the fourth century to the accounts of Western observers who travelled with huge crowds of Russian pilgrims at the beginning of the twentieth century, to the profusion of pilgrims' manuals available today. Many national communities, such those of Armenia and Ethiopia, and in previous centuries Georgia, have established centres at Jerusalem, and a visitor to the Holy Sepulchre is able to share in a variety of liturgies being celebrated simultaneously. Each country also has a large number of its own local centres of pilgrimage. Often these will be the places where the bodies of saints are buried, or it may be a miracle-working icon or a healing spring.

Pilgrimage can often be casual about boundaries between religions, and in particular can be a point of union between Christians and Muslims. It is an expression of religious devotion deeply rooted in the culture of regions, especially in the Middle East. Pilgrimage is an essential devotion of Islam, and the pilgrimage to Mecca is a focus for the identity of the Muslim faith community. Holy places, the pilgrimages to them and the festivals around them are common to both faiths. The tradition of the *maulana* in Egypt attracts members of both faiths. A delightful story is told of the visit to the Virgin of Seidnaya (a miracle-working icon at a monastery near Damascus) by Syrian Muslim cosmonauts who, after their safe return from the perils of a space journey, went to Seidnaya to sacrifice a sheep to the Virgin.[3]

Another important expression of popular faith is fasting. Fasting is an ancient and universal religious discipline, but its significance shifted as a result of the influence of the monks. In the early Church, abstaining from food was a part of eucharistic celebration. The believer turned away from earthly food and drink, as part of his sharing in the eschatological meal, which looked forward to the banquet in the age to come, and showed that the new spiritual food and drink mattered more than material nourishment. For the monk, though, fasting was a way of disciplining the self, through a continuing effort to regain a spiritual freedom from the tyranny of the insistent physical demands of the flesh. This showed itself as the avoidance of certain foods on a regular and legislated basis, and the prescription of when food might be taken.

Fasting practice varies in different parts of the Orthodox Church. A usual pattern is the avoidance of animal products – meat and dairy produce – and, when the fast is stricter, oil as well. Fish is usually permitted. Fasting days are Wednesdays and Fridays, the periods before Easter and

---

[3] The story is in W. Dalrymple, *From the Holy Mountain* (London 1997), p. 191.

Christmas, before the feast of the Apostles Peter and Paul, and before the feast of the Falling Asleep of the Mother of God. Some of the non-Chalcedonian Churches add their own stricter disciplines, such as the three days of total abstention from food and water of the Syrian Church, and the extra fast days of the Ethiopian Church, which appoints over 250 days in the year as fast days.

This discipline, practised by the early Christian communities and by the monks, has become a shared, corporate discipline, with rules laid down by the Church, and integrated into the culture of Orthodox communities. The keeping of the fasts has a great importance in defining who the Orthodox are, and the recognised taboos on eating certain foods at certain seasons give cohesion and identity to the local community. In many areas with a strongly Orthodox population, meat is hard to obtain during the fast seasons, and a member of the Orthodox Church found eating any of the prohibited foods may be subject to strong community disapproval. I have heard it convincingly argued that for many people fasting takes the place of the Eucharist as the main sacrament of God's presence – not a totally strange idea given the eschatological nature of fasting mentioned above. Since Western Churches generally prefer privately chosen methods of ascetical discipline rather than corporate customs, the Eastern emphasis on fasting becomes an argument in the controversy between East and West, seen by many Orthodox as an indication of the superiority of their Christian tradition.

These expressions of popular piety are given a visible location in the monasteries, where holy objects and icons are often found, where pilgrimages are drawn, and where the rules of fasting are kept most assiduously. Monasteries are the link between the two levels of piety – the official and the popular. Monks have been drawn from all levels of society, but there has been a respect for the peasant monk. The scholar Arsenius was seen consulting a simple Egyptian monk. 'How is it', he was asked, 'that you, with such good Latin and Greek education, ask this peasant about your thoughts?' He replied, 'I have indeed been taught Latin and Greek, but I do not know even the alphabet of this peasant.'[4] At various times the distinction between 'intellectual' and 'popular' monasticism has emerged, for example in the fifth- and sixth-century debates between the followers of the learned writer Evagrius, who had an intellectual

---

[4] Arsenius 6, in *Sayings of the Desert Fathers*, trans. B. Ward (Oxford 1975), p. 8.

understanding of the nature of God, and the simpler 'anthropomorphites' who took the physical language used of God in the Bible literally. But generally the monastery brought together both the cultured monk of the large cities and the simple ascetic of the countryside. If anything there has been a bias to the countryside, since the ascetic leaves the city behind and settles in a remote 'desert', which rapidly develops into a spiritual centre as local people are attracted to it.

The central place of the monasteries in popular Christianity has ensured that revival movements have remained firmly within the Church. In Serbia the *bogomoljci* (literally 'God-pray-ers') movement emerged in the region around Ohrid in the 1930s under the leadership of the popular preacher Bishop Nikolai Velimirović (1880–1956), and spread north into other parts of Serbia. It produced a popular literature, with an emphasis on the sharing of experience, personal testimony, simple instruction in the doctrines of the Church, classes formed in towns and villages, but always within an ascetic and monastic atmosphere. It has resulted in a revival in monastic life and influenced many later bishops and monks. Reminiscent of the Methodist movement in eighteenth-century England, its firm monastic roots ensured that it remained within the Church rather than leading to a division. Another example is the Lord's Army, founded in 1923 by the priest Iosif Trifa in Romania. However, this group presented a challenge to the episcopal hierarchy, which it accused of being too strongly controlled by the government, and Fr Iosif was removed from the priesthood in 1935.

A different form of semi-monastic revivalism were the theological brotherhoods in Greece of Zoe (life) and Soter (saviour), which was a conservative off-shoot of Zoe. The Brotherhood of Theologians, or Zoe, was founded by a monk, Fr Eusebios Matthopoulos, in 1907, as a fellowship of teachers and preachers in the service of the Church. Members of Zoe have been unmarried men, many of them graduates of the Theology Faculty of the University of Athens, who share in a missionary and educational task, living a life of simplicity and holding property in common. Some were monks. The brothers preach, and run catachetical schools, providing a missionary and evangelistic ministry. A typical weekend in the life of a lay theologian in around 1950 is described by Peter Hammond.[5] He travelled by truck a distance of 55 km, followed

5 See P. Hammond, *The Waters of Marah* (London 1965), p. 130.

by an hour's walk to the village of Lechovo, where he gave an evening address; on Sunday morning a sermon in church was followed by a talk to the youth; then a hasty meal and another walk to a neighbouring village, for a talk given in the town square; then he climbed to another village high in the mountains for a further two talks in the evening. In some villages it was over ten years since a sermon had been preached. After the Second World War, Zoe was at its most effective, assisting the Church in its struggle against Communism, but the movement has declined since then. The brotherhoods have been responsible for revival in Church life in post-war Greece, and many of those who are now monks were influenced by Zoe and Soter.

The flexibility and versatility of the monasteries of the East have enabled them to retain an openness to the community they serve. It remains common to find a variety of people living within a monastery: students, workmen, visitors, pilgrims. Often there may be only one or two monks within a community of a dozen or so who live in or around the monastery and share in its work and its life. The editors of the *Philokalia* were well aware of the popular and open nature of monastic life, and made it clear that their work was intended for all Christians. The author of a little book which has introduced the Jesus Prayer to many purports to be just such a layman. An anonymous Russian pilgrim described his search for the true silence, his wanderings around Russia, and his efforts to discover a guide to the use of the Prayer, in a book entitled the *Candid Narrations of a Pilgrim to his Spiritual Father*, which was published in Kazan, in south-east Russia, in 1884, and translated into English as *The Way of a Pilgrim* and *The Pilgrim continues his Way*. In fact the book is written in an elaborate literary style, in spite of its simple appearance, and contains theological and philosophical sections which suggest that the author is being a little disingenuous in claiming to be a wandering peasant. Perhaps a more learned author – even the spiritual father of the title – revised the original material narrated by the pilgrim. It seeks to show that not only monks but all classes of society can respond to the challenges set by the classics of the spiritual life and become not only adept at the practice but also popular teachers.

The history of Orthodox spirituality has produced a succession of holy men who have built up a reputation for holiness or miracle-working and have become popular among believers. The continuing significance of these popular holy men can be seen from two examples from pre-Revolutionary Russia.

Grigorii Rasputin (1869–1916) has come to be seen as a personification of all that is evil, manipulative and demonic, but he is a good example of the figure of the wandering holy man, who was nurtured within a popular religious culture. He began his life in a Siberian village, near the capital of Tobolsk. He was married, then his first child died, and he entered a local monastery. His spiritual father advised him to go to Mount Athos to save his soul, and he walked from Siberia to Greece. He was shocked by what he saw as a weak monastic life – filled with 'moral dirt and vermin', as his daughter recounts – and walked back to Russia.[6] He was said to have been associated with the sect of the Khlysty, which was one of several heterodox groups at the edge of Church life, alternately rigorously celibate and unrestrainedly promiscuous. So from a background of peasant life, visions, monasteries and pilgrimage emerged the figure who came to exert such a fateful influence on the imperial family. He represents the huge chaotic underworld of Russian religion, steeped in faith and superstition. But he was also a figure rooted in the life of the popular Church and respected by it. He was sponsored by the Rector of the St Petersburg Theological Academy, Theophan, and had the support of Metropolitan Pitirim of St Petersburg (1915–17) and Makarii of Moscow (1912–17). The style of popular spirituality represented by Rasputin was part of the religious life of pre-Revolutionary Russia.

Another influential figure from this period was Fr John Sergiev (1829–1908). He became a parish priest at Kronstadt, a naval garrison town on the Baltic Sea, in 1855 and remained there for the rest of his life. He read the Bible, celebrated the liturgy, distributed alms to the poor. But in addition he had a reputation as a healer, and people not only came to seek his help but even sent him telegrams from all parts of Russia, asking for his prayers. For him the liturgy was an intense personal encounter. He required all who attended to receive communion with him, and in order for the many thousands in church to confess their sins before communion, as the Church required, he established the unusual practice of communal spoken confession. 'It was an impressive, even a terrifying spectacle: thousands of people shouting aloud their most secret

---

[6] M. Rasputin, *My Father* (London 1934), p. 47.

sins and sobbing for forgiveness; all the barriers of ecclesiastical order and propriety were transgressed.'[7] While John was the first married priest to be canonised in Russia and so set an example for a new type of saint, his life illustrates the vitality and energy of popular religion, at a time when the Orthodox Church was firmly under the control of the Tsar.

Orthodox spirituality is corporate. It is shown not through individual study or commitment, nor through private prayer, but rather its expressions are deeply rooted in the culture and experience of the community. Faith is shown by keeping the fasts, celebrating the festivals, and going on pilgrimage to the holy places. All of these things are done together. Above all they are not only done together with other Church members but in communion with the saints and with the Mother of God. In the church building, the saints are present in their icons which confront the worshipper; or remain in their burial place, with the uncorrupted body as a sign that their presence and protection is maintained. The communion of saints is not only a doctrine but a part of the living experience of Orthodox Christians.

[7] See G.P. Fedotov, *A Treasury of Russian Spirituality* (London 1950), p. 349.

8

Mission: incarnation as proclamation

THE FIRST CHRISTIAN MISSIONS AND THE FIRST CHRISTIAN NATIONS

The concept of mission is usually associated either with the early Church, especially with the Apostle Paul and his extensive preaching journeys around the Mediterranean Sea, or with the valiant labours of Western missionaries in Africa and other non-Christian territories. As a result, mission has come to be seen as part of the expansionist self-confidence of Western Europe, and goes hand-in-hand with nineteenth-century imperialism. But mission has always been a part of the life of the Church. One cannot conceive of a Church that is not directed towards the world it seeks to serve and that does not include the making of new members as part of its life – whether by conversion, persuasion, conquest or simply by birth. The Orthodox Churches have produced some of the greatest missionaries in the history of the Church, but most of these are little known and the mission strategies are overlooked.

It is usual to date both the birth of the Church and the beginning of the mission of the apostles to the same event in the New Testament. On the day of Pentecost the apostles were given a power which they described as that of the Holy Spirit enabling them to preach with conviction, and to go out on a series of daring and far-reaching – literally – missionary journeys, in the course of which the new Christian Church was established in the cities of the Empire, and even beyond. Western missionaries see Pentecost as a paradigm, a normative theological statement, rooting their preaching in the activity of God. But for the East it was the start of a historical process to which many Eastern Christians look back as the start of the life of the local Churches.

Many major Churches of the East claim to have been founded by the apostles: Antioch by Peter and Paul, Alexandria by Mark, Constantinople by Andrew, Cyprus by Barnabas, Ethiopia by Matthew, India by Thomas, Edessa in eastern Syria by Thaddeus, Armenia by Bartholomew, Georgia by Simon the Zealot. The Syrians manage to claim an even earlier origin through the gift to King Abgar the Black of the cloth with the image of the face of Christ on it. Since the claim of being an apostolic foundation gives prestige and authority to the Church concerned, these traditions clearly have an apologetic motive. As a result, we cannot be too confident in the historical reliability of many of the accounts of the founding of the Churches. But we cannot be too confident, either, in dismissing claims of apostolic foundation as legendary.

Transport by road or by sea was not difficult. Not only was there a well-developed road transport system around the Roman Empire, but there were also well-established trade routes connecting the Middle East with India and China. It is also easy to forget how short many of the journeys were. For example, the distance from Jerusalem to Alexandria is around 300 miles. According to the evangelist Matthew, the infant Christ was taken along this road by Mary and Joseph, presumably on foot or by donkey, to escape the wrath of Herod. Even if we question the historicity of this episode, its inclusion in the gospel suggests that the journey was manageable and the story plausible. It has been incorporated into the memory of the Egyptian Church, and many sites commemorate events on that journey of the Holy Family. As well as travel by road, journeys could be undertaken by sea. If the Apostle Paul could travel by boat to Rome, then Matthew could sail the similar distance to Ethiopia, and Thomas could undertake the journey, of about twice the distance, to India. The Acts of the Apostles and New Testament Epistles present a picture of an infant Church spreading naturally and unobtrusively along sea routes and roads, later exported by the merchants and soldiers who travelled across the known world. Traditions of apostolic foundation of national or urban Churches suggest that the first wave of missionary expansion could have been rapid. While there is no historical or archeological evidence for the existence of Churches in sub-apostolic times, this cannot be taken to indicate that they did not exist.

1. The Church of the Haghia Sophia or Holy Wisdom in Istanbul, the interior of the dome. The church was built between 532 and 537. People were amazed by the dome suspended in the air, with the light of heaven pouring in. See Ch. 2, p. 5 and Ch. 3, p. 57.

2. A boy receives communion at a church in Crete. At the liturgy heaven and earth meet, and enter the experience of the faithful. The baptised of all ages share in this great gift. See Ch. 3, pp. 39–40, 45–6.

3. Epiphany procession at a monastery near Addis Ababa, Ethiopia. Festivals are popular expressions of faith. Here the priests carry on their heads the *tabots*, representing the Ark of the Covenant. See Ch. 7, pp. 136–7.

4. Fresco of Bishop Nikolai Velimirović at Kaona, Serbia. The iconographic tradition remains an expression of devotion. This fresco of the preacher Nikolai Velimirović, who died in 1956, shows local veneration of the holy man in the region around his birthplace. See Chs. 5 and 7, p. 139.

5. The church of the monastery of Anba Bishoy, wadi el-Natrun, Egypt. Monks have lived in this place at least since the early fourth century. Many hermits' cells surround the monastery. The monastery is now a centre of modern monastic revival. See Ch. 6, p. 112 and Ch. 11, p. 244.

6. The remains of the column of Symeon Stylites at Qala'at Sima'an, Syria. The column once reached a height of over 15 metres, and today a single boulder rock marks the place where it stood. The vast church surrounding it was built between 475 and 491. See Ch. 6, p. 121.

7. The domes of St Sergius' monastery, Sergiev Posad, Russia. Large monasteries quickly grew in the places where monks settled. The monastery of St Sergius has become a centre of Church life with a large monastery and theological academy. See Ch. 6, p. 118 and Ch. 8, p. 152.

5

8. The burial place of the head of John the Baptist at the Ummayad Mosque, in Damascus, Syria. According to tradition the head of John the Baptist is buried in what was once a church and is now a mosque. Christianity and Islam share many holy places and revere many of the same saints. See Ch. 7, p. 137 and Ch. 9, pp. 170–2.

9. Monument to the dead of the Second World War, Kraljevo, Serbia. The inhabitants of this town in central Serbia are continually reminded of the day in 1940 when almost 2,000 local people were rounded up and shot. Violence is deeply rooted in the memory of peoples in all parts of the Christian East, and fuels further fear and hatred. See Ch. 9, pp. 192, 198.

10. The door-keeper of the church in a village in the Tur Abdin, on the left. One of the few remaining Christians in this once-Christian village in the Tur Abdin keeps the key of the church, where services are no longer held. See Ch. 1, pp. 31–2 Ch. 9, p. 190 and Ch. 11, p. 240.

11. A monk planting a tree on Mount Athos, Greece. The concern for ecological issues is not restricted to academic conferences. Here woodland is being replanted following a forest fire. See Ch. 6, p. 133 and Ch. 11, p. 246.

7

12. The Syrian Orthodox Archbishop of the Euphrates visits a Catholic Chaldaean family. Archbishop Matta is liked and respected by members of all Churches and is concerned for the welfare of the Christians in his area. See Ch. 1, p. 2 and Ch. 10, p. 219.

A new stage in the history of the Church began when not just localised communities but nations became Christian. The stage is associated with the conversion of Constantine and the beginnings of a Christian Empire, but the Byzantine Emperor was not the first ruler to lead his people into Christianity, thus setting up the first Christian state. That honour traditionally goes to the church of Armenia. Armenia (Hayastan, in the Armenian language) is in the Causcasus, between the Black and Caspian Seas, on the borders of the great empires of Rome and Persia. The existence of Syrian influence on the ecclesiastical vocabulary of Armenia suggests that Syrian missionaries were active before the life of the great bringer of the faith to the region, Gregory the Illuminator. According to later sources, Gregory was a Parthian who fled to Caesarea in Cappadocia to escape a feud between his family and the king. He was baptised a Christian and returned to Armenia in 298. Then he was imprisoned in a pit by the pagan king Trdat, but he was secretly fed by a kind-hearted widow. After his release he converted the king and returned to Caesarea, where he was consecrated as bishop of Ashtishat in 314. Armenians date their conversion to 301, thus claiming to be the first Christian kingdom, although this seems a little unlikely and a date closer to 314 is to be preferred. Gregory was a tireless missionary who, it is said, baptised four million persons in one week – which does at least suggest a vigorous strategy of incorporating the people into the Church even if the figure seems inflated. In 387 Armenia was divided between the Byzantine and Persian Empires, with the larger part of it in Persia. Etchmiadzin, near modern Yerevan, became the seat of the bishop, and the Armenian script was devised by the ascetic teacher Mesrop Mastoc, who was resident at the time in northern Syria. Many Christian texts were translated out of Syriac and Greek into the new language, and so the Armenians developed their culture and sense of nationality. Alongside this process, the Christian faith also reached neighbouring Georgia, or Iberia. St Nino, a Christian slave woman, is said to have performed healings, and included among her patients the wife of the king, Mirian. The clergy ordained by Gregory extended their ministry among the Georgians too.

In the same century, Ethiopia was converted to Christianity, again through the influence of Syrian missionaries. Two Syrian boys from Tyre, Frumentius and Aedesius, were shipwrecked on the coast of Ethiopia in the early fourth century. Both were brought up at the royal court at Axum, impressed the members of the court by their learning and then became tutors to the Prince Ezana. Once crowned, Ezana adopted his teachers' faith and, while Aedesius returned to Tyre, Frumentius went to Alexandria, where he was consecrated archbishop of Ethiopia in around 340 by Athanasius of Alexandria. Frumentius was known in Ethiopia as Abba Salama (the Father of Peace) or Kassate Berhan (Bringer of Light). Frumentius, however, did not bring Christianity to Ethiopia, but found it there already in communities of merchants and others who had settled in the kingdom. His achievement was to organise the Christian communities which already existed, and to ensure that the king and his court were converted to the Christian faith.[1] Coins from the reign of Ezana testify to the introduction of Christian symbols into the kingdom. Later, in the sixth century, the Ethiopians extended Christian rule into Arabia, and parts of the Scriptures were translated into Ethiopic (known as Ge'ez).

It is clear that in both these instances, Christianity was already present. The result of these missions was to root the ruling house in the faith, set up an ecclesiastical hierarchy, and incorporate people into the Church through baptism.

JACOBITES AND NESTORIANS

In the expansion of the Church towards the east, monasteries became the centres of mission. An example of monastic mission comes from the life of Euthymius (377–473), an early hermit and ascetic in the desert east of Jerusalem. Aspabet, the king of one of the Arab tribes, known to the Greeks as Saracens, had a son who was sick. He brought him to the holy man, who cured him, and as a result Aspabet adopted the faith of the saint and instructed his tribe to follow his example. So they pitched their tents by the monastery to benefit from the teaching of Euthymius, and this settlement became a centre of Arab Christianity, with an Arabic-speaking bishop arranged for them by Euthymius.[2] The holy man conveys the gospel through a life of ascetic endeavour and works of power which can speak across cultural and religious boundaries. In the Eastern tradition the roles of ascetic and missionary are closely associated.

---

[1] Rufinus, *Ecclesiastical History* 10.9–10.
[2] Cyril of Scythopolis, *Life of Euthymius* 10, 15, trans. Price, pp. 14–17, 20–1.

Several of the Arab tribes became Christian, and this led, indirectly, to the career of one of the most remarkable missionaries of the history of the Church, Jacob Baradeus, sometimes referred to as James or Jacob bar-Addai (*c*.490–578). In 543 a king of a confederation of some Arab tribes, named al-Harith, decided to attach himself to the Monophysite groups, and requested that the Emperor Justinian I (527–65) send a bishop. Seeing an opportunity for strengthening a useful alliance and securing his eastern frontier, Justinian sent Jacob as one of two bishops to serve the Arabs. Jacob had been born at Tella and had became a monk in the great Syrian monastic centre of Mount Izla, at the edge of the Tur Abdin. He then travelled to Constantinople to join a group of Monophysites, under the protection of the Empress Theodora, and so was in the capital when the request from al-Harith was received. He was given an extensive but indeterminate area of operation. It was a time when the ideological gap between Chalcedonian Orthodox and Monophysites was widening, and the two tendencies were evolving into separate communities. Until then they had been members of the one Church, and the leader of the Monophysites in Constantinople, an exiled Patriarch of Alexandria, Theodosius, had been reluctant to ordain clergy for Monophysite communities.

The ordination of clergy was Jacob's great contribution. He travelled first to Alexandria, where his two companions Conon of Tarsus and Eugenius of Seleucia were consecrated as bishops to work with him. Then for the next thirty-five years he made long and arduous journeys, visiting Syria, Armenia, Asia Minor, Egypt, Cyprus, Rhodes, in fact most of the Empire. As well as teaching, he carried out ordinations for the emerging Monophysite Church. His biographer says that he 'caused the priesthood to flow like great rivers over the whole world of the Roman domains'.[3] He is said to have ordained a total of twenty-seven metropolitan bishops and one hundred thousand clergy, and was given the title of 'ecumenical metropolitan' by later sources, to indicate that his authority and jurisdiction extended through the whole of the known Christian world.

The Emperor Justinian realised that the act of co-operation with a potential Arab ally had gone badly wrong and that a new Church was

---

[3] John of Ephesus, *Life of James bar-Addai* Patrologia Orientalia 18, p. 696.

being created which was to undermine rather than cement the unity of his Empire. He resolved to capture Jacob, but his quarry kept on the move. He travelled constantly, often covering thirty or forty miles a day, dressed in an old horse cloth, known in Syriac as a *burd'ata*, which was the origin of his nickname *burdana*, or in Latin *baradeus*. He seems to have evoked great loyalty for he was never betrayed by the local people. There are some extraordinary stories of the ordinations of this period. On one occasion a colleague of Jacob's, John of Hephaistos, celebrated a Monophysite liturgy at which he ordained fifty new priests in the gallery of the cathedral at Tralles at the same time as the Chalcedonians were holding their own liturgy in the main body of the church below – a story which also suggests a far less ordered and decorous form of liturgical celebration than that familiar today.

Out of these journeys of Jacob and others the character of the Monophysite Church was formed. It had its strongholds in rural areas and was based on monasteries. One Monophysite Patriarch of Antioch, Peter of Callinicum, claimed that he had never been able to visit Antioch, although he was supposed to be its bishop. The church had a strong Syriac tradition since Jacob selected as bishops many of his fellow-members of the large monasteries in northern Syria. As a result of Jacob's huge labours, the Monophysite or Syrian Orthodox Church came into existence, with its ordered hierarchy of bishops and other clergy. It is still sometimes called the Jacobite Church as a testimony to its great missionary founder.

While Jacob was setting up the structures of a new Church on the frontier of the Empire, an even more remarkable missionary expansion was taking place to the east. Asia was being evangelised by the Church of Persia, or the Church of the East. Sadly the evidence for this most dramatic period of the missionary history of the Church is scanty. We know that there were bishoprics at Merv and Herat in Transoxiana, east of the Caspian Sea and south of the Aral Sea, by 424. The Egyptian traveller, Cosmas Indicopleustes, writing a century later, described churches in Sri Lanka and southern India, with bishops and priests of these churches ordained in Persia, suggesting that by the early sixth century a diocese had been established by the Church of the East in India. By the seventh century the Church had arrived in China. This is shown by a stele (discovered in 1625) at Sian-Fu in western China, which has inscriptions in Chinese and Syriac describing how A-lo-pen – a name in the Chinese part of the text – brought the scriptures of the 'luminous religion' about 635. These scriptures were translated into Chinese. The stele was erected in 781. In 850 there was a Metropolitan of Samarkand, and remains of a tenth-century monastery have been discovered in China. From 500 to 1000 this huge Church spread through much of Asia.

The Church of the East was vibrant and confident. Abraham of Kashkar carried out a programme of monastic reform in the sixth century, based on his monastery on Mount Izla, at the edge of the Tur Abdin. This contributed to the strong tradition of monastic spirituality which produced among others Isaac of Syria. The Church was also known for its scholarship. Thus armed, its missionaries set out across the central Asian steppe to engage in spiritual combat with the forces of paganism. In 644 Elias, Metropolitan of Merv, engaged in a trial of strength with pagan priests. They conjured up violent storms, which he then dispelled by making the sign of the cross. The local people were then baptised in the river Oxus. All the evidence for this mission is consistent with patterns already noted: a strong ascetic tradition (as with Euthymius), the setting up of a hierarchy (as with the journeys of Jacob), and the reputation for scholarship (as with Frumentius, who had so impressed the Ethiopians).

CYRIL AND METHODIUS

The great missionaries of the Orthodox Church are Cyril and Methodius, known as the *isoapostoloi* or 'the equals to the apostles'. Their labours in the missions during the late ninth century are seen as being responsible for the great expansion of the Byzantine Orthodox Church into the Slavic regions of east and north-east Europe. Their missionary careers were short – in Cyril's case only six years (863–9) – and the main work for which they are remembered was in the field of translation. Oddly for one of the great Orthodox missionaries, Methodius was, at least for the latter part of his work in Moravia, the legate of the Pope of Rome, and he used the Roman form of the liturgy.

They were brothers. Methodius (815–85) and Cyril (in fact named at baptism as Constantine) (826–69) were brought up in Thessaloniki, a city in an area with many Slav inhabitants, as a result of which they became familiar with the Slavonic language. Constantine travelled to Constantinople and became an official (*chartophylax*) in the Church of the Haghia Sophia and then, around 850, a teacher of philosophy at the

University, hence he was known as 'Constantine the Philosopher'. He was also, significantly for his later work, a formidable linguist, being familiar with Greek, Latin, the form of Slavonic spoken in Macedonia, Hebrew, Syriac and Samaritan. Political conflict drove him from the capital, and he joined his older brother at a monastery on Mount Olympus in Bithynia.

The Slav tribes had settled in the Balkans in the sixth century, but the Russians burst upon the scene in the ninth century. The Patriarch Photius wrote that 'this sudden hailstorm of barbarians burst forth'.[4] The presence of these new arrivals to the northern frontier set a challenge for the missionary work of the Church. The Emperor Michael III (842–67) sent an embassy to the land of the Khazars, between the Black and Caspian Seas, in 860, which included within it Constantine and Methodius. Later came a request for missionaries from Rastislav, the ruler of Moravia. Christianity was not new to Moravia, as is shown by the discovery of stone churches from this period which had been built by earlier missionaries from Frankish Germany and Latin Rome. The brothers' innovative work was in teaching and translating. Constantine invented an alphabet in which the sounds of Slavonic languages could be accurately transliterated, and so was able to translate liturgical books, the four gospels and the liturgy of St John Chrysostom. Having made the translations, they then taught people how to use the new books.

After only three and a half years they left and went to Italy. In Venice they were challenged by an assembly of bishops who were 'trilinguists', convinced that the liturgy could be celebrated only in Greek, Latin or Hebrew (the three languages in which the inscription on the Cross of Christ was written). In Rome they lived in a Greek monastery, where Constantine became ill, was received as a monk, taking the name Cyril by which he has been remembered, and then died. Methodius, meanwhile, gained the approval of Pope Hadrian II for his Slavic liturgy, and was sent back to Moravia as papal legate and archbishop of Sirmium. He was imprisoned by Frankish missionary rivals from 871 to 873, but was freed by the orders of the Pope. His links with Rome did not cut him off from Constantinople. He visited the capital in 881–2 and was warmly

---

[4] The remark of Photius is in C. Mango, *The Homilies of Photius, Patriarch of Constantinople* (Cambridge, MA 1958), p. 98.

received by the Emperor Basil I and Patriarch Photius. After this he returned to Moravia and continued his herculean task of translation: all the necessary liturgical books, the canons of the Church, and (probably) the Old Testament, although this text no longer survives. He died in 885, and was buried in his cathedral church (possibly the basilica discovered at Mikulcice, near Velehrad, in Moravia).

The work of the brothers in Moravia seemed to come to an ignominious end. The Frankish clergy, who had persistently opposed the brothers, gained the favour of the ruler, Svatopluk, and many of Methodius' followers were imprisoned and then expelled. Shortly afterwards the Moravian kingdom was overrun by Hungarian invaders and disappeared from history. Although there is evidence of a Slavonic hierarchy in Moravia in the tenth century, it did not last and Moravia was lost to Orthodoxy. However, some of Methodius' disciples travelled to Bulgaria and carried on the work of establishing a Slavonic Christianity. Clement set up a school at Ohrid, as did Naum at Preslav. Clement is said to have trained 3,500 disciples at his school – sometimes referred to as the first Slavonic University – and then sent them out in groups of three hundred to a total of twelve different areas. From Ohrid, Slavonic Christianity entered Serbia, since the bishopric of Ras, the historic centre of the young Serbian kingdom, was dependent on Ohrid. There was also cultural exchange with the Christian communities of Russia.

The originality of Cyril (to give him his customary monastic name) and Methodius lay in their linguistic work. At this time, the Church was becoming more centralised and the newly confident papacy was introducing the use of Latin as the liturgical language of the West. Against this trend the brothers gave to new Slavonic Christians the opportunity to worship in their own language. Their contribution has received its memorial in the use of the name Cyrillic for the script used for writing many Slavic languages, although this is somewhat misleading since modern Cyrillic characters are based on Greek uncials while Cyril's alphabet was the very different Glagolitic. It is also worth noting that this original work received the support of both Rome and Constantinople. The brothers lived through the Photian schism and a century or so before the Great Schism, and their lives demonstrate the underlying – yet fragile – unity of the Church.

RUSSIAN MISSIONS

The missionary tradition of the Eastern Church was continued by the Russians. A glance at a map shows the huge extent of the growth of Russia from its modest beginnings as a Muscovite statelet in the fourteenth century, when it defeated a superior Tartar army at the battle of Kulikovo Field in 1380, to its expansion into a huge empire that extended to the Pacific Ocean and into the Alaskan region of North America, with significant communities in the western USA, China and Japan. The missionaries of the Church shared in, and often led, this process of colonisation. It was a creative and sustained mission enterprise, carried out by ascetic and brilliant churchmen, several of whom have been canonised, with alternating support, indifference and hostility from the Church authorities and government.

As was the case with the Syrians, the most effective colonisers and missionaries were the monks. Sergius of Radonezh (1314–92) founded a hermitage in the forests to the north of Moscow, which he dedicated to the Holy Trinity. It grew rapidly, and he found himself persuaded to become the abbot of a monastery which developed into a thriving community with a *typikon* based on that of the Constantinople monastery of Stoudion. His lonely hermitage in the forest is now the large monastery called Sergiev Posad, a short train journey from Moscow, and a centre of Russian Christianity, where today a choir sings continually by the grave of the holy founder.

Sergius' ascetic zeal lived on in his community, and some of his disciples moved on, penetrating the northern forests beyond the river Volga, in search of solitude, only to find that, like Sergius' Trinity hermitage, their simple settlements quickly became the centres of growing commercial and agricultural life. Sergius' disciples founded a total of thirty-five monasteries. Paul of Obnora, a disciple of Sergius, was a devout lover of silence and chose to live in the hollow of a linden tree, at peace with his companions the animals. But before long his ascetic life was disturbed by settlers. The disruption of his silent life is shown by the expanding size of the monastery. In 1489 it was granted a territory of thirty square *versts*, an area large enough to support four villages, and by 1539 the monastery lands supported forty-five villages. The modest man of peace found himself transformed into the founder of an agricultural and commercial outpost of a growing empire.

In 1429 two monks, Sabbatii and German, settled on Solovkii, an island in the White Sea. This was at the furthest northern edge of the territory colonised by the missionary monks. Here, as elsewhere, the simple ascetic life of the monk led him to seek harsh and isolated living conditions, enabled him to survive and provided an example of spiritual endeavour for others to follow. The place of ascetic struggle on the remote island in the arctic north became a large community, a trading centre, a strategic fort, and later, under the Communist regime, a prison in which many bishops and other clergy were incarcerated. This distant outpost of the religious life has now been returned to the Church and is once again a growing monastic community, with a reputation as a centre of contemplative prayer.

A contemporary of Sergius was Stephen of Perm (1340–96). A priest and a scholar, he lived in a frontier area not finally absorbed into Russia until 1472. In 1378 he travelled east, across the Ural mountains into the forests of Siberia, preaching to the local Zirian people. Like Cyril and Methodius, he invented an alphabet in which to write the local Zirian speech, based on runic signs; and then translated the Scriptures and liturgical texts into it. He hoped to form a Zirian Orthodox Church using the local language and developing its own traditions, and he trained young men for service as preachers. Sadly, this initiative did not develop, and the infant Zirian Church was absorbed by the Russian Church; within a century of Stephen's death, the books were destroyed and Church Slavonic imposed. The ideal of transposing the Orthodox faith into the language and culture of varied peoples, and of encouraging an indigenous ministry, however, remained at the heart of Russian missiology, and was repeated in the centuries that followed.

Both Stephen's missionary ideals and Sergius' ascetic life-style become the models of the dynamic forces behind the expansion of the Church several centuries later, during the golden age of Russian mission of the nineteenth century. The focus of this movement was the city of Kazan, once a Tartar capital, and conveniently placed to provide both reasonable access to Moscow and also a base for expeditions into the east. The Kazan Theological Academy was founded in 1842, and it opened a centre of missionary training in 1854. With the support of the Russian Bible Society, the Academy produced translations of the liturgy in twenty-two languages of the eastern part of the Russian Empire by the end of the

nineteenth century. Strangely, among the last groups to receive a translation of the Bible into its own language were the Russians, owing to
conservative elements in Church and state. This had to wait until the
reign of Alexander II (1855–81).

The movement was a sign of the creativity and vision of a series of
remarkable missionaries. The Synod of the Russian Church was happy
to receive the benefits of the expansion of Russian influence, but they
were not responsible for initiating it.

The Altai region of south-west Siberia became the home of Makarii
Glukharev (d. 1847), who settled there in 1830. In his youth he had taken
care to equip himself with a variety of useful skills – studying natural
science, anatomy and botany – and he advised a woman colleague to
train as a midwife. He lived in great poverty and shared everything with
his companions, not only out of necessity but also to develop a unity
of mind and intention among the missionaries. Makarii was a pioneer
of ecumenism and inter-faith co-operation, although he would not have
known these terms, at one stage sharing a church with Muslims, and
dreaming of a cathedral with Orthodox, Roman Catholic and Lutheran
altars within it. He translated, of course, and even asked to be allowed
to produce a Russian translation of the Bible. For this presumptuous
desire he was punished by being required to celebrate the liturgy daily
for six weeks – a punishment which he enjoyed to the full, unable to see
any hardship in this discipline. The canonisation of such an unusual and
open-minded churchman as Makarii by the Russian Bishops' Council in
2000 can be seen as a cautious endorsement by the Patriarchate of the
attitude he lived by.

Russian missionaries also brought the Orthodox faith to America.
Russians had explored Alaska from the seventeenth century, and had set
up trading posts for the export of furs. They had then intermarried with
the coastal Indians and had baptised some of these into the Orthodox
Church. The first missionaries who arrived to serve this infant Church
were ten monks from Valaamo monastery in the north-west of Russia
who arrived in Alaska in 1794. The leader, Ioasaph, was summoned to
return to Russia five years later and was consecrated bishop for the mission. Unfortunately he was drowned on the return trip, and this resulted
in the closure of the cathedral until 1811, and left only three monks out
of the original ten. About ten years later one of them, Herman, set up
a hermitage on Spruce Island, just north of the centre of the mission on

Kodiak Island, some time between 1808 and 1818. He called it New Valaamo and lived there until his death in 1837, at the age of 81.

Shortly before Herman died, a young married priest named John Veniaminov (1797–1879) volunteered to go to Alaska and arrived with his family in 1824. A large and powerful man, he covered huge distances to visit the scattered Aleutian Islands in a light Alaskan kayak, a form of transport which left him with severe arthritis and continual pain in his legs as a result of the cold and exposure to the elements. While he was on a visit to Moscow to report on his missionary activities, his wife died, and he was immediately persuaded to become a monk, with the name Innocent, and was then consecrated bishop, with responsibility for a huge diocese covering Kamchatka in east Asia, Alaska, and California. He advocated frequent communion and encouraged his clergy to celebrate the Eucharist regularly, which, he observed, strengthened the faith of the converts. His writings were popular, and his *Indication of the Way to the Kingdom of God*, written originally in Aleut in 1833, was translated into Russian and was reprinted forty-six times. 'The unlearned one', as he liked to describe himself, was surprised when, in 1868, he became Metropolitan of Moscow. From this position he continued to encourage mission, and in 1870 he revitalised the Orthodox Missionary Society, which had been founded five years earlier.

The account of the Russian missionaries would not be complete without mention of Nikolai Kasatkin (1836–1912), sent in 1860 to Japan as a chaplain. He began his work by spending four years in study, prayer and – predictably – studying Japanese. He was attacked by a Samurai who suspected him of being a spy, but his non-violent and patient response amazed the Samurai so much that he was converted, ordained priest and became a leader of the mission. There were only two Russian priests in Japan and so the work of mission was carried out almost entirely by indigenous Japanese. By 1883 the Orthodox Church in Japan was served by 311 Japanese priests and 106 evangelists. In 1906 Nikolai was consecrated archbishop but still chose to live in one small room attached to the cathedral. 'We cannot be poorer than Father Nikolai', his congregation commented.

A famous director of the seminary at Kazan and a preacher among the Tartars, Nikolai Ilminskii (d. 1891), wrote 'we believe that the evangelical word of our Saviour Jesus Christ, having become incarnate in the living tongue of the Tartars, and through it having associated itself most sincerely with their deepest thoughts and religious consciousness, would produce the Christian revival of this tribe'.[5] This model of the Incarnation describes the style of the Russian missions, and of the missionary method of the Orthodox Churches, which set out to root the Christian Church within the culture concerned, rather than – as has happened in some other examples of missionary work – supplying a complete cultural package of which the Christian message is simply the spiritual component. The elements encountered through the history of Eastern mission contributed to this Incarnation missiology: the ascetic life-style and healing gifts of the monk; the monastic community rooted in the life of the local people; the simple and rudimentary ecclesiastical structure based on the ministry of the bishop; the translation of texts into the local language and the process of instruction in using them. These methods enabled the development of an indigenous form of Orthodox Christianity which produced an independent local Church.

THE CHURCH IN AMERICA

In 1867 the Russian government sold Alaska to the United States of America. Most Russians returned home, leaving around 12,000 local Orthodox grouped into nine parishes. Since then the life of the Church has continued, with strong lay leadership. In 1991 there were thirty clergy, of whom twenty-three were local Alaskans, leading a Church rooted in local Indian society.

After the sale, the episcopal seat was moved to San Francisco by Bishop John Mitropolskii, who spoke English and recognised that not only could the Alaskan mission be better cared for from the more accessible centre on the west coast, but also that the Church could grow in other parts of the USA as well. This 'missionary diocese' spread rapidly. By the time of the Russian Revolution in 1917 there were 350 parish churches and chapels, a seminary, monasteries, a women's college and even a bank. It attracted Orthodox immigrants of many nationalities. Among them were Greek Catholics, or Uniates, who came to work in the coal fields and other industries. They found the Roman Catholics were unsympathetic to their traditions and required them to adopt Latin practices. Large numbers became Orthodox, perhaps as many as a third of

---

[5] For Ilminskii, see G. Florovsky, 'Russian missions, a historical sketch', in his *Aspects of Church History* (Belmont, MA 1987), p. 154.

the total number of 350,000 Uniates who settled in the USA. Fr Alexis Toth (d. 1909) was a Uniate priest who found himself in the diocese of a strongly Latinising bishop. He has left a vivid account of a conversation in which he reported, 'The Archbishop lost his temper. I lost mine just as much. One word brought another so that the thing has gone so far that our conversation is not worth putting on record.'[6] Later Fr Alexis led sixty-five Uniate parishes, consisting of 20,000 people, into the missionary diocese of America.

In 1898 a new bishop arrived from Moscow. Aged only 33, Tikhon Bellavin realised that the missionary diocese needed to evolve into an American Church – multi-ethnic and self-supporting. He formed a new Russian diocese of New York, an Arab diocese of Brooklyn, a Serbian diocese of Chicago and a Greek diocese. In addition, Romanians and Albanians were included. In 1907 the diocese held its first 'All-American Council' of both clergy and laity, with decisions taken on a democratic basis. Tikhon was recalled to Russia in the same year, and in due course became the first holder of the restored Patriarchate in 1917, at another Council which had a democratic character to it. He had the heavy responsibility of leading the Church through the early years of Communist rule and died under house arrest in 1929.

The Communist Revolution in Russia led to a straining and then a breaking of the links and the financial support which bound the missionary diocese to Moscow. The American diocese was faced by a legal challenge to its status launched by Bolshevik sympathisers within the Church, known as the 'Living Church', which sought to gain control of the parishes. In 1925 the courts awarded the diocesan cathedral in New York to this Communist 'Living Church'. As a result, the American diocese declared the individual parishes independent with control over their own property, thus becoming a voluntary federation of virtually independent parishes. This had the result of protecting parishes from any legal action taken against the diocese, but it also broke up the already somewhat fragile unity of the diocese. The parishes had always had a strongly independent streak because they were set up by groups of immigrants, rather than through the initiative of the diocesan authorities, and as immigration continued it was not unnatural that ethnically based dioceses developed.

---

[6] See C. Tarasar (ed.), *Orthodox America* (New York 1975), pp.50–1.

The alternative pattern of forming members of ethnic groups into their own dioceses had developed alongside the multi-ethnic structures of the missionary diocese. Many immigrants preferred to maintain their links with the Mother Church. Most Greek communities, and also Bulgarians and Macedonians, set up their own independent parishes, looking to their home Churches for support. By 1920 there were 150 Greek parishes, dependent either on the Greek Church or on the Ecumenical Patriarchate. These Greek parishes were formed into an archdiocese by Meletios Metaxakis, who was – remarkably – bishop of the Church of Cyprus and then of Greece before becoming Ecumenical Patriarch and then Patriarch of Alexandria. Toppled from his archbishopric of Athens in 1920 by changes in political fortunes, Bishop Meletios fled to the USA and proceeded to shape the independent Greek parishes into a diocese, which was inaugurated in September 1921. Two months later he was elected Ecumenical Patriarch and hastily transferred the Greek archdiocese of America from himself – as Archbishop of Athens – to himself – as Ecumenical Patriarch. He pointed out that the Council of Chalcedon made the Patriarch of Constantinople head of all Orthodox in 'barbarian lands'. His action – not unreasonable from the perspective of the Ecumenical Patriarchate – was challenged over the next ten years but ultimately prevailed. Unity within the Greek parishes was strengthened by Athenagoras Spyrou (1886–1972), archbishop from 1931 to 1948, and then Ecumenical Patriarch.

Other national groupings followed this example, and the American diocese disintegrated into ten different dioceses, each recognising the authority of a different Church. There were three Russian groups: the original American diocese, by now independent of Moscow and calling itself the Metropolia since it was governed by a Metropolitan; then parishes set up by the Moscow Patriarchate; and others loyal to the conservative monarchist Church of the Karlovci Synod (which was known as the Russian Orthodox Church Outside Russia and in 1946 moved its headquarters from a war-torn Serbia to New York). There were two Arab bodies, one under the Patriarchate of Antioch and one independent; and also Serbian, Romanian, Albanian, Ukrainian, and Carpatho-Russian groups. Other jurisdictions were established, including a further two separate Ukrainian groupings, both under the Ecumenical Patriarch, which were not united until 1997. Thus the Orthodox Church in the USA withdrew from its missionary task and retreated into national and often inward-looking ghettos.

The American missionary diocese did not disappear. Among the priests who had served with Bishop Tikhon at the start of the century was Leonid Turkevich. He became a monk on the death of his wife in 1925 and took the name Leonty. In 1950 he became head of the Metropolia. Metropolitan Leonty was a true successor to Bishop Tikhon. While other Church leaders were establishing a centralised control over their Churches, Leonty encouraged decentralisation, lay initiatives, the use of English in the liturgy, and the admission of women into the seminaries. It was said of him that he 'blessed everything'. He died in 1965, and the momentum which he had encouraged continued under his successors. In 1967 the 13th All-American Council voted by a show of hands to change the name of the Church from the Russian Orthodox Greek Catholic Church of America to the somewhat simpler Orthodox Church in America, although no action was taken at that stage. Then three years later closer relations with the Patriarchate in Moscow led to the granting of autocephaly to the American Church, which rapidly adopted its new name and canonised its first saint – the hermit Herman of Alaska. It has been joined by the Romanians, Albanians and Bulgarians. In 1995 it had over 600 parishes and a million members.

The autocephaly of the Orthodox Church of America carried with it the hope that this movement towards multi-ethnic American Orthodoxy would continue. But there were problems. The Greek archdiocese, by far the largest Orthodox Church in North America with 1,500,000 members, was not involved and the Ecumenical Patriarchate did not accept the autocephaly of the new Church. Most other Patriarchates followed the example of the Patriarch of Constantinople. From the point of view of the Ecumenical Patriarch, the way to an American Church was through the development of the Greek archdiocese, much the largest Orthodox community and under his jurisdiction, rather than the smaller autocephalous Church set up unilaterally by Russia. Other Patriarchates were concerned for the identity and contact with their own diaspora, expressed through being an American diocese of the home Church. The longing for a united, English-speaking American Orthodox Church remains and has produced several joint inter-Orthodox agencies and initiatives. In 1994 twenty-nine bishops met together at Ligonier in Pennsylvania and affirmed their commitment to move towards a united Church. This was not accepted by the Patriarchates – apart from Moscow – and the Orthodox Church of America remains unrecognised by most Orthodox Churches.

The confusion of many jurisdictions remains and the hopes for an indigenous American Orthodoxy, expressed as long ago as 1867 by Bishop Innocent Veniaminov, remains unfulfilled.

9

Church and state: the dream of God's kingdom on earth

To realise why the Eastern Churches are as they are, we have to begin to grasp what they have been. This task requires imagination and understanding. As in most areas of the life of the Churches, the political experience of the Eastern and Western Churches has been dramatically different. In the West, the Enlightenment political virtues of freedom, democracy, liberalism and tolerance are taken for granted. It is assumed not only that these are the hall-marks of a civilised society, but also that they are taught by the Bible. But these attitudes have come to be accepted only as a result of a specific history. This history has not been shared by the peoples of the East, and as a result the post-Enlightenment attitudes are not shared either, at least not always.

The history of the Eastern part of the Christian world followed a radically different course, and so has produced different values and ideals. It falls into three periods, each with its own characteristics. They form three political configurations, which have placed differing demands and presented differing opportunities. The three are, first, that of the Christian Empire, in which universalism combined with Christian rule to produce a vision of a Christian world order; second, that of oppression, when a non-Christian foreign power, often with universal aspirations, dominated and sometimes oppressed the Churches; and third, the growth of nationalist consciousness. These three great communal experiences of controlling, being controlled and independence should be incompatible, but in reality they exist together in the self-consciousness of the Churches and shape the present attitudes to the state. To develop a coherent and creative role for the Churches in a modern state, which both builds on the experiences of the past and responds to the demands of the present, is an intensely challenging and problematic task.

The successful discovery of an authentic Orthodox attitude to political authority is important not just for the Churches and states concerned, but for the witness of the Church as a whole. It may be that a grasp of the Western concern for the individual and his or her rights and freedoms may need to interact with an Eastern understanding of the corporate and religious nature of society to produce a wholesome synthesis and with it a creative influence of the Church on the political world order.

THE CHRISTIAN EMPIRE

The project of establishing and maintaining a Christian Empire was initiated by the Emperor Constantine, who was declared Emperor, or Augustus, at York in 306, and Emperor of the whole Roman Empire in 324. In 313 he issued the edict of Milan (in fact neither an edict nor proclaimed at Milan), as a result of which the Church found that it had suddenly become a legal institution. So Constantine proclaimed the toleration of Christianity, ending years of intermittent persecution and initiating a new era. However, although he favoured the Christian religion, he did not always act according to Christian morality, but continued as Roman Emperors had done before him. Following familiar Roman imperial practice, he ordered the killing of his sons to ensure they did not become rivals to the throne. He maintained his use of the pagan imperial title of *pontifex maximus* and was not baptised until he was on his deathbed in 337. A better candidate for the title of the first Christian Emperor is Theodosius I (379–95), who was far more active in rooting out pagan practice. From his reign onwards, the Empire was more deliberately Christian.

But the way events are remembered is as important as what actually happened, and Constantine is remembered as a saint. His biographer, Eusebius of Caesarea, is in no doubt that he was chosen by God to establish the Church as the basis of the Empire. It all began in 312, when as Constantine prepared for the crucial battle of the Milvian Bridge, he had his celebrated vision of the cross. 'About noon when the day was already beginning to decline he saw with his own eyes the trophy of a cross of light in the heavens above the sun, and bearing the inscription "by this sign conquer" [in Greek, *en touto nika*]. At this sight he was struck by amazement.'[1] He enquired of wise men as to the meaning of this sign and discovered it was the Christian symbol. From that moment on his Christian vocation, we are told, remained central to his self-awareness. He referred to his imperial task as having episcopal qualities of oversight, but exercised outside the boundaries of the Church, saying, 'I am a bishop ordained by God to oversee whatever is external to the Church.'[2] This remark shows both the claims made by his theory of divine kingship, since he is a bishop or overseer set in place by God, but also the limitation – since this does not place him over the Church, which has its own bishops, but only extends to those outside the Church. He constructed in Constantinople the Church of the Apostles, with twelve sarcophagi and in the centre a magnificent tomb in which he was eventually to be laid. This visual statement was echoed by the title given to him in the Church of *isapostolos*, or 'equal of the apostles'. So whatever his personal conduct was like, he inaugurated a new period of Church history: a Christian Empire, which was to last for over a thousand years and to shape the nature of the Eastern Church.

Within this Empire, Church and state worked together, according to a *symphonia* or harmony of interests, both seeking to uphold Orthodoxy, oppose heresy, extend the Empire, and protect the Church. This harmony of interest is shown by an incident from the life of the Palestinian holy man, Sabas. He visited Constantinople as part of a delegation to the Emperor Justinian (527–65). The party was admitted to the presence of the Emperor and made a number of requests on behalf of the Church around Jerusalem. The Emperor agreed to these petitions with alacrity, and immediately gave orders that they should be carried out. While this was being done, Sabas retired to a corner and proceeded to pray the monastic office. One of his companions was shocked at this lack of respect and remonstrated with the old man to be more attentive to the Emperor, who was being so co-operative. Sabas gave this reply: 'They are doing their work, let us do ours.'[3] This anecdote conveys something of the understanding of the Byzantine state. It was a unity under the

---

[1] Eusebius, *Life of Constantine*, 1.28–32.   [2] Eusebius, *Life of Constantine*, 4.24.
[3] Cyril of Scythopolis, *Life of Sabas*, 73, trans. Price, p. 187.

final authority of God. Each person had his part to play in it, and the Emperor had a special vocation to govern in a godly fashion, promoting well-being in civil affairs, while the Church promoted the Orthodox faith.

The Emperor received his power from God, and had an absolute authority. 'God gave you to us; God will guard you.' So the crowd welcomed the Emperor Leo I (457–74). His divinely given vocation was expressed in legal texts and also in descriptions of court ceremonial, in which ecclesiastical and secular elements were blended. In the palace a throne containing an open gospel book proclaimed the source of his authority, and in the church he shared with the Patriarch in presiding at liturgical celebration. On entering the church, the Emperor met the Patriarch at the Royal Door from the Narthex, and only then did the court officials, clergy and people enter the church. Legal texts produced by various Emperors express this conception further. Classic expressions are in the *Sixth Novella* of Justinian and the *Epanagoge* of Leo III the Isaurian, probably written by the Patriarch Photius. In the novella, Justinian wrote that 'the greatest blessings of mankind and the gifts of God which have been granted us by the mercy on high are the priesthood and the imperial authority. The priesthood ministers to things divine: the imperial authority is set over and shows diligence in things human but both proceed from one and the same source and both adorn the life of man.' Then the Patriarch Photius, who wrote the *Epanagoge*, added that 'the Lord, having entrusted the realm to the Emperors, hath likewise commanded them to tend Christ's faithful flock, after the example of Peter, the chief of the Apostles'.[4]

The practice of this theory varied. Sometimes Emperors controlled and deposed Patriarchs. Sometimes Patriarchal or, more often, popular pressure led to changes in imperial policy. Shortly after the end of the iconoclast controversy, in 795, the Emperor Constantine VI divorced his wife Mary and married Theodote. This gave rise to the so-called 'moechian', or adultery, controversy since there were inadequate grounds for the divorce and it was held that the Emperor should not be married a second time. The Patriarch turned a blind eye (a strategy often resorted to and justified under as 'economy' or an act of discretion exercised in the administration of temporal responsibility), but punished the priest who

[4] For these texts, see E. Barker, *Social and Political Thought in Byzantium* (Oxford 1957), p. 174.

officiated at the wedding. The monks were furious at this convenient overlooking of Christian standards, and so the Emperor exiled some of them. Then the Emperor's mother caused her son to be blinded and reinstated the monks. The officiating priest's fortunes went up and down, being excommunicated, reinstated, and excommunicated again, depending on who was in power. Within the power politics of the Byzantine court, it would be rash to claim either that the Emperor had supreme power and controlled the Church, or that he bowed to the authority of the Patriarch in matters ecclesiastical.

The view that the Emperor was ordained by God could have unexpected results. It could contribute to the difficulties faced by an unpopular Emperor, assisting in his deposition and downfall, as well as authenticating and upholding his authority. A successful military *coup* could be interpreted as a sign of God's approval of the successful claimant, and so inevitably a sign of disfavour towards the outgoing Emperor, who had obviously been rejected by God and should be viciously punished, with the anger of the people seen as the instrument of God's judgment. This led to instability and made being Emperor a dangerous privilege. Of the eighty-eight emperors – from Constantine I (324–37) to Constantine XI (1449–53) – thirty died a violent death and a further thirteen had to flee to a monastery for protection. One of the most grisly imperial ends befell the last Comnenian Emperor, Andronicus I, in 1185. He was overthrown and suffered a death of horrifying brutality, chained in the stocks for several days, dragged through the streets with his head held under the tail of a sick camel and his eye cut out by a furious bystander as he passed, then tortured to death in the Hippodrome. Mutilation was always a more popular penalty than death since capital punishment should be reserved to the will of God. There were surprisingly few cases of the death penalty within the Byzantine Empire. It was a violent society but was recognised to be also a Christian Empire in which all life was a gift of God and the state did not have the right to interfere in God's provision or withdrawal of his gift.

The notion of an autocratic Emperor with power given directly by God is not a common view of kingship today, but it can claim persuasive credentials. Not only did it have its roots in Greco-Roman political theory, but more significantly in the Jewish traditions of the Old Testament. The kings David and then Solomon were anointed by God to lead the chosen people, and so their secular and religious roles were indistinguishable.

In the fourteenth century, Nicholas Cabasilas pointed out in his *Life in Christ* that both the priest and the king were anointed with holy oil and the Church now follows this Biblical example. As a result both these offices 'have the same intent and the same power'.[5]

For some, the idea of a Christian state through its very nature subjects the Church to a secular authority. The phrase 'caesaro-papism' describes the action of an Emperor who takes to himself the ecclesiastical and spiritual power that rightly belongs to the Patriarch, or his equivalent, and so rules both Church and state. As a result the Church becomes a department of the administration of the state. This is a misunderstanding of Byzantine history. Church politics and imperial ambition could become confused, but the notion of the Christian Empire required that the Patriarch and Church on the one hand, and the Emperor and civil administration on the other, co-operated and worked together. While the theory of symphony could be distorted, it remained as the expression of the Byzantine ideal. A more substantial comment is that in a Christian state the Church loses its nature as a community called out by God and becomes absorbed into an earthly political order, providing ritual, doctrine, moral teaching and religious legitimisation of authority, but losing its character as an eschatological community. In Byzantium, the monasteries inherited the eschatological dimension of Christian life, providing both a distinctive community and a political opposition.

During the final siege of Constantinople by the Ottomans, in April 1453, the Emperor Constantine XI wrote to his enemy, the sultan Mehmet II, expressing his conviction that he held his rule under God's authority. 'I turn now to God and God alone. Should it be his will that the city be yours, where is he that can oppose it? I will defend my people to the last drop of my blood. Reign in happiness until the All-Just, the Supreme God, calls us both before his judgment seat.'[6] Six weeks later, on 28 May, the Emperor attended the liturgy for the last time, prostrated himself before the icons, asked forgiveness for any wrongs he had committed, embraced all the clergy, and then received the holy mysteries. The congregation wept. By 8 o'clock the next morning the long siege ended, he had died in battle, the city had fallen and the last liturgy had been celebrated in the Great Church of Constantinople.

[5] Nicholas Cabasilas, *Life in Christ* 3.1, trans. de Catanzaro, p. 103.
[6] Michael Dukas, *Historia Byzantina*, ed. I. Bekker (Bonn 1834), p. 245.

Moscow, the Third Rome

Although the fall of Constantinople brought to a final conclusion the long history of the Christian Empire of Byzantium, the imperial ideal remained in the hearts of the people of Eastern Christendom. It is a dream that has never disappeared. The natural inheritor was the growing Christian state to the north, in Russia.

The Kievan period of Russian history began in 988 when Prince Vladimir of Kiev was baptised and ended in 1188 when the city of Kiev fell to the Mongols. Its rulers tried to model their conduct on Christian values. Prince Vladimir Monomakh (d. 1125) left instructions on the art of kingship to his sons. 'My children, please God and love men. Feed the poor. Be fathers to orphans, be judges in the cause of widows and do not let the powerful oppress the weak. Put to death neither the innocent nor the guilty, for nothing is so sacred as the life and soul of the Christian.'[7] Among the saints of the Kievan period were Boris and Gleb, princes who refused to resist the fratricidal attacks of their brother Sviatopolk and preferred to accept death, thus modelling their conduct on the patience of Christ. They were not, strictly speaking, martyrs since they did not die for their Christian faith but are described as 'passion-bearers', a description to be used nearly a thousand years later of the Tsar Nicholas II and his family, killed by the Bolsheviks.

As in the history of the Byzantine Empire, many rulers did not show these Christian qualities. Ivan IV (1547–84), called the Terrible (although the Russian *groznyi* would be more accurately translated 'awesome'), set up a secret police force called the *oprichnina* to remove all opposition to the Tsar. The Metropolitan of Moscow, Philip, one day refused to allow Ivan to approach the cross. 'Sir, don't you fear God? We are here rendering the bloodless sacrifice for the salvation of the world, but beyond the sanctuary the blood of innocent Christians is being shed.'[8] Before long Philip too died at the hands of the *oprichnina*. The belief in a divinely appointed Emperor did not prevent the Church from opposing state policy when it fell short of Christian standards.

It has been suggested that, after the fall of Constantinople, the new Muscovite state saw itself as inheriting the divine vocation to rule over

[7] The Admonition of Vladimir Monomakh is assessed in G.P. Fedotov, *The Russian Religious Mind*, vol. 1 (Cambridge, MA 1966), pp. 244–60.

[8] See D. Pospielovsky, *The Orthodox Church in the History of Russia* (New York 1998), p. 66.

the Christian Empire. The monk Philotheus of Pskov wrote to Prince Basil III, 'All Christian empires bow down to you alone, for two Romes have fallen, but the third stands fast; a fourth there cannot be; your Christian empire shall not be given to another.' This text has been often quoted to suggest that Russia saw itself as a successor to the Byzantine Empire, with Moscow as the next Rome, but some caution is necessary over claiming too much. In the context in which it was written, it was intended as an apocalyptic warning. It was a time of deep uncertainty, when many believed that the fall of Constantinople was a sign of the coming end of the world. The glories of the first and second Romes had passed and the Third Rome – Moscow – would also be the Last Rome. The message was that the world must soon end, not that Moscow was destined to rule for ever into the future. The idea of the Third Rome did not pass over into political ambitions. Unlike some of the German rulers, from Charlemagne onwards, the Russian Tsars never claimed the title of Roman Emperor. Nor did the Patriarchate of Moscow claim to be first in rank among Patriarchs, but often saw itself as the fifth Patriarchate, being added to the Pentarchy to replace the Pope of Rome who had, it was clear by that time, definitely slipped into heresy.

Russia was, however, conscious that it was the largest Orthodox kingdom which was not subjected to the domination of the alien faith of Islam. This sense of religious vocation combined with the desire for political advantage to shape foreign policy and encourage expansion. As its influence extended in the nineteenth century, some Russians hoped to see the Empire embracing all Orthodox, especially including the old Constantinople. Among them was the novelist, Dostoevskii, who commented: 'Constantinople is Orthodox and all that is Orthodox should be Russian.'[9]

Today it is hard for us to imagine the possibility that the longing for a just, universal, Christian ordering of society could be a political reality. In the East, it was the foundation of the political ordering of society for over a millennium, and then a powerful dream, which has remained deeply ingrained in the heart and the imagination of the Orthodox Church. Many Orthodox churches contain two thrones. One is for the bishop, used when he visits, and the other is for the king. Often there is no king

---

[9] F. Dostoevskii's comments on the vocation of Russia are in 'Sooner or later Constantinople must belong to us', in *Politische Schriften* (Munich 1923).

to sit in the throne, since especially in formerly Communist states the monarchy has been abolished. But the throne is still in place awaiting the Christian ruler who will be a new Constantine and order the affairs of the state in co-operation with the Church to uphold a godly and Christian society.

THE ISLAMIC EMPIRES

The second great political experience of the Eastern Churches is that of being within an empire, but an empire ruled by a non-Christian power – that of Islam. There were two great periods of expansion relevant to our theme. First was the extraordinarily rapid series of conquests by the Arabs. Within a decade of the death of the prophet Muhammad in 632, the Arab tribes occupied Damascus (635), Ctesiphon, the capital of Persia (637), Jerusalem (638, following the decisive battle of the Yarmuk in 636) and Alexandria (642). This brought the Syriac and Coptic Churches under Islamic rule, a situation that has continued to the present day. The conquests extended westwards through North Africa and into Spain; and east and north into India and Central Asia, but did not defeat the Byzantine Empire in Asia Minor. The Arab Empire had exhausted itself by the tenth century.

The second period of expansion was that of the Turkish peoples. These were a group of nomadic tribes living on the Asiatic borders of the Empire who were infiltrated by the teachings of Islam when, from the ninth century, they provided slaves for the army of the Abbasid dynasty. When these slaves returned home they brought back their new faith with them, and so Islam became adopted by the peoples of the Asian steppe. There were three waves of Turkish invasions: the Saljuqs who occupied Asia Minor after the battle of Manzikert (1071); the Mongols who came within a hair's breadth of accepting Christianity (as a result of Nestorian mission – a possibility that stretches the imagination with the tantalising fantasy of a Christian Asian Empire); and then the Ottomans, named after the founder of the dynasty, Uthman I (died *c*.1299). The Ottomans conquered Bulgaria (1308–11), Thrace (after 1326), the city of Constantinople (1453), Serbia (1459), Bosnia (1463), and were not halted until their unsuccessful attempt to capture Vienna in 1683. They extended Islamic government over most of the Orthodox peoples, with the notable exception of Russia, and they retained control until the nineteenth century, when new nationalist aspirations led to a wave of revolts against a by then enfeebled Ottoman Empire. Although Arabs and Turks came from different racial stock, they shared a common religion and pattern of government based on Islamic principles, so the chronicler Michael the Syrian (1126–99) could write: 'Turks and Arabs were mixed together like a single people.'[10]

The religious movement that was Islam developed in the seventh century in a land where Christians and Jews were well established, and so it shared a common religious background with these monotheistic faiths. The Quran tells of Adam, Noah, Abraham, Ishmael, Lot, Joseph, Moses, David, Solomon, Jonah – and of course Jesus. The prophet Muhammad (c.570–632) was influenced by Christian priests, among whom were the monk Bahira, who recognised Muhammad's prophetic status when the young man was accompanying a caravan expedition into Syria, and also a priestly relative of the prophet's wife Khadijah named Waraqah, who helped the Prophet to identify the voice which revealed the Quran as that of the angel Gabriel or Jibril. Some have suggested that Muhammad came from a family of Nestorian priests. At first Islam was seen as a brand of Christianity in a shifting and syncretistic religious culture, and even the poet Dante places Muhammad among the schismatics, rather than pagans, in the *Divine Comedy*, which is seen by some as modelled on Muhammad's night journey into heaven.

Islam can be described as a monotheist reforming movement among the tribes of western Arabia. It was simple and uncompromising in its worship of the one God, clear and straightforward in its religious practice, and totalitarian in its regulation of the legal and civic institutions of the state. It grew among – and was especially suited to – the needs and characteristics of a militant, warlike and nomadic people. As such it had immediate and devastating success. Among its institutions were the *jihad* or holy war. This regularised and codified the traditional Arab practice of the *ghazw* or *razzia* (or raid), modifying its destructiveness but also exalting it into a religious duty and a political institution. The *jihad* became a method of propagating Islam, dividing the world into the *dar al-islam* (land of Islam) and *dar al-harb* (land of war). Another institution was the *dhimma*, or covenant or agreement, which gave a legal but clearly subordinate status to a subject people, and provided a framework for governing these peoples. These two institutions shaped

[10] Michael the Syrian, *Chronicle* 3.176.

the relationship of the new Muslim governments with their subject peoples, the principal of which were the Christian Orthodox. Islam was first a religion, but quickly developed into a state polity, and in due course became a culture.

Since its rapid arrival in the mid seventh century, Islam has remained a religious, political and cultural world power. From their shared Middle Eastern homeland, the encounter between Orthodoxy and Islam has expanded across three continents and extended over thirteen centuries. There have been a variety of experiences of this relationship. Some accounts have emphasised the tolerant and universalist tendencies of Islam, which have ensured a generous and benevolent regime, overall more favourable to Christians than some more intolerant Christian governments. Others have a darker view, attacking Islam as setting in place an imperialistic and totalitarian state which combined a parasitical dependence on Christian economic prosperity and hard work with a progressive destruction of the Churches, carried out alternately by vicious pogroms and by a more oblique strategy of penalising legislation.

The *dhimma*

If the *jihad* or holy war, carried out with the exuberance and aggression of an expanding nomadic people, overcame the Christian Churches, then the *dhimma* maintained them in a state of subjection. *Dhimma* means covenant, or treaty, or agreement. The equivalent in the Ottoman Empire was the *millet*, or nation, which defined the subject peoples, among whom was the Christian *millet*. The origin lies in an event in the life of the prophet Muhammad, when the armies of Islam defeated a community of Jews at Khaybar. A treaty was drawn up which allowed the conquered people the two choices of converting to Islam or paying a tribute. Ominously for generations of Jews and Christians, they were later ejected after it was decided to tolerate only Muslims within Arabia.

This principle was extended on a larger scale as the conquests continued. It gave to the Churches a recognised legal status and protection from the government, as well as requiring them to pay the tribute as a subject people. The *dhimma* was based both on religious grounds, since the Christians and Jews were 'people of the Book' and so probably not to be numbered among the polytheists, and also on pragmatic grounds, since the minority of Arab, and later Turkish, tribesmen needed the resources of the Christian communities to help them to govern effectively. Since Islam was a system of law and government which applied only to Muslims, the *dhimmi* communities enjoyed considerable autonomy, functioning as semi-autonomous national groupings, under their own religious leaders. The *dhimma* locked Muslim and Christian into a symbiotic interdependence, but it was a relationship not of equals but of conquerors and conquered, of first and second class citizens.

By giving the Church a legal and recognised place within Islamic society, it enabled the Christian communities to survive. Even in Middle Eastern countries where the Churches have been under Islamic rule since 650, there are still vigorous and sizeable Christian communities. The Coptic Church of Egypt accounts for about 15 per cent of the total population and is involved in government and in many aspects of society. Once the protection of the *dhimma* was removed in Turkey in the nineteenth century, persecution on a large scale began, removing ancient communities which had survived for centuries.

Many Church communities welcomed the Arab invaders. Monophysite and Nestorian Churches had been branded as heretics by the Ecumenical Councils of the Byzantine Empire, and had been the object of continued imperial attempts to incorporate them into the unified structure of the Empire. For these groups, the Arabs came bringing freedom from the hated Byzantine oppressor. Michael the Syrian, a Patriarch of the non-Chalcedonian Syrian Church, spoke for many: 'The God of vengeance, seeing the evilness of the Romans [= Byzantines] led the sons of Ishmael from the region of the south to deliver us from Roman hands.'[11] Many welcomed the Arabs as deliverers, or at least as no worse than the distant Greek overlords from Constantinople. In 635 the city of Damascus was handed over to the Arab general Khalid ben Walid by a group of influential Chalcedonian Christians, including Mansur ibn-Sarjun (Sergius), who was the grandfather of the future St John of Damascus. John himself was a friend in his youth of the future caliph Yazid, and was a poet, a scholar, and an official in the Umayyad court before he decided to retire to the monastery of St Sabas near Jerusalem – also, of course, within the Arab Empire. The continuing power and

---

[11] Michael the Syrian, *Chronicle* 2.412, although generally Michael is less harsh to the Byzantines.

influence of the Christians is a reminder that the Arabs were a small minority, and for a century at least the conquered countries remained Christian, with agriculture done by Christian peasants, government done by Christian leaders, scholarship continuing in Christian schools, and workmen building Christian churches. The medical profession was a virtual monopoly of Christians.

An example of a Christian who retained an influential position was Hunayn ibn-Ishaq (809–73), called by one scholar 'the greatest figure of the ninth century' and 'one of the most impressive intellects and characters that we encounter in history'.[12] He was a Nestorian Christian from al-Hirah and trained as a dispenser for a local doctor. He then learned Greek, and was appointed by the caliph as superintendent of the library and academy in Baghdad. A translator of the writings of Aristotle, Plato and Hippocrates into Arabic, Hunayn also produced an Arabic version of the Old Testament. Like many Nestorian scholars, he was learned in medicine and was appointed as the caliph's doctor. When asked to prepare a poison to dispose of one of the caliph's enemies he refused and spent a year in prison for his lack of co-operation. The caliph asked him why he would not do this, and Hunayn replied 'Two things. My religion and my profession. My religion decrees that we should do good even to our enemies. And my profession is instituted for the benefit of humanity and limited to their relief and cure.'

A similar collaboration was established by the Ottomans after the fall of Constantinople (1453). It was widely expected that the Ottomans would suppress the Orthodox Church along with the Byzantine state, but the sultan Mehmet II chose to support the Christians. He selected Gennadios Scholarios as Patriarch, saying to him, 'Be Patriarch, with good fortune and be assured of our friendship, keeping all the privileges that the Patriarchs before you enjoyed.' The result was that the power of the Patriarch was significantly enhanced. He now had control over the Chalcedonians throughout the Ottoman Empire, a considerable extension to the tiny area which had been all that was left of the Byzantine Empire in 1453, and he also enjoyed precedence over the other Eastern Patriarchs. In addition, he had civil and legal authority over the Christians.

---

[12] This remark is from I. Leclerc, *Histoire de la médicine arabe*, vol. 1 (Paris 1876), p. 139. The incident when Hunayn was doctor is in P. Hitti, *A History of the Arabs*, 10th edn (London 1979), pp. 312–14.

This constitution established by Mehmet served the Church well, providing it with some protection against later sultans who were hostile to the Church, and increasing the Greek population of Constantinople from 50,000 to 150,000 in the century following the fall of the city. A group of wealthy Greeks gained increasing amounts of power. Referred to as the Phanariots, a name derived from the Phanar region of Constantinople where many Greeks lived, these families, many tracing their descent from old Byzantine nobility, acquired their wealth from commerce, especially shipping and trade. One, Michael Cantacuzenus, was the richest man in the Middle East. Known as *Shaitanoglu*, or the Devil's son, by the Turks, he had the monopoly of the Russian fur trade. His wealth, however, did not give him security and he was arrested by the Turks on a trumped up charge and executed in 1578.

Throughout the period of Islamic rule, the Christians were an integral part of society, providing agricultural produce, commercial expertise and, above all, money to maintain the Arab, and then Turkish, state and to support the war effort. Without the Christian *millet*, or nation, the income from taxation would have diminished and the state would have ceased to be viable. It was in the interests of the governments to protect Christians from the aggression of local tribes, so that the Christians in turn could provide the supply of money and slaves on which the Empire depended.

While it was in the interests of both sides to maintain the status quo, for the Christians the reality was that they were identifiable as groups of second class citizens. They suffered occasional bouts of persecution and a consistent process of lingering civil disadvantage. There were some cruel and fanatical governors who unleashed outbursts of ferocious attack. A governor in Egypt, Abu Ja'far al-Mansur (750–4), who happened to be Armenian, was hostile to the Christian Church and ordered the destruction of many monasteries. A later Egyptian caliph of the Fatimid dynasty, abu-'Ali Mansur al-Hakim (996–1021), had a reputation for cruelty and madness. He destroyed many churches, including the Holy Sepulchre in Jerusalem in 1009. But he was not discriminating in his violence and all suffered at his hands. These formed brief interludes, however, and cannot be considered normal.

The Churches suffered more from taxation. As *dhimmi* communities, they were required to pay the *jizya*, or poll tax. This could be levied on men, women, children, and even on corpses. Then further taxes and tribute were levied from the Christians. An Ottoman levy on the Balkans was the infamous *devshirme*, or collection, which was introduced in the fourteenth century and was not officially abolished until 1656. This required that one fifth of male children in the Balkans were collected up, converted, educated as Muslims, and formed into the janissaries, or élite troops of the sultan. Some of these boys rose high in government and could provide an influence sympathetic to their homeland.

As members of a separate *millet*, Christians had their own law courts, with the result that they could not participate in trials within Islamic legal process. They were not permitted to testify in a court against Muslims, so that they could not defend themselves against accusations of, for example, blasphemy. Then there were daily humiliations to be endured. Christians were allowed to ride donkeys or asses, but not horses; their graves had to be level with the ground; they had to wear distinctive clothing; churches had to be lower in height than mosques and could not show crosses; bells could not be rung.

More significantly, the Church was weakened from within, and in this the members of the Christian communities connived. This process applied throughout the Muslim centuries but is best documented under the Ottomans. Since the function of the Christians was to pay taxes, corruption and bribery were the methods by which power could be obtained. Each new Patriarch had to pay a sum of money to the Sublime Porte, or government of the Empire, and so it was in the sultan's interest to ensure frequent changes of Patriarch and the highest possible sum of money to be paid by the person elected. As a result, high office in the Church was effectively auctioned, and the elections were controlled by wealthy Phanariot businessmen, who had the financial resources to arrange for the succession. Frequent changes were the order of the day. From 1595 to 1695 there were sixty-one changes of Patriarch, although, since some were expelled and reinstated several times, only thirty-one persons were involved in this serious game of musical chairs. Cyril I Lucaris was Patriarch a total of seven times between 1620 and 1638. Cyril II was Patriarch for seven days, before being ejected and replaced by another candidate. The average length of a Patriarch's tenure of the office was a little under twenty months. It was expensive too. In 1726 Callinicus III paid 36,400 piastres, or 5,600 gold pounds, for the Patriarchal throne and in his excess of joy, died of a heart attack the following day. Looking back over this period, a historian compares the corruption of absolute power among the Ottomans, but also 'the corruption of absolute impotence among the Greeks'.[13]

Connivance with the Turkish rulers was not the only reaction of the Christians. Many refused to co-operate, and took the path of remaining true to their faith, witnessing to the message of the gospel. Several offences could incur the death penalty. A Christian who preached to Muslims or a Muslim who became Christian was liable to the death penalty. The Church reveres the memory of many martyrs, among them Demetrios Doukas (d. 1657), who became Muslim while a child but decided to return to his original faith as an adult. He was beaten to death. The presence of martyrs continued to witness to the truth of the gospel and provided examples which encouraged Orthodox to remain loyal to their faith.

Characteristics of the Church under Islam

During the centuries of Muslim domination, some distinctive trends can be seen emerging in the Christian communities.

First, the Churches became more closely associated with the national groups rather than with the Empire. The *millet* system was the Ottoman equivalent of the Arab *dhimma*, by which a religious group was formed into a nation or *millet*. The Christian *millet* was a subordinate body, even though consisting of several ethnic groups, and so Christians came to identify with each other, rather than with the universal Empire. During the nineteenth century loyalties became narrowed still further, as the Patriarchate of Constantinople became identified with the aspirations of the Greek-speaking peoples, a process encouraged by the Phanariots who controlled the succession of the Patriarchate. The Greeks, and so also the Ecumenical Patriarch, became perceived as oppressors by the Slav Churches of Serbia and Bulgaria.

The position of the Patriarch as head of the Christian nation placed him in an impossible position when the nationalist movements emerged in the nineteenth century, since these both provided a challenge to the Patriarch's authority and also set up revolutionary insurrection for which the Turks held him responsible. Greek nationalists were fighting for a Greek state within the Greek land. While they did this, the Patriarch was forced to support the Ottoman authorities and to watch his power

---

[13] S. Runciman, *The Great Church in Captivity* (Cambridge 1968), p.187.

dwindling as Greeks gained independence, set up their own autocephalous Church, and emigrated from Turkey to the new homeland.

In the east of the Empire, nationalism has tended to unite the Churches. In the Middle East, Christians identified themselves with the new nations. Syrian Christians, for example, became more aware of their common Syrian roots and ecclesiastical divisions became less important. So in these areas national consciousness led to an overcoming of division on the basis of a common cultural and national identity.

A further consequence of the *millet* system was the hardening of the division between Constantinople and Rome. In 1453 the movement towards unity between the two, which had made some progress, was brought to an abrupt halt. The removal of the Emperor and his supporters, never popular among much of the population, brought an end to attempts at reunion. Clearly the Ottomans wanted a Church which would support them in their plans to expand westwards, and had no interest in good relations with the papacy. Since the Christian *millet* was under the Patriarch, there was no obvious place within the system for a non-Orthodox. Ottoman administrative convenience helped to exclude Western Christians from the territory of the Empire.

Language became more important as a way of ensuring the survival of the community. Amidst the decline of study, candidates for the priesthood would still be taught Greek, or Syriac, or Coptic, or Serbian, or Bulgarian, as well as a basic acquaintance with the service books. Language became a vehicle of nationhood, ecclesiastical identity and national aspiration. Much Orthodox education today retains this concern for language, for example in the Syrian monasteries of the Tur Abdin.

The legacy of the long centuries of what one writer termed 'dhimmitude' was a network of apparently weaker and more divided churches.[14] However, these have demonstrated remarkable resilience. The absence of central leadership or educational standards has led to a reliance on the worshipping life of the local church, the power of local saints, and the celebration of local festivals. This has produced an adaptable and popular form of faith which had the capacity to sustain its people through a long period of unsympathetic government. In order to survive, the Church

[14] The word 'dhimmitude' was coined by Bat Ye'or in *The Decline of Eastern Christianity under Islam, from Jihad to Dhimmitude* (London 1996).

needed strong local roots. It found that it possessed these, indeed had always had them.

NATIONALISM

The breaking up of the former empires and the growth of new nations has resulted in the emergence of a number of distinct national Churches. So, to the two political experiences of ruling a Christian Empire and being subject within a Muslim Empire, must be added a third experience. This is the development of the nation, or nationalism, a process which is continuing.

While the idea of a national Church may seem to be a modern concept, it is not necessarily contrary to Orthodox teaching, and indeed has been present within Eastern Christianity as long as the universal ideal. The absence of a centralised administrative Church structure has, as we have seen, allowed ecclesiastical organisation to mirror political reality. So at periods of history when the universal empire has been in the process of disintegration or diminishment, it has been inevitable that the one Church should also break up into smaller units. Nationalism begins when empire stops. The phenomenon of nationalism among the Orthodox Churches has a long history, characterised by opposition to the unifying centripetal tendency of imperial ideology.

The first stages of the Byzantine Empire were dominated by the long-drawn-out work of the Ecumenical Councils in combating heresy. It has been suggested that the great Christological heresies of Nestorianism and Monophysitism should be recognised as nationalist movements.[15] First, the Churches that adhered to these doctrinal positions used mainly the local languages of Coptic and Syriac instead of the Greek of the Empire. Then they had their power base in the rural monasteries rather than in the episcopal churches of the cities, and these monastic centres provided protection and resistance against the demands and control of the imperial authorities. When the Arabs arrived they were greeted warmly by many Monophysites as liberators from the Byzantine yoke, and independent Coptic and Syrian Churches rapidly took shape. This nationalist thesis has been criticised for not doing justice to the social and linguistic complexity of the new separatist Churches, but if the Councils were – at

[15] A.H.M. Jones, 'Were the ancient heresies national or social movements in disguise?', *Journal of Theological Studies* NS 10 (1959), pp. 280–98.

least in part – imperial political programmes in disguise, then the heresies were – also at least in part – national movements in disguise. The identification of these Churches with national and ethnic groups is one of the reasons for their extraordinary tenacity in surviving centuries of hostile discrimination.

The next wave of nationalism happened after Constantinople fell to the Crusaders in 1204, and the Byzantine Empire retreated into three small enclaves at Nicaea, south-east of Constantinople; at Epirus in the north of Greece; and at Trebizond, on the Black Sea coast of Asia Minor. This left a power vacuum at the heart of the Empire which the buoyant and emergent Balkan states were not slow to exploit. The Bulgarians acted fast, setting up a patriarchal bishopric in Trnovo, which survived until the Ottoman conquest of Bulgaria in 1393. The Church of Serbia was given self-governing status in 1219 by the Patriarch of Constantinople, based in Epirus. Later, in 1448, the Church of Russia was finally granted the same status after the Ottoman capture of Constantinople. These new Churches combined an ethnic identity, an Orthodox faith, and imperial ambitions, as each hoped to supplant the Emperor and perhaps even gain the ultimate prize – the conquest of the glittering capital city of Constantinople.

In the two centuries that have passed since 1800, the great Empires of both Constantinople and Russia have disintegrated. Independent and national Churches have been formed in the place of the large and multinational Patriarchates, so changing the face of Orthodoxy. The nationalist tendency which had been an alternative to imperial government now displaced the universal ideal. This was helped by the fact that both of the once great Christian Empires of Constantinople and Russia had become clearly non-Christian – one Islamic and the other atheist – and so there could be no nostalgic longing for the good old imperial days. In addition, nationalism was the prevailing political philosophy across Europe. The French Revolution provided the clearest expression of the new political philosophy of nationalism – where national identity became the basis of the state, and was expressed through a shared language and culture – although with a certain flexibility in accepting those from a different ethnic group who nevertheless felt themselves to be included within the national culture. As a result, ethnic groups asserted their language and culture, claimed the right of national self-determination and recognised that the source of political authority lay within the people rather than in a divinely appointed ruler. A wind of national consciousness was sweeping across Europe, and reached into its eastern corners.

The impact of nationalism is shown clearly by the example of the great commercial centre of Thessaloniki, known then as Salonika. It was the capital of Macedonia, and was a cosmopolitan, multi-cultural, multi-ethnic city. The largest ethnic group were the Jews – mainly Sephardic Jews who had been expelled from Christian Spain and Portugal between 1492 and 1497. They had found a home in the more tolerant Ottoman Empire, and as a result Salonika had the largest Jewish population of any city in Europe, dominating commerce and trade and sometimes politics. Next came the Turks, the wealthiest sector of the community. The Greeks were only the third largest community, followed by the Bulgarians. When in 1908 the Ottoman sultan fell to the Young Turks of Kemal Ataturk (himself a native of Salonika), all communities were united in celebrations. The people of the city hoped that the new ruler would bring the reconciliation of races and the dawn of a new era.

Their optimism proved misplaced and the harmony was not to last. In 1917 a fire destroyed much of old Salonika, and the rebuilding both modernised and hellenised the old town. Then in 1921 came the population exchange when Turks were expelled and replaced by shiploads of destitute Greek refugees expelled from their homes in Turkey. The 50,000 Jews of Salonika disappeared in 1943 in train loads bound for Auschwitz and other final destinations. The transmutation of multi-ethnic Salonika into Greek Thessaloniki illustrates a process that was changing the face of Eastern Europe. To the *millet* system of the Ottomans which asserted religious and national distinctiveness within one Empire was added a new element: that of territory, with each group fighting for control of its own land. The result in the case of Salonika was the unscrambling of a cosmopolitan and tolerant commercial centre and the setting up of a Greek city.

In the case of the new Greek nation, of which Thessaloniki was a part, the national Greek identity gradually displaced an older Greek Byzantine internationalism. Greek-speaking people in the Empire remembered their Byzantine past and tended to refer to themselves as 'Christians' or 'Romans' – and Chalcedonian Orthodox in the Middle East are still known as Rum (or Roman) Orthodox. They were scattered throughout the Ottoman Empire, and were especially numerous in western Turkey. The Phanariot Greek élite of Constantinople controlled not only the Ecumenical Patriarchate but also the Romanian principalities of Moldavia and Wallachia. Greeks controlled shipping and commerce, and it was even a Greek admiral who led the Ottoman fleet fighting against the Greek rebellion that led to an independent Greece. So as the Greek state began its struggle to exist, it was fighting not only the Ottoman Empire but also much of the Greek community within the Empire too. A new nationalistic Greek identity was replacing the old Byzantine Christian universalism.

The beginnings of this process came with the foundation in 1814 of the *Philike Hetairia* or 'friendly association', with its dream of reconstituting a new Greek civilisation in the eastern Mediterranean. An abortive uprising in Romania in 1821 sparked off a more spontaneous and serious revolution in Greece. Bishop Germanos of Old Patras was a leader of the rising, which was centred on the monastery of the Megalospelaion in the Peloponnese. Priests and monks were fully involved, including the monks of Mount Athos, of whom around half participated actively in the struggle. Along with Greek conquest went enforced baptism of Turks into the Orthodox faith. Many of the Greek soldiers refused to fight on religious holidays. In June 1822 the Acropolis in Athens was reconquered, and the Parthenon rededicated to the Mother of God. To this Greek urge for self-determination was added support from the European powers. Allied European ships destroyed the Turkish navy at the battle of Navarino (1822), and the independence of Greece was secured. As well as supplying military support, the allies also gave the Greeks a king in the person of Otto I of Saxe-Coburg, who brought with him European ministers of state, including Georg von Maurer, who helped to draw up a constitution for the Church and the state. This was opposed by the Ecumenical Patriarch, who, living in Constantinople, had little choice but to oppose Greek national aspirations.

The influence of the West led to the Church being seen as subject to the state, following Protestant models. In 1834 all monasteries with less than six monks were dissolved, and the lands appropriated by the government, so the number of monasteries was reduced from 412 to 148, with convents down from about thirty to just two. In 1843, the 'year of revolutions', a Greek army successfully demanded the removal of German advisers, a new constitution, and an Orthodox king. Soon after that, in 1850, Constantinople recognised the Greek Church.

The present boundaries of the Greek state were formed through a traumatic event, sometimes known as the Great Catastrophe. By the end of the First World War, the Ottoman Empire had disappeared and the new Turkish state had retired to the depths of Anatolia. In 1919, with British encouragement – but no practical help – an invading Greek force landed in Smyrna (today, Izmir), on the west coast of Turkey. At first the Greeks made steady progress, but then a resurgent Turkish army won a decisive victory in Anatolia in 1922. Greek retreat turned into massacre, and a peace was rapidly brokered at the Treaty of Lausanne in 1923 at the terrible cost of the Great Population Exchange. By this arrangement 1.3 million Greeks were forced to leave Turkey for Greece and 800,000 Turks travelled in the opposite direction. In addition to those forcibly ejected must be added the number who left Turkey voluntarily, so that the Greek state, exhausted by war, was forced to absorb over 4 million refugees, or around a half of its total population. This had a devastating effect on the young Greek state.

Each of the new nations of the Balkans followed its own path to independence. But some characteristics, shown vividly in the experience of the emerging modern Greek state, were common to all. As infant states trying to survive in a Europe where the militarised and imperialistic Great Powers were bristling on the edge of armed conflict, national boundaries, economic survival and political stability often depended on decisions taken in Western European capitals. Several of the Balkan states gained independence in 1878, namely Serbia, Romania and Montenegro. This was achieved at the Congress of Berlin, when the Great Powers met to decide on the shape of the south-east part of Europe. Here, according to the formula stated by the Hungarian delegate Julius Andrassy: 'The decisions should in the first instance be based on geographical and strategical considerations and only on ethnographical grounds if no other basis for decision could be found.'[16] The countries whose borders were effectively being pencilled onto blank maps were of course not consulted. This pattern continued at future international deliberations. Generally speaking, Romania did quite well, being awarded Transylvania and Bessarabia, at the Treaty of Paris after the First World War, and Bulgaria did quite badly, having its territories reduced from

---

[16] Cited in M. Glenny, *The Balkans 1804–1999* (London 1999), pp. 145–6.

176,000 sq. km to 96,000 at the earlier Congress of Berlin, and never regaining its pre-1878 extent.

The nations thus created were sometimes offered around the royal houses of Europe, and kings and princes were arbitrarily installed. Otto I of Greece (1832–62) came from Bavaria; Prince Alexander of Bulgaria (1879–87) came from Hesse and when he proved to be too successful in expanding Bulgaria's borders was replaced by Ferdinand of Saxe-Coburg (1887–1912).

The beginnings of the Greek state also contains an ominous example of a strategy to be used all too often in modern Balkan history. The Population Exchange between Greece and Turkey solved the problem of civil war through mass deportation, otherwise known as ethnic cleansing. Britain has to bear some of the responsibility for this, since not only did a British Prime Minister encourage the Greek invasion of Turkey, but another British government minister, Lord Curzon, presided over the Treaty of Lausanne which arranged the pioneering example of ethnic cleansing. A modern historian comments: 'Under the eyes of Britain's senior diplomat, two Balkan nations agreed to end a conflict that British diplomacy had inspired by setting a dreadful precedent.'[17] The Western powers have been involved in the sad history of the Balkan states, and have to acknowledge some responsibility for the tragic and bloody events which have taken place.

The second characteristic which all Balkan nations shared was the extreme level of violence. Massacre, intimidation and intrigue became the most readily available methods of political discourse and action. No area of the Balkans escaped the persistent waves of violence. In the case of Bulgaria and Macedonia, there was the quasi-independent state set up by Pasvanoğlu Osman Paşa in 1795, which was controlled by armed thugs; the arrival of hundreds of thousands of Circassian refugees expelled from the Caucasus by the advancing Russians in the 1860s, eager to take revenge on any Christian they could find; vicious reprisals by the Turkish irregular *basi-bozoks* (broken heads) after the 1876 Bulgarian uprising; the struggles between competing nationalist groups after 1893; the extreme violence of the First and Second Balkan Wars of 1912 and 1913; and then the slaughter of the First World War; the arrival of the

---

[17] M. Glenny, *The Balkans*, p. 392.

Nazis and the extermination of Jews in the Second World War; and so it went on. The British journalist H.N. Brailsford travelled in the region in 1906 and sent reports home:

> Fear is the great fact of their [the Macedonian and Bulgaria peasants'] daily lives. Looking back upon my wanderings among them, a procession of ruined minds comes before the memory – an old priest lying beside a burning house speechless with terror and dying slowly; a woman who had barked like a dog since her village was burned; a maiden who became an imbecile because her mother buried her in a hole under the floor to save her from the soldiers; a lad who turned ill with fear when a solder put a knife to his throat. The human wreckage of a hurricane which usurps the function of a government.[18]

The legacy of violence is fear, and the legacy of fear is more violence.

From this period a new word entered the theological vocabulary of the Orthodox Church: *phyletism*, from the Greek *phyle* or tribe. The occasion was the Bulgarian independence struggle. In order to retain some form of control over Bulgaria the Turks accepted the setting up of a Bulgarian Orthodox Church under an exarch. The north of the country was given to the exarchate and the other regions could choose between the Ecumenical Patriarchate and the exarchate; a two-thirds majority in a referendum was required to secede from Constantinople. Villages switched from being Greek (Patriarchate) to Bulgarian (exarchate) depending on promises of aid or of education, or under threats from armed gangs, including sometimes the local bishop.

In 1870 a Council met at Constantinople at which the Patriarch excommunicated the Bulgarians, stating that they should not sacrifice the obedience due to the Church to the 'new and destructive principle of nationality'. The Council's objection was not to the new Church, but to the ethnic basis of the new Church. In many areas the people were faced with a choice between two Churches, of different ethnic composition, but this offended against the inclusive nature of the Church, which should include people of any nationality who live in the area concerned. The Council pointed to the difference between a local Church and an ethnic Church. The Patriarch was right to point to the danger which nationalism posed to the Church, but his strictures in this instance are somewhat lacking in moral authority since his Church was as fully

---

[18] H. N. Brailsford, *Macedonia, its Races and their Future* (London 1906), pp. 36–7.

involved in the struggle as the Bulgarians he was excommunicating. The squabble festered on, and a Bulgarian Patriarch was not elected until 1953 and not recognised by Constantinople until 1961.

The concept of *phyletism* has come to define the darker side of modern Orthodoxy: its support of nationalism, its participation in discrimination and even massacre of other ethnic groups, its involvement in intrigue and power grabbing. In reality the Churches' involvement has been varied and complex, including examples of both clear moral leadership and also incitement to racial hatred. The different and even contradictory nature of the Churches' involvement can be seen in their attitudes to Jews. They can claim both credit and blame. There are examples of xenophobic, anti-Semitic movements within the Church, such as the Legion of the Archangel Michael. This was founded in 1927 by a Romanian peasant, Zelea Codreanu, and later developed into the nationalist Iron Guard. Codreanu was a charismatic figure who dressed in white and rode on a white horse, inspiring fanatical devotion and a campaign of rural reconstruction to improve the lot of the peasants. His organisation was motivated by two principles: reverence for the Romanian peasant and hatred of the Jews. 'They are the arch-enemies; we shall destroy the Jews before they can destroy us', he said. His movement gained considerable power in the next few years before the government arrested many of its leaders in 1932. On other occasions the Church has provided clear humanitarian leadership. In 1941 the head of the Bulgarian Church was Metropolitan Stefan. His fearless and persistent advocacy of the cause of the Jews is seen as one of the main reasons for the cancellation of the order to transport Bulgaria's Jews to the death-camps of Germany in 1943.

New nationalisms: three examples

Nationalism as a movement has by no means run its course. The end of the twentieth century has seen the break-up of the Soviet Union and of Yugoslavia, both of which were federations of national groups linked for political convenience and through military conquest, and both of which disintegrated in the 1990s. As a result a number of new states have claimed their independence, producing further fragmentation within the Churches. The three examples of Macedonia, Estonia and the Ukraine show the tensions and difficulties the nationalist process produces for the Churches.

Macedonia was a recognised national grouping within the Ottoman Empire which failed to gain self-determination as the Empire faded. A strategically significant region in the centre of the Balkans, with the port of Salonika as its capital, its history is distinguished by figures such as Alexander the Great (d. 323 BC) and the missionary saints Cyril and Methodius. It is an ethnically mixed area, with Slavs, Greeks, Albanians, Turks (until the Population Exchange), as well as large numbers of Roma, or gypsies, and other smaller groups. As a result of the ethnic mix, the territory had many claimants and has now come to be divided between modern Greece, Bulgaria and Yugoslavia. Since the Second World War, national aspirations developed in the northern region, which had become a separate Macedonian republic within the former Yugoslavia. The three Orthodox dioceses in the republic were under the jurisdiction of the Patriarch of Serbia, but no bishops were appointed due to difficulties in finding candidates acceptable to both local Macedonians and the Serbian Church. In 1958 the Macedonians took unilateral and uncanonical action by electing bishops to these sees without the consent of the Serbian Patriarch. This produced an uneasy relationship with the Church of Serbia and led to a self-proclaimed autonomy by the Macedonians in 1967. The new Church was not really viable – with one diocese, and no monasteries or seminaries – and the Serbs rightly objected that it was, in part, a political movement encouraged by the Communist government, with the aim of dividing and weakening the Church. The Church has grown since then, and there is now, as in many countries, a revival of monastic life. But since Serbs claim the Church, and Bulgarians consider Macedonian to be a dialect of Bulgarian and rightfully theirs, and Greeks consider Macedonia to be part of northern Greece, both the newly independent Republic of Macedonia and its national Church have a precarious existence. The Church is not recognised by any of the Patriarchates, but is in the process of regularising its status by becoming an autonomous Church within the jurisdiction of the Patriarchate of Serbia.

Estonia is one of several states which gained independence during the break-up of the Soviet Union. While the Lutherans are the largest denomination, the Orthodox Church in the region has a long history, with missions being active from the tenth century. After the Bolshevik take-over in 1917 and the assassinations of several Church leaders, the Orthodox Church sought the protection of the Ecumenical Patriarch and was granted autonomous status in 1923. In 1940 Russia conquered Estonia, and the Church once again became part of the Moscow Patriarchate, then it was returned to the Ecumenical Patriarch from 1942–4, then back to Moscow from 1944 to 1990. Many Estonian Orthodox, including the Metropolitan Alexander Paulus, fled to the West and established an Estonian Church Abroad under the Ecumenical Patriarchate. Thus, at independence, both the Moscow Patriarchate and the Estonian Church (now able to return from exile) had grounds for claiming to be the legitimate Estonian Orthodox Church. Uncertainty led to conflict, which led in turn to the extraordinary situation in which, for a few months in 1996, the two Patriarchates of Constantinople and Moscow were not in communion with each other. An agreement was quickly reached – as it had to be – whereby each individual Estonian church could choose which Patriarch it would be under. A larger number of parishes chose Constantinople, but a majority of individual believers have opted for Moscow.

The most complex, violent and intractable dispute is found in the Ukraine. Not only is the Ukraine the second largest country in Europe, but it has a long Christian history since the centre of the Russian Church was in the Ukrainian capital of Kiev before it moved to Moscow. It is also the home of the largest Greek Catholic Church. After the Communist Revolution in 1917, the Ukrainian Autocephalous Orthodox Church was set up by local bishops; this survived until 1930, when the Church was reunited with the Moscow Patriarchate by Stalin. Then in 1946 the Greek Catholic Church 'decided' at the Council of Lviv to reunite with Moscow, although this decision was required by the Russian government. These two Churches continued to exist both in the diaspora and also in an underground form within the Ukraine, and so were ready to re-emerge when the control of Moscow relaxed after 1990. The situation was further complicated by the controversial figure of Metropolitan Philaret Denisenko, the Moscow Patriarchate's Metropolitan of Kiev. He decided to become independent of Moscow but was expelled from the episcopate in 1992, for a number of disciplinary reasons. Metropolitan Philaret enjoyed the support of the President of the new Republic of the Ukraine and was able to establish his own Church, the Patriarchate of Kiev. At present there are four main Churches in the Ukraine. The largest is the Moscow Patriarchate with, in 1998, 6,300 parishes mostly in the east of the country; then comes the Kiev Patriachate, with 1,901 parishes;

then the Autocephalous Orthodox Church, with 1,063 parishes in the west; and there is also the Greek Catholic Church, with 3,151 parishes in the western Ukraine. The possession of church buildings has been bitterly contested, often with violent clashes between opposing groups.

From the beginning the Orthodox Churches have not developed a clear political philosophy and have instead allowed ecclesiastical organisation to respond to political reality. This has been the strength of the mission strategy, with the Christian faith expressed and articulated in the language and culture of a national group. But it becomes a problem when disorder, conflict and extremism are present in the nation, and then the Church shares in these features of the society.

The Biblical traditions of peace, harmony and justice are also present within the Churches, and the close identification of the Church and the people has the potential for the Church to provide a creative leadership as well. So just as the Church shares in the sometimes destructive nationalistic fervour which drives a people to demand statehood, so it can give to the new nation the Christian traditions of peace and reconciliation. Churches have a level of popular support and influence far greater than in the West and so have the capacity to provide political as well as religious leadership within new nations as they seek to develop stable and viable structures.

A moment of democracy

Orthodox Churches have lived in corporate rather than individualistic societies. The Byzantine, Ottoman and Russian Empires can be described as totalitarian in that power is seen as residing in the Emperor, Sultan or Tsar, who rules over all aspects of the life of the Empire. Traditions of democracy, tolerance, individualism and freedom have emerged in post-Enlightenment Europe and are less familiar in an Eastern context. Within the two thousand-year history of Christianity, these democratic traditions should be recognised as a relatively new arrival, although Western Christianity has found them compatible with the Christian faith. The East has not inherited the same traditions. So the question arises as to whether democracy and Orthodoxy can co-exist.

For just over a month, from 15 August to 17 September 1917, the Russian Church enjoyed a brief and heady moment of freedom. The Tsar had abdicated, ending the centuries of state control, and the Bolsheviks had not yet initiated the years of persecution. During this month the

Council of Moscow carried out a series of rapid reforms, which are significant both because they demonstrated the democratic potential of the Church and also because they gave the beginnings of a structure to strengthen the Church in the difficult years ahead. It enacted a rapid pro-gramme of legislation including the re-establishing of the Patriarchate; the setting up of a system of elected councils or *sobors* at diocesan and national levels; new rights for parishes, including the right to elect their own priest. This Council was made up of 564 members: eighty bishops, 149 priests, nine deacons, fifteen sextons and 299 laypersons. This broad spectrum of Church opinion had emerged out of old and sometimes ide-alised Russian communal village traditions; from structures developed in the missionary diocese of the USA, under the bishop and future Patriarch Tikhon Bellavin; from socialist agitation of radical groups of politicised clergy in St Petersburg and Moscow; and in the views of many bish-ops and clergy. It was the moment of glory of what one writer, Nicolas Zernov, has referred to as the Russian Religious Renaissance of the twentieth century. It set up a structure of Church government which ref-lected the will and responsibility of the people. This gave the Church a strength and resilience that helped it to withstand the onslaught to come.

While the Orthodox understanding of the Church sees power as be-longing to the bishop, and as expressed in practical terms in the synod or council of bishops, it also recognises the responsibility of all Church members to 'receive' the decisions of a Council. This spirit-given right and responsibility can show itself in democratic institutions as well as in a more prolonged process of accepting or rejecting decisions made by somebody else. Orthodox Churches have not had much opportunity to practise democracy, but the Moscow Council of 1917 shows that the potential is there.

Nationalism among the Oriental Orthodox

The Oriental Orthodox experience of nationalism has been very differ-ent. While nationalism led to the establishing of new national states and Churches in Eastern Europe, it was disastrous in areas where the Church was a minority faith, especially in Turkey. Under Western pressure the Ottoman Empire initiated a programme of liberal and administrative reform in the nineteenth century. This included equality of rights for all citizens of the Empire. These reforms seemed at first to be of benefit to Christians, but they badly backfired. In the years that followed, around

3 million Muslims fled from the Balkans back to Turkey and the Arab provinces, feeling resentment against the new Christian states which had forced them to leave. In addition, traditional Muslims saw the reforms as a dismantling of the *dhimma* which had given a legal – if subordinate – status to the Christians, so removing the protection given to Christian minorities. The new Turkish state, led by Kemal Ataturk and the Young Turk movement, was secular in religious affiliation but based on Turkish ethnic identity, and so providing no recognised place for non-Turks. All these factors combined to produce a series of massacres of the large Christian minorities of Turkey.

The first massacres were directed against Armenians in 1895–6 in which up to 200,000 lost their lives. Further killings followed in 1909 and in 1915–17, and then sporadically up to 1922, Syrians, Assyrians and Armenians were all slaughtered, but the genocide of Armenians was more systematic, since their larger numbers and wider dispersion led the Young Turks to see them as a potential threat to the new state. Altogether, over 1,500,000 Armenians were killed. Hitler noted this genocidal policy, and used it an example for his own pogroms, and also noted how little concern was expressed by Western European states. In addition, the Greek population has declined, many moving to Greece after the war of 1920–1, and then as a result of ethnic tension after the partition of Cyprus.

TSAR AND COMMISSAR: THE CASE OF RUSSIA

Russia, alone among Orthodox countries, was beyond the reach of Arab or Ottoman invasion. As a result it does not quite fit into the categories and experiences described here. Its history shows both similarities and differences from that of the Byzantine and Ottoman Empires, and needs to be discussed separately from them.

The first period of subjection to a non-Christian power began in 1240 when the great city of Kiev, with its twelve monasteries and 400 churches, fell to the Mongols. Mongol rule continued for the following two centuries, although persecution was slight.

A different kind of captivity came three centuries later in 1700. Peter the Great determined to rule Russia as a modern Western state, and part of his strategy was to follow the example of the West in reducing the status of the Church to that of a government department. He was helped in his task of redefining the Church by two bishops: Stephan

Yavorskii, a young professor from Kiev who was promoted to become the youngest bishop in the Church; and then later Feofan Prokopovich, who was consecrated bishop of Pskov in 1718 and who drew his ideas from Lutheran sources. Prokopovich had a large library of 3,000 volumes of which three-quarters were Lutheran. In 1720 with the help of an English lawyer, Francis Lee, he produced the *Spiritual Regulation*, which was, as Georges Florovsky commented, neither spiritual nor a regulation. It defined the Church as 'an association of the people of God into a society or republic of citizens for the purpose of knowing each other better, being of help to each other, and so that, with God's help, they might defend themselves better from their enemies'.[19]

Government was to be in the hands of a College for Spiritual Affairs, with a Chief Procurator or, since the Tsar preferred a German title, *oberprokuror*, providing communication with the Tsar. At its first meeting in 1721 the bishops complained that this title was not known in the Orthodox Church and it should be called a Holy Synod. They got their way over the name, but the nature of the body ensured that the Church was firmly under the control of the Tsar. It consisted of about twelve members, mostly bishops, who were appointed by the Tsar and could be dismissed by him. They could not initiate any discussion, and could only vote for or against matters presented to them by the Chief Procurator, and if the vote displeased the Procurator, he would not present it for the Tsar's approval.

Over the next two hundred years the *oberprokuror*s included men of a wide variety of opinions. There was Melissino, a free thinker; Chebyshev, who denied the existence of God; Prince Golitsyn, a pietist and freemason; Nechaev, another freemason. The most notorious and, from the point of view of his legacy, disastrous was Konstantin Pobedonostsev (1827–1907), who was to play an important part in the end of the old Empire in Russia. He was *oberprokuror* from 1880 to 1905. A professor of law and a devout man, he translated Thomas à Kempis' *Imitation of Christ* into Russian. He was a friend of Dostoevskii, but also a man with a deeply pessimistic view of human nature, which, he felt, needed strong and paternalistic government, and the strict elimination of any corrupting hint of a progressive or liberal movement. He was a good civil servant who helped to promote an ineffective episcopacy

---

[19] Cited in D. Pospielovsky, *The Orthodox Church in the History of Russia*, p. 112.

and a stagnant theological education. Under his guidance bishops were kept on the move, with the average length of stay of a bishop in any one diocese being two and a half years, with the result that the huge Church of Russia with its 100 million members divided into 63 dioceses was run on a state-imposed episcopal rota system. It was one of the tragic elements of nineteenth-century Russia that a man of such talent and ability, but of such conservative convictions, should have dominated the Church during a critical period of its history and frustrated every attempt to restore and renew it.

PERSECUTION

The recent history of the Orthodox Churches has been marked by extreme suffering and persecution. Accurate figures are not available – since the victims were nameless and unknown Christians whose martyrdoms went unrecorded – but it is clear that more Christians have died for their faith in the last century than in any other, and that the overwhelming majority of these have been in the eastern parts of Christendom. Between 1918 and 1940 it is estimated that 40,000 clergy, 40,000 monks and nuns, and many millions of laypeople died in Russia. To these can be added the numbers who have died since then in Russia; those who suffered in the extension of Communism to the countries of Eastern Europe after the Second World War; 1.5 million Armenians, hundreds of thousands of Greeks and many Syrians in Turkey between 1895 and 1925; around 750,000 Serbs in the Nazi concentration camps of the Second World War; and attacks and deaths at the hands of militant Islamic groups, which is still the experience of many in the Middle East and especially in Egypt. While the experience of Russia dwarfs the other persecutions by virtue of its unbelievably huge scale, the other waves of persecution should not be overlooked. The self-consciousness of the Orthodox Churches in this century has been shaped by suffering.

Why should this have happened? While there are many ways that such a huge phenomenon can be interpreted, it is essential to recognise that there has been a conflict between two religious faiths. Marx had stated that Communism begins with atheism, and since atheism is a religious conviction, then it becomes an attitude of faith (since the question of the reality of God falls outside the range of scientific demonstration). It has sometimes been spoken of as an eschatological heresy, with its roots in the Judaeo-Christian tradition. In place of the promise of a transcendent heaven, resulting from faith in God, Communism believes in an earthly paradise created by just and communal human social structures. So, once the material base of the Church, which is its legal protection and economic support, has been removed then it follows that the Church will wither and die, since it has no other basis for its existence. The problem for the Soviet government was that it didn't. The phases of extreme persecution, from 1928 to 1939 and then from 1959 to 1964 (the Krushchev years), arose in part because of a sense of desperation that the expected demise of religion was just not taking place. From 1926 to 1927 it was noted that the number of churches in the Soviet Union actually grew, in spite of legal restriction, from 27,126 to 29,584. And in the 1950s sociological surveys showed a growing interest in religion, especially among young people. In both these periods, it was clear that the Church was not dying, and so it had to be killed.

The seventy years of persecution in Russia went through phases. Its beginning can be dated precisely, to 23 January 1918, when a decree separating Church and state was issued. This led to confiscations of Church goods and attacks on churches, followed by attempts to divide the Church by supporting groups hostile to the Patriarchate. In 1927 the new leader of the Church, Sergei, was imprisoned. After some negotiation he was released and promptly issued a Declaration of Loyalty to the Soviet government, and also required Russian refugee parishes to do the same. 'We want to be Orthodox and at the same time recognise the Soviet Union as our civic motherland. Her [note that motherland is feminine in Russian, while Soviet Union is masculine – clearly the use of the feminine form points away from the Communist state towards the country] joys and successes are our joys and successes, her misfortunes are our misfortunes.'[20] This statement did not prevent the tightening of the laws against the Church, with a new law in 1929 forbidding all forms of religious 'propaganda' and restricting the Church to liturgical acts of worship within the walls of the churches. It also did not prevent the onset of a decade of intensified persecution which left, according to one estimate, no more than 300 churches open in Russia, and 40,000 priests, and a similar number of monks and nuns dead. The words of Patriarch Tikhon on his deathbed in April 1926 were proved true: 'the night will be very long and very dark'.

[20] Cited in ibid., p. 251.

There was a respite during the Second World War. The Church adopted a nationalist position giving full support to the national war effort. As a result, Stalin – who was, like many Bolsheviks, a product of the Church education system – summoned the Patriarch and two senior bishops to a personal meeting in September 1943. The benefits which resulted from the meeting were immediate and dramatic. Within four days bishops were transported to Moscow for a Council, churches and seminaries then started to be opened and some imprisoned bishops and clergy were released. The position of the Church was further strength-ened by Soviet military success in the West, which regained large areas of land in the Ukraine, Belarus, the Baltic states and elsewhere. These had around 4,000 Orthodox – and Greek Catholic – Church communities which were absorbed into the Russian Church, which as a result found itself vastly increased in size. This situation persisted so that, as late as 1988, official Patriarchate figures stated that over 4,000 of the 6,893 Orthodox parishes in the Soviet Union were located in the Ukraine.

A further wave of persecution began with the rise of Krushchev in 1959, and continued less virulently after his death in 1965. Gorbachev, it might be noted, was in charge of anti-religious persecutions as head of the KGB. So this would suggest that he decided on his policy of relaxation of persecution in 1988 because of his need of support for his policies of *perestroika* and *glasnost*. At a meeting with a group of bishops he spoke, remarkably, of 'our common cause'. In 1990 a new law proclaimed freedom of religion and permitted religious instruction in schools. The law, however, has become slightly less liberal since then, with a new law in 1997 setting restrictions on the work of many Churches, especially those from the West and new sects.

Various strategies were used against the Church. The most obvious was violence. The first casualty among the bishops was Metropolitan Vladimir of Kiev. A band of sailors attacked the Monastery of the Caves in Pskov, where he was living, dragged him out and killed him, as the monks watched powerless to intervene. Millions more deaths were to follow.

Then there was taxation. After 1929, clergy were classed as benefiting from private enterprise (taxed at 81% of income), and were not allowed to vote or serve in the army (for which a further tax of up to 50% of income could be levied). A tax of 10% of the value of the home could also be charged. Often the tax payable by clergy exceeded their total income. In 1930, to give one example, Bishop Sinezi of Izhevsk, with an income of 1,440 roubles per year, was served with a tax bill of 10,703 roubles.

Then there was division. In the early years the Soviet government set up an alternative, compliant, radical Church, called the 'Living Church' or Renovationists, led by a left-wing St Petersburg priest, A. Vvedinskii. Its purpose was to lure believers away from the Orthodox Church, and initially it was quite successful, claiming the allegiance of 400 out of the 404 churches in Moscow in 1922, the year it was set up. It quickly declined and within a few years had become a negligible force, but the government remained keen to support any schism.

Then there were legal restrictions on the constitution of churches, with many pretexts available for removing the legal registration of a church and so closing it, and reasons for preventing the opening of new churches.

Many, however, would claim that these penalties were not the most serious form of persecution. More damaging was the requirement to live a lie. In order to stay in existence at all, the Church authorities had to proclaim loyalty to an atheist regime which was persecuting the Church, and to deny that this was taking place. The Romanian theologian, Dumitru Staniloae, who was a prisoner for seven years, was once asked what were the worst features of the Communist system, to which he replied 'There are two things. The first is the fear and the second is the lie.' Commentators sympathetic to the Moscow Patriarchate have spoken of a new form of martyrdom, in which the Patriarch and bishops voluntarily accepted that they must collude in the attack on the Church and so, from the perspective of faith, were placing their immortal soul at risk of damnation in order to maintain some form of existence for the Church. They made the greatest sacrifice to enable the Church to remain in some kind of existence as a part of Russian society. Others have been less charitable and have condemned the leadership as collaborators with an atheist regime.

In assessing the effects of this period, it is tempting to suggest that little changed. The faith of the Russian people before the rise of Communism should not be overestimated. The vitality of the Church had been stifled by two centuries of state control by the Synod established by Peter the Great, and by being associated with the repressions of the Tsars. A delegate at the 1917 Church Council commented, 'We say we have 110

million Orthodox Christians, but what if we have as few as 10 million?'
Military chaplains reported that when the government made the receiving of Holy Communion voluntary in 1917 the proportions of soldiers
taking communion fell from 100 per cent to 10 per cent. Another chaplain reported that the soldiers built a church while on campaign, only for
an officer to use it as a shelter, with a lavatory in the sanctuary, and the 2–
3,000 soldiers of the regiment seemed indifferent to this desecration. So,
while it seems that we should be cautious about assuming that Russian
society was deeply Christian before the Revolution, so we should be
cautious about assuming it to have been rigidly atheist afterwards. By
1990, after seventy years of persecution, the situation of Russian society
was volatile and questioning, like a simmering pot, waiting for a pretext
to boil over in a dramatic demonstration of religious fervour which had
been building up for years.

A CASE STUDY: YUGOSLAVIA

Within a few years of the end of the Cold War, when the West was
optimistically talking about a new world order, a series of bloody and
destructive civil wars, of the utmost brutality, broke out in a European
country which had been seen as the acceptable face of Communism and
a model of ethnic harmony. Apart from the suicidal bloodthirstiness and
the sinister concept of ethnic cleansing, one of the shocking aspects of
the wars was the element of religious hatred. In the West, one of the main
causes was often seen as being the nationalist aspirations of Orthodox
Serbia, although the countries of the East, especially Greece and Russia,
had a different viewpoint.

The recent history of Serbia shows how the three forms of political
experience are all present, shaping how people perceive their Church and
nation, and influencing their actions. The three political configurations
of this chapter – and a few more besides – have all contributed to the
destructive and self-destructive cocktail which is the self-consciousness
of the Serbian people.

The great founders of the Church and state were devout kings and
archbishops, for whom the idea of '*symphonia*' was a controlling ideal.
Stephan Nemanja (1169–96) founded the Nemanjid dynasty which was
to last for 200 years. The king presided over a council of government in
which both civil and ecclesiastical representatives sat together. In 1196
King Stephan abdicated, to become a monk with the name of Symeon,

and went to Mount Athos, where he founded the monastery of Hilandar, which remains a Serbian monastery. His son Sava assisted him in this foundation and then became leader of the Church in Serbia. He is revered as the true founder of the Serbian Orthodox Church. He was consecrated as first archbishop by the Byzantine Emperor Theodore I Lascaris, and went on to found both monasteries and institutions of state.

The Serbian kingdom continued to expand until, during the reign of King Stephan Dušan (1331–55), it extended over most of the former Yugoslavia, and much of Bulgaria and Greece, and threatened the city of Constantinople. Stephan died young; some have claimed that had he lived, he might have built a kingdom strong enough to defeat the Ottomans.

The medieval Serbian kingdom, with its vivid expression of *symphonia*, lives on in the churches and monasteries founded by the kings which remain as monuments to this period, but more especially it lives on in the relics of the royal saints: St Symeon Mirotočivi (literally 'Myrrh-oozer', since his uncorrupted body still exudes the sweet odour of sanctity), and many others. St Sava's body is no longer present in the midst of the Serbian people, since it was burnt by the Turks in 1594 to stamp out the cult which surrounded it. Far from being a piece of history, the medieval state is a part of present national culture and the saintly kings still watch over their people, suffering with them and caring for them. For Serbs, the renewal of this holy state is both a hope and a duty.

In 1389 came the battle of Kosovo Polje in which King Lazar (or rather St Emperor Lazarus, as he is known in Serbia) was killed fighting the Turks. The battle is remembered as a heroic defeat, but historical evidence suggests an inconclusive draw. More significant than the historical battle is the powerful myth which developed of King Lazar's dream, in which, on the night before the battle, he was offered earthly victory or a heavenly kingdom. He chose the latter. This helped to build up a sense of the Serbian vocation of sacrifice and suffering for the sake of others, shown in their self-sacrifice in stemming the tide of Muslim advance and absorbing the national pain of 500 years of slavery (a national slogan) under the Turks which somehow saved the rest of Europe. Under the Turks, the Serbs bore the brunt of being the people on the frontier.

After a century when a Serbian ruler was again on the throne (1830–1945), the nation suffered a further onslaught. This time it came from neighbouring Croatia, which was ruled by a puppet Nazi regime, the

Ustaše, during the Second World War. The Ustaše unleashed a campaign of genocide against the Serbs, with Muslims and gypsies added for good measure. Probably about 750,000 Serbs were killed in Jasenovac and the other death-camps.

During the war Tito's Partisans rather than the Serbian Mihailović's Chetniks gained the upper hand (partly due to Western support), and as a result Tito, the Croat atheist Communist, came to power. He built a federation of republics out of the multi-ethnic region. Since it would have poisoned the atmosphere to re-live old conflicts, a veil was drawn over the death-camps and war crime trials did not feature in Tito's Yugoslavia. It was also important to ensure a balance between the ethnic groups, and so, since the Serbs were numerically the largest group, the boundaries of the republics were carefully drawn to ensure that there was a measure of equality; as a result, large Serb minorities found themselves in territories now part of Croatia and Bosnia.

Of course, the other ethnic groups of the former Yugoslavia would tell the story differently – and we cannot claim that the Serb version of the history is the only account that is valid. But we should recognise how these elements have contributed to a powerful folk memory, and have given to both Church and people a longing and a determination to build a Serbian state which, at long last, will be truly Orthodox, as it was under St Sava. The longing for a truly Christian Orthodox state, the resentment and fear of Croat and Muslim neighbours (with the concentration camps a very recent experience), and the opportunity presented at long last after the death of Tito to realise the dream, are a powerful combination of deeply held feelings, waiting to be exploited by an unscrupulous leadership. The Serbian past is also the Serbian present and is one of the factors that has led to the tragic destruction of the region, in which Serbs have been both aggressors and victims.

The Serbian Orthodox Church contains members and leaders of all shades of political opinion. Love for the Church and loyalty to the nation are inextricably linked. Some of the Serb leadership during the wars of the 1990s, especially in the Bosnian Serb Republic, were close to the Church. The Republic's founder, Radovan Karadzić, was respected by many Orthodox in Serbia and elsewhere. Others have tried to find constructive and peaceful solutions. So in 1999 Bishop Artemije of Raška-Prizren diocese, which includes Kosovo, supported democratic structures for the province; sadly, this aroused little interest or support in

the West, which saw no alternative to war. Bishop Artemije was attacked verbally and physically by Serb nationalists for his conciliatory
approach. The Patriarch of Serbia, Pavle, is a man of simplicity and asceticism who seeks to build relations with those of other faiths. Within
the Republic of Serbia, it might also be noted, there is a greater diversity
of Churches than in many parts of the country, with Roman Catholics
and Protestants maintaining a Church life.

The tragic history of modern Yugoslavia shows the problems faced
by Orthodox countries in coming to terms with their past, in finding
ways of living in an unfamiliar political order dominated by the ideals
of the West, and in sharing in the creation of stable and peaceful states in
economically dysfunctional nations. Fortunately history does not stand
still, and we can only hope that the creative and peace-making elements
within the Serbian Orthodox Church will share in the building of a new,
stable and just society.

10

East and West: the division of Christendom

The Churches of Europe are divided between the Orthodox East and the Catholic West. This has been a tragedy for the Christian faith. It seems to be a contradiction of Christian teaching, in which unity is both a characteristic of the godhead – the three distinct persons are also a unity of love – and also of the ministry of Christ, which brings reconciliation to what is divided. There is a fundamental inconsistency or, to put it another way, scandal that the Church which teaches unity should have been split by schism for most of its history.

On a practical level the consequences of division have been devastating. The hostility of Chalcedonians and non-Chalcedonians in the sixth century led to the alienation of Monophysites in Syria and Egypt, which in turn created an opening for the Arab armies. For two hundred years a Muslim minority was able to retain power over a Christian majority, thanks to the co-operation of Christian Churches in the governance and economic life of the area. Gradually, as we have seen, the Muslims grew in number until they formed the majority of the population, but until then they were able to retain power only because of the division of Christians. Later, the failure of West and East to build up an alliance against the Ottoman Turks led to a situation that permitted the defeat of the Christian Empire of the East. Instead of providing the military support so badly needed by the East, the Western Crusading armies preferred to occupy Constantinople themselves and so further weakened the Byzantine state and deepened antagonism into irreconcilable hostility.

This set the scene for the fall of Constantinople to the Ottomans. Had there been a united front combining the forces of East and West, then Christendom, and its Holy Places, could have been preserved and even extended. These should not be seen as pieces of imagination and might-have-been fantasy, but rather as a realistic estimate of the causes of the political ascendancy of Islam in the Middle East and Balkans.

Many would argue that in our own time the two halves of the Christian world still need each other. The West badly needs to strengthen its roots in the patristic doctrinal and ascetical tradition, and the East needs to share in the experience of the West in witnessing and ministering in a secularised society. And so suspicion and division continue to sap the vitality of the Body of Christ.

The traditional date for the formal beginning of the schism between the Churches of East and West is 1054. The dispute which led to the act of mutual excommunication involved participants on both sides who were deeply concerned for the integrity and purity of their respective Churches, and also uncompromising and intransigent in their attitudes to the other. Pope Leo IX (1049–54) had insisted that Greek churches in parts of Italy ruled by the Norman Angevins should follow Latin liturgical practice and customs, while the Patriarch of Constantinople, Michael I Cerularius (1043–58), ordered Latin churches in Constantinople to conform to Greek practices and, when they declined to do so, he closed them. A group of three papal legates were invited by the Patriarch to try to settle the quarrel. One of them, Humbert, bishop of Silva Candida and a monk of Cluny, was a determined Church reformer and advocate of papal power, as well as being rigid and overbearing in his attitude. Their discussions did not go well, and one afternoon the three legates went to the Great Church of Haghia Sophia just as a service was starting, marched to the altar, placed a Bull of Excommunication on it and then left. A deacon hurried after them and asked them to take the Bull back. It fell to the ground and was eventually picked up and passed on to Michael Cerularius. Shortly afterwards the legates left Constantinople. A synod was summoned by the Patriarch which refuted the charges made in the Bull, and in turn excommunicated Humbert.

Both sides in the dispute affirmed their respect and support for the other, and the excommunications were confined to Humbert and the legates, on the one hand, and Michael Cerularius, on the other. The condemnations did not extend to the Churches as a whole. Pope Leo, the Pope in whose name the Bull was delivered, had died shortly before, so it is doubtful whether the Bull signed by him retained its validity. The event was not considered to have been significant by many contemporary historians. Byzantine chroniclers scarcely mentioned it, and relationships between subsequent Popes and Patriarchs were often good. Many since then have been disinclined to take it too seriously. The Russian theologian Vladimir Soloviev considered that the mutual excommunication was only between Byzantium and Rome and did not extend to the Russian Church, and the schism between these two Churches did not have a legal basis. He was reconciled to the Catholic Church by a Russian Roman Catholic priest, Nikolai Tolstoy. Patriarchs of Antioch often took a similar view. It might be more accurate to describe what actually happened as an unsuccessful attempt to resolve a problem rather than the creation of a definitive schism. But in spite of all these factors mitigating the significance of the event, the mutual excommunications remained in force for over nine hundred years, from 1054 until 1965, when Pope Paul VI of Rome and Patriarch Athenagoras I of Constantinople simultaneously revoked them.

Rather than seeing the so-called Great Schism of 1054 as a decisive moment of division, removing a communion which had been there hitherto, we should consider it as one event in a long and troubled history.

A GROWING DIVISION

The continent of Europe has been divided into two halves since the end of the third century. The decision to draw this line across the map was made by the Roman Emperor Diocletian (284–305), who solved the problem of controlling an unruly and rebellious Empire through a system of four Emperors: two in the west and two in the east. The boundary was the Adriatic Sea and the river Syrtis to the north. This line has become a fact of European history, and has remained in place since then, shifting a little to the east to reflect a slow expansion of the West. It has been referred to as a fault line, separating East from West, Catholic and Protestant from Orthodox, the so-called free world from the Communist bloc, and now the European Union from the newly independent states. There is discussion about expansion of the European Union which could lead to a Europe that is able to transcend this great division.

After the administrative arrangement of Diocletian that was to have such momentous consequences, there was an attempt to recreate the universal Roman Empire, reuniting Eastern and Western Europe during the reign of the Emperor Justinian (527–65). In a series of military campaigns the Emperor extended his power into Italy, North Africa, Spain and the Balkans in the west, as well as to Syria, Palestine, Egypt and parts of Armenia in the east. But this huge effort drained the resources of the Byzantine state, and his territory began to disintegrate after his death.

From then on the hope for a Christian world order was gradually eroded. In the East, the Arab advances in the seventh century removed the eastern shores of the Mediterranean from the orbit of the Christian world. Then, in the West, the Frankish kingdoms had adopted Christianity, and had established a new Christian power in the northwest of Europe. The Roman Church found itself increasingly oriented towards the Franks of the West, until on a momentous Christmas Day in the year 800 a second Roman Empire came into existence with the coronation of the Frankish king Charles the Great, known as Charlemagne, as the Emperor of the Holy Roman Empire. So there were now two Roman Empires, and each required its own Church. The Empire was both reduced in size and divided between two centres of political power.

Byzantine horizons became further narrowed with the advance of Turkish tribesmen. In 1071 the Turks defeated the Byzantine army of Romanus IV Diogenes (1068–71) at the battle of Manzikert, and took the Emperor prisoner. This led to the inauguration of a Turkish kingdom based on Iconium and the beginning of the end of Byzantine power in Asia Minor. The Emperors became increasingly preoccupied with survival. The Popes, on the other hand, while they did not lose sight of their ambitions to extend their authority into the Byzantine world, found themselves drawn into the Germanic world of northern Europe.

The political re-orientation encouraged separate cultural development. The new Universities of the West were producing exciting new theological works, based on the philosophy of Aristotle, which contrasted with the more conservative world of Constantinople. From this new spirit of enquiry came a movement of philosophical, cultural, religious and scientific change. A new Western Christian culture was emerging which would help to foster the Renaissance, Reformation and Enlightenment. All of these were Western in origin and character, and passed by the East.

The growing gap between them is shown by the surprising lack of interest on the part of both Greeks and Latins in understanding each other's languages. In the classical world theological writing had been transmitted quickly around the Mediterranean. For example the *Life of St Martin* was written in Gaul in the fourth century and was being read in Syria within a few years. By contrast the works of St Augustine, written in the fifth century, were not being read in Constantinople until the fourteenth century. And when they were read, they were often misunderstood. Important words could not be translated accurately. So for example the Latin infallibility (*infallibilitas*) was translated by the Greek impeccability or sinlessness (*anamartetos*) – a very different idea. And the word *vicarius*, as used in the phrase 'Vicar of Christ', had no Greek equivalent. Thus for the Greeks, the Pope was claiming a sinlessness more appropriate to the Virgin Mary, and they did not know what was meant by being Vicar of Christ. Communication became more difficult, and in reality was not a high priority for either side.

There was a sadly predictable succession of quarrels and disagreements and excommunications. Early signs of trouble to come emerged at the Council of Serdica in 343, when claims were made by the Pope of Rome to act as a court of appeal for ecclesiastical disputes in other dioceses – a suggestion which did not impress the Easterners with their more egalitarian approach to episcopal relations. Then in 484, there was a schism when Pope Felix III broke off relations with the Patriarch of Constantinople Acacius, and this lasted for thirty-five years, until 519.

A more significant schism occurred in the late ninth century when Photius was Patriarch. He was a *protoasekretis* or president of the Imperial Chancery, a layman and a scholar, who was made Patriarch in 858, having been speedily ordained reader, subdeacon, deacon and priest, in time for a pre-Christmas consecration as Patriarch. Unfortunately his predecessor Ignatius was still alive and had been deposed on account of his hard-line approach to the imperial family, an intransigent stand which had led the Emperor to favour the more flexible Photius. Relationships with Rome deteriorated when Pope Nicholas I in 863 declared Ignatius to be the rightful Patriarch, and Photius to be deposed. Then quarrels broke out between Rome and Constantinople over the recently converted land of Bulgaria, where Frankish missionaries had been active and had propagated some Roman practices, including the *filioque*. Photius dispatched an encyclical attacking these practices, and, for good measure, deposed the Pope. The schism was concluded in 867 when a change of Emperor led to a change of Patriarch, and Ignatius was reinstated, thus satisfying the extremist supporters of Ignatius and Rome at one stroke. Photius was Patriarch for a second term from 877 to 886, and there is some suggestion in contemporary anti-Photian sources that there was a second schism, but this has been shown to be a misunderstanding of the evidence.[1]

This first early schism between East and West contains the ingredients of later conflict: claims by the Pope to act as arbitrator in disputes outside his diocese, missionary competition, and doctrinal differences, here the *filioque*. It proved relatively easy to heal the breach – a new Pope and Patriarch being all that was needed.

The disagreement between Michael Cerularius and Leo IX, in the person of Humbert, led to the mutual excommunication. Although this excommunication remained in force, it did not bring about an end of cordial relations. Later in the century both Theophylact of Ochrida and Anselm of Canterbury wrote about the differences between East and West. Both agreed that there were issues to debate, notably the *filioque* and the claims to papal primacy, but neither concluded from these that there needed to be, or even was, a schism between the Churches.

It was the Crusades that sharpened antipathy to hatred, and brought about a situation in which reconciliation proved impossible to achieve. They were launched by Pope Urban II with the best of intentions. He was a great friend to Byzantium and recognised the importance of providing military assistance to the Empire in its struggle against the Turks. This aid would, he hoped, help towards the reunion of the Churches, while regaining the Holy Places at the same time. The Byzantine Emperor, Alexius I Comnenus (1081–1118), was involved in the preparations for the Crusade, and sent legates to the Council of Piacenza in 1095 exhorting Western armies to send aid.

It quickly became clear that the two sides had different goals. For the Byzantines, the immediate priority was the security of the Empire, which would provide a base for the recovery of the Holy Places. The Crusaders, on the other hand, wanted the adventure, the glory, the heavenly reward of reclaiming the Holy Places, while also gaining plunder, power and personal wealth. From a military point of view the First Crusade achieved its objective by recapturing Jerusalem in 1099, although at

---

[1] This question was settled by F. Dvornik, *The Photian Schism, History and Legend* (Cambridge 1948).

the cost of dreadful and indiscriminate slaughter of both Muslim and Christian inhabitants. In the course of this Crusade, Bohemond captured Antioch and decided to keep it for himself instead of restoring it to the Emperor Alexius as agreed. The Patriarch of Antioch, John the Oxite, returned to Constantinople and died in 1100. Both the Latins in Antioch and the Greeks in Constantinople elected successors, thus putting in place two rival patriarchal lines in Antioch. Pope Paschal II unhelpfully decided to support Bohemond and declared a holy war against Constantinople.

And so the sad succession of events was carried inexorably forward. In 1147 the Second Crusade was a miserable failure. The Byzantines hurried the Crusaders through their territories as fast as possible, and when the campaign failed, the Crusaders and the Byzantines blamed each other. In 1182 there were riots in Constantinople in which Latins were killed. In the course of the Third Crusade, in 1191, Richard I of England captured Cyprus, and Frederick Barbarossa of Germany launched an attack on the Emperor Isaac II Angelus (1185–95) with the help of Serbs, Bulgars and dissident Byzantines. Frederick died before any battle was fought and the alliance disintegrated. So the relations festered and deteriorated, until the ill-fated Fourth Crusade.

The armies of the Fourth Crusade reached Constantinople in June 1203. It so happened that there was a struggle between two claimants of the imperial throne, Alexius IV and Alexius V. Alexius IV persuaded the Crusaders to support him for a money payment. He was then expelled by Alexius V, and so was unable to pay the Crusaders for their help. Deprived of their expected profits, the Crusaders decided to attack Constantinople instead, and captured it in 1204, with the inevitable orgy of pillaging and destruction, directed by Christians against fellow-Christians. This led to the Latin occupation of the capital, and a Latin Patriarch of Constantinople for fifty-seven years. The great adventure of the Crusades, which had begun as a shared initiative by West and East, ended by establishing a hostility that is vividly remembered by the Orthodox Church to this day.

By this time relations were strained to breaking point. Writing in the late twelfth century, the canon lawyer and Patriarch of Antioch, Theodore Balsamon, considered that Latins and Greeks were no longer in communion. The popular feelings behind this statement are put by the Greek historian Nicetas Choniates, who had been an eye witness of the Latin conquest of his capital city: 'The accursed Latins lust after our possessions and would like to destroy our race . . . between them and us there is a wide gulf of hatred, our outlooks are completely different, and our paths go in opposite directions.'[2] It was a fair summary of the popular attitudes at the start of the thirteenth century. Relationships had deteriorated to such an extent that, at this time, it can be said that the Churches were no longer in communion.

DIVERGENCE IN DOCTRINE: THE *FILIOQUE*

In addition to the growing hostility and distrust, there were two serious differences over doctrine. These are the *filioque* and the papal claim to authority. Both had developed gradually and both had become serious obstacles by 1204, adding to the distance between the Churches caused by the political disaster of the Crusades.

The *filioque* is an addition to the Nicene Creed which was made unilaterally by the Churches of the West. While in the East the faithful affirm that they 'believe in the Holy Spirit . . . who proceeds from the Father', their counterparts in the West confess that they 'believe in the Holy Spirit who proceeds from the Father *and the Son (filioque)*'. This alteration reflects a different tradition of Trinitarian theology which emerged in Western Europe, especially in Spain and Germany. So the *filioque* controversy has two aspects. The first concerns the status of the Creed as an agreed Conciliar statement and a focus for unity, and also whether it can be altered and if so by whom. The second concerns the correct description of the relations between the persons of the Trinity. Since the *filioque* refers to belief in the nature of God, it is seen as having a vital importance, although the difference is generally viewed more seriously in the East than in the West.

The Nicene Creed was produced as part of the process of doctrinal formulation carried out by the Ecumenical Councils. It was drawn up at Constantinople (381), using the doctrinal statements of Nicaea (325), and was re-affirmed at Chalcedon (451). It contains the Nicene teaching that the Son is of the same substance as the Father, and is 'begotten' by him. It then goes on to speak of the Spirit – a main topic at Constantinople – who 'proceeds' from the Father. This Creed gives a clear definition of the relationship between the Father and the Son, and the Father and

---

[2] Nicetas Choniates is cited in G. Ostrogorsky, *History of the Byzantine State*, 2nd edn (Oxford 1968), p. 390.

the Spirit, but it remains silent on whether there is any relation between the persons of the Son and the Spirit, and how this might be spoken of. The *filioque* debate can be seen as a continuation of the process of definition of the nature of the Holy Trinity, a proper and inevitable continuation of the work of the Councils, dealing with the next phase of Trinitarian theology, which is how the relationship of the Son and the Spirit is to be described.

The *filioque* teaching of the West states that the Spirit proceeds from the Son as well as the Father. This gives the Son a certain logical priority over the Spirit. It is an inevitable consequence of using the title Father, since to speak of God as Father must mean that he is Father of somebody, and that somebody is of course the Son. So it could be – and was – said that the Spirit proceeds from the Father-of-the-Son. 'His very being presupposes the existence of the Father as well as that of the Son because the Holy Spirit proceeds from the Father and the Father is Father only of the Son.'[3] This approach can be discovered in a style of thinking about the Trinity which is found in influential figures in Western theology, especially Augustine and Anselm of Canterbury, and which has roots in early Latin theologians such as Marcellus of Ancyra and Tertullian. These theologians emphasised the unity of the godhead (indeed Adolf Harnack once commented that Augustine would never have thought of the Trinity if the tradition he inherited had not forced him to do so), and therefore wanted to keep the bonds that united the persons as close as possible. From this they argued that the Son is united to the Father and is a positive and necessary condition for the proceeding of the Holy Spirit. In addition to this concern to preserve the unity of the godhead, they did not distinguish clearly between the immanent Trinity (God as he is in himself) and the economic Trinity (God as he acts towards his creation). So, since the sending of the Spirit follows on after the earthly ministry of Jesus (the historical sequence expressing the work of the economic Trinity), it follows that this order is a reflection of the nature of God (the immanent Trinity), in which, therefore, the Son is begotten first, and so shares in the procession of the Spirit which, logically, is consequent on the generation of the Son.

The use of the phrase *filioque* spread gradually in the West. It is encountered first in Spain as early as the fifth century, and then a little

[3] See B. Bolotov, 'Thèses sur le *filioque*', *Istina* 1972 (3–4), pp. 261–89.

later in the canons of the Council of Toledo in 589, and then in the Athanasian Creed (nothing, of course, to do with Athanasius but a traditional formulation of faith in the West). It is sometimes maintained that the *filioque* was adopted as an anti-Arian strategy, since it affirms uncompromisingly the divine nature of the Son by placing him alongside the Father in the proceeding of the Spirit, but there is no evidence for this and it is more probable that it was simply a part of local tradition. By the ninth century it was being used in the Frankish Church, although not in Rome. At the Synod of Rome in 810, as an instance, Pope Leo III declared the *filioque* to be orthodox but deliberately did not include it in the Creed. The gradual intrusion of the *filioque* into the Creed took place as part of the growth in influence of the Franks, at the expense of the Byzantine Empire. It was Frankish missionaries who were active in Bulgaria and who used the interpolation and so in 866 precipitated the conflict between the Patriarch Photius and Pope Nicholas I, which was the context of a sharply polemical statement of the Eastern position by Photius. In 1009 Pope Sergius IV included it in the statement of faith that he sent to Constantinople on the occasion of his consecration. Then in 1014, on the occasion of the coronation of the Frankish Emperor Henry II, Frankish influence led to its first use as part of the Creed said at a Mass in St Peter's in Rome. The adoption of the *filioque* was a long process, with five hundred years elapsing between its first recorded use in Spain and its inclusion in the Creed as recited at Rome. By the time of the mutual excommunications of 1054, the *filioque* had found its way into the Western Creed.

The Eastern understanding of the relation of the Spirit to the Son is that the Spirit proceeds from the Father only. This definition can be traced back to the Trinitarian theology of the Cappadocian Fathers, who made a clear distinction between *ousia* (or substance) and *hypostasis* (or person). The procession of the Spirit from the Father was articulated with greater clarity by Patriarch Photius with his statement that the Spirit proceeds from the Father *only* (*ek tou patros monou*), and was further developed by Gregory of Cyprus and Gregory Palamas. The latter's distinction between essence and energies enabled him to say that according to essence (the immanent Trinity) the Spirit proceeds from the Father, but according to energies (the economic Trinity) the Spirit proceeds from the Father through the Son.

The root of this language about the Spirit lies in the different levels of relationship within the Trinity. There are two kinds of relationships in the Trinity: substantial, which are those common to all the persons; and hypostatic or personal, which are unique to the person concerned. The nature, substance or *ousia* of the persons of the Trinity is identical, since there is clearly one nature which the three persons share. Since the persons of the Trinity have this one identical nature, it follows that the only conceivable difference between them concerns how they relate to each other – the hypostatic relations. The Father's distinctive characteristic is that he is the origin of the other two, and this characteristic belongs to his *hypostasis* and so cannot be shared with the other persons. So to say that the Holy Spirit proceeds from the Father and the Son introduces two origins into the Trinity, removes the Father's distinctive personality, and distorts a central doctrine of the Christian faith.

Some modern Orthodox exponents of this view suggest that the implications of this error are far-reaching. Misunderstanding of the nature of God leads to distortions in all parts of the life of the Church. The *filioque*, they suggest, subordinates the Spirit to the Son, and perhaps even reduces him to a function of the divine unity, and removes his personal hypostatic reality. This prevents a proper appreciation of the work of the Holy Spirit in the Church, subordinating the charismatic Spirit-inspired nature of the Church to the institutional nature. This encourages a formal, hierarchical papal style of Church government, rather than a more charismatic, unstructured, conciliar form of government. While this stern critique, associated in our own times with Vladimir Lossky, reminds us that Trinitarian theology cannot be dismissed as irrelevant to the life of the Church; it simply does not seem to be true that ecclesiastical distortions of this kind can be traced back to Trinitarian theology. There are other theologians – B. Bolotov, Paul Evdokimov or Sergei Bulgakov – who have a less strict view of the creeping and pernicious nature of the *filioque*.

The Eastern position was expressed with clarity by the Patriarch Photius, in the course of whose writing the question of the procession of the Spirit developed from being a matter of speculation to a polemical position. It was further developed by Gregory of Cyprus, Gregory Palamas and Mark of Ephesus. But other writers explored ways of expressing the relationship between the Son and the Spirit in a more conciliatory way. John of Damascus wrote: 'The Spirit is the Spirit of the Father, but he is also the Spirit of the Son, not because he proceeds from him, but because he proceeds through him from the Father.'[4]

Gradually the two approaches to understanding the place of the Spirit within the Trinity developed from being a debate within the Church to being a way of defining two opposing sides. After the career of Photius, the issue was discussed at the Councils of Lyons (1274) and Florence (1438–9). By this time the *filioque* had become an accepted part of the Latin faith which the delegates of the Eastern Churches were required to accept. On both occasions the Eastern representatives subscribed to the doctrine, with the significant exception of Mark of Ephesus at Florence, but their decision was not supported by the majority of the inhabitants of Constantinople, and the union was officially ratified for only a short period from 1452 until the fall of Constantinople on 29 May 1453.

The more tranquil climate of the modern ecumenical movement has enabled the question to be debated more openly and eirenically. As far as the text of the Creed is concerned, there is a growing consensus that the West should restore the text drawn up at the Council of Constantinople. At the Bonn Reunion Conferences of 1874–5 the Old Catholic Churches agreed that the insertion of the *filioque* into the Creed was illegitimate, and since then the Old Catholic Churches have gradually removed the offending clause. The Anglican Lambeth Conference of 1978 asked its member Churches to consider doing the same, although this request has as yet resulted only in occasional omission of the offending phrase.

The theological debate is being explored by some theologians, although it is difficult to see it making much progress. There are various possible formulae for the definition of the relationship, such as the Spirit proceeds from the Father through the Son, or from the Father and receives from the Son, but if this is not to be incorporated in the Creed it will remain peripheral to the relations between the Churches.

PAPAL PRIMACY

The place of the Pope is the second main point of disagreement. This has become a doctrinal question, concerning the unity of the Church and the nature of authority, but was rooted in politics and culture. Since,

---

[4] John of Damascus, *On the Orthodox Faith* 1.12, PG 94.849b.

first, the eastern and the western parts of the Empire were divided, and since, secondly, the Emperor resided in the East, it followed that there was a power vacuum in the West. While in Constantinople there was an Emperor and a Patriarch to share power, in Rome there was no Emperor. There was, therefore, every encouragement for an exploration and expansion of the nature of papal authority.

The Eastern view of authority within the Church has already been discussed. It locates the presence of Christ in the Eucharist as celebrated by the bishop. Since this is the source from which the Church comes and is the fullness of its being, there can be no higher authority over the bishop. In the ordering and administration of the Church, the bishops of an area work together in harmony, with none in authority over the others. On the occasions when a more far-reaching authority has been exercised by the Patriarch, as, for example, when the permanent synod of bishops (who thus did not reside in their own diocese) or *synodos endemousa* was set up in Constantinople to assist the Ecumenical Patriarch, this is usually felt to undermine the simple understanding whereby each bishop presides over his own Church.

An alternative view of authority and of unity emerged in the West, based on Rome. We might call this a 'universal' approach to authority. This view understands the whole Church as the Body of Christ, and local Church communities as parts of this one body. It follows almost inevitably from this that there must be a 'head' to the 'body' and that this head must govern, in order to maintain the unity. So unity is expressed in the whole Church, rather than in the local manifestation of it – as in the East. This is an organisational understanding rather than a eucharistic understanding, since the fullness of the Church is present in the totality of the whole Church rather than in each eucharistic assembly. A result of this is that the Church can be seen as functioning on two levels. There is the mystical or sacramental level, in which it is recognised that the Church is a spiritual reality governed by Christ and led by the Spirit; but there is also the human or earthly level, on which the Church is a human reality with the Pope as its head. This alternative view was a consequence of the growing importance of the structure and administration of the organisation of the Church.

The different views have resulted in a different dynamic of Church life and a different understanding of how unity and order are achieved. It is hard to imagine the Roman Catholic Church today continuing to exist if all the administration in the Vatican were removed, yet it is one of the surprising achievements of Eastern Church life that the Orthodox Church continues as an identifiable unity without any single authority over the whole Church, nor the opportunity for bishops to continue to meet in Ecumenical Councils, nor any universal legislative or juridical authority.

The teaching that the Pope is the head of the Church is, so Rome believes, derived from passages of the New Testament which portray the Apostle Peter as the leader of the apostles, the rock on which the Church is built, the one who receives the commission to strengthen the others. Since Peter, and Paul, taught in Rome and both were martyred there, the church of this city, and its bishop, has a position of pre-eminence over the other churches and power over them. Thus the order and unity of the universal Church is maintained.

This theory of papal primacy developed gradually. At the Council of Chalcedon, Pope Leo I mediated between the different sides, and con-tributed a decisive statement of faith, the Tome of Leo, greeted with the acclamation 'Peter has spoken through Leo.' Then, as Byzantine power waned in the West and the Franks grew stronger, the Pope developed into a temporal ruler of the parts of Italy around Rome. Around this time there emerged a notorious forgery called the Donation of Constantine, probably composed in the eighth century, which purported to record the gift from the Emperor Constantine to Pope Sylvester I (314–35) of temporal control of the city of Rome and the surrounding areas, and pre-eminence over the Patriarchates of the East. This doctrine was developed further in the eleventh century with the Gregorian Reform. Although this concerned papal control over pastoral government of the Church, it re-sulted in a series of synods that proclaimed the 'universal jurisdiction' of the Pope – to use the later language of the First Vatican Council. Pope Boniface VIII (1294–1303) proclaimed in the papal Bull *Unam Sanctam* (1302) that it was necessary to salvation to obey the Roman Pope. While such an extreme view was not generally accepted, papal claims to authority gradually extended. At the First Vatican Council of 1869–70 the dogma of papal infallibility was defined. The Melkite Patriarch Gregory II Yusuf (1864–97) opposed this, and when he next visited Rome was pushed to the floor in front of the Pope, who placed his foot on the Patriarch's head, thus providing a vivid image confirming all that the East feared and hated.

While Easterners agreed that the Pope had a certain priority, they held that this derived from his occupation of the ancient imperial city of Rome, as expressed by the 28th canon of Chalcedon. The papal claims which developed through the medieval period, and have further developed since, are, in their view, heretical. In theory, if the Pope renounced his heretical views – mainly over the nature of his primacy and also over the *filioque* – he would re-assume his place as the senior bishop of Christendom, East as well as West, speaking with the authority of love as a witness to the unity of the Church and assisting the maintenance of unity by giving an opinion on matters of dispute. Pope John Paul II (1978–) has acknowledged that the papacy itself has become a stumbling block in the way of unity, and has declared his desire to express the role of the papacy in a new way that can contribute to the reconciliation of the Churches. The teaching of papal primacy is more than a doctrinal difference but proposes a different and incompatible understanding of how the Church works.

LITURGICAL DIFFERENCES

Liturgical usage developed along different lines, and some of the variations were seen as having doctrinal significance, and entered into the debate between the Churches.

There were different understandings of how the elements at the Eucharist were consecrated. Both sides agreed that the elements of bread and wine became the body and blood of Christ. But the West believed that this was accomplished through the priest speaking the words of Christ at the Last Supper, 'this is my body . . . this is my blood', known as the words of institution. For the East, on the other hand, the prayer to the Holy Spirit or the *epiclesis* (part of the prayer of consecration) was seen as the focal point of the prayer, which accomplished the transformation of the elements. The Easterners justified their position by claiming, first, that since prayer to God is the way in which the Holy Spirit works and is how other sacraments are administered, this is true also of the Eucharist. Then, second, at the Last Supper, the words of institution were spoken by Christ as he gave the bread and the cup to the apostles; this took place after he had given thanks and broken the bread, and therefore the mysterious transformation had already taken place. So to understand these words as consecrating is a misunderstanding both of the Biblical narrative and of the nature of sacramental worship.

Then the West used unleavened bread, or *azymes*, thus reproducing the tradition of the Jewish Passover, while the East used leavened bread, holding that the Last Supper was not a Passover meal, and that yeast or leaven gives life to the bread, showing that Christ is the bread of life. This, along with other points of debate, such as the Latin customs of priests' shaving and fasting on Saturday, were the causes of the disputes between Michael Cerularius and Cardinal Humbert which led to the schism of 1054, and the *azymes* question was debated at the Council of Florence.

ATTEMPTS TO ACHIEVE UNION

Attempts to undo the damage of disunity began immediately. The Byzantine Empire still needed Western help, and the Popes still hoped to reunite the Church under their leadership. It was in nobody's interest for the schism to persist, and both sides realised that they needed to enter into negotiations to reunite the Churches. This suggests both that the schism was clearly in place and also that it was recognised as an abnormal situation.

The first attempt at reunion between the Churches of East and West was held at Lyons in 1274. It is surprising that it was held at all. Constantinople had been under Latin occupation, with a militantly un-compromising Latin Patriarch of Constantinople, and was not liber-ated until 1261. Yet only thirteen years after this humiliating experi-ence the Greek Church was prepared to send delegates to a reunion Council at Lyons (for the West, the Second Council of Lyons), and these delegates agreed to accept the Pope's authority. But the Emperor Michael VIII Palaeologus (1259–82) was unable to persuade the people of Constantinople to accept this union.

Over one and a half centuries and considerable deterioration in the political situation in Constantinople had to pass before another meet-ing was held. The next Council of reunion took place when the Ottoman forces were drawing close to the walls of Constantinople and the situation of the Empire was precarious. This time the Greek delegation was large, with more than 700 members, and was led by both Emperor and Patriarch. Discussions lasted from 9 April 1438 until 6 July 1439, first in Ferrara and then, when plague afflicted Ferrara, in Florence. The subjects discussed were the procession of the Holy Spirit (the *filioque*), the doctrine of Purgatory, the *epiclesis* and use of unleavened bread in the Eucharist, and the papal claims. The conversations were long, leading the frustrated Emperor John VIII Palaeologus to exclaim: 'you drown us in words and then claim victory'. The delegate George Scholarios' address to his colleagues shows the pressure that they were under. 'Remember the gravity of the situation, the strength of the enemy, the weakness of our defences, the length of the wall to be manned, the size of our population halved by plague. Union immediately and then away. Remember wives, families, and what conquest by the infidel will mean for them who look to us as their saviour. We are the advance-guard of Christianity.'[5]

It was not therefore surprising that the union was agreed, and that it was on Latin terms, albeit with some compromises to accommodate Greek sensibilities. So, for example, the *filioque* was accepted but a Greek theological understanding of the Trinity was permitted. The union was proclaimed at Mass in the Cathedral at Florence with only one voice of dissent, the significant figure of Mark Eugenicus of Ephesus. It was also not surprising that opposition as well as support greeted the delegation on their return home. The union was not proclaimed in Constantinople until 12 December 1452, although the cause of union was not helped by the indecision of the Emperor, who did not take any action to prevent opponents of the union such as Mark Eugenicus from preaching against it; nor by the lack of support given to the besieged city by the Pope, who sent no military help to the hard-pressed Byzantines. Less than six months after the proclamation of the union, the city fell to the Ottoman Turks – for many, clear evidence of divine disapproval of a policy of compromise.

The fall of Constantinople ended the formal and short-lived union between the Churches. The experiences of Latin occupation after the Fourth Crusade, combined with a determination not to compromise over contested dogmatic teachings, led to a solid popular opposition in Constantinople to any form of union with the West. In addition, the imperial government, with its hope that Rome and the West might provide much-needed military support against the Ottoman, had been replaced by the Ottoman enemy, who took care to ensure that the Patriarch and Church would not develop any alliance with a Western power that could destabilise the new regime.

---

[5] John's words are in J. Gill, *The Council of Florence* (Cambridge 1959), p. 244. George Scholarios, *On the Need for Aiding Constantinople*, PG 160.385–437.

But contacts were maintained. The Pope longed for the Church to be reunited through acceptance of Roman primacy, and Catholic nations, especially France, were happy to co-operate in this aim in order to extend their political influence in the East. The Churches of the Ottoman Empire were kept in a subordinate and weakened position by their Muslim rulers, and they were ready to accept any help – money, education, preaching, hearing confessions – even from Western Christians.

GREEK CATHOLIC CHURCHES

The beginning of Catholic mission to the East can be dated to 1576 when Pope Gregory founded the Greek College of St Athanasius in Rome. Here students were taught Latin Catholic traditions in the Greek language, and graduated either as missionaries dedicated to spreading the Catholic faith in the Greek East, or as confirmed enemies of all things Roman. In 1583 five Jesuits arrived in Constantinople, the first of a huge number who were to teach and preach throughout the Christian East. Among Catholic missionaries, the Jesuits were the most sensitive to the needs and traditions of the indigenous Churches. They were followed by Capuchin friars four years later. These various initiatives were brought firmly under papal control through the foundation of the Congregation for the Propagation of the Faith, usually referred to as Propaganda, in 1622. In the following century Catholic missionaries worked throughout the Orient.

Conversions could be individual or corporate. The individual approach has been called, by Bishop Kallistos Ware, the Trojan Horse policy.[6] Its intention was to persuade individual Eastern Christians to make an act of submission to Rome but to continue to worship in their own Church. It was hoped that if enough people thus became reconciled to Rome, especially if they were bishops, then one day the Church concerned would wake up to find itself Catholic and a reunion by stealth would have been successfully and surreptitiously achieved. This policy had significant success. In 1681 the monastery of St John on Patmos became Catholic for a while and two French Capuchins became monks. In 1656 a Syrian Orthodox convert was consecrated as a bishop, taking the

---

[6] K. Ware's image of the Trojan Horse is in 'Orthodox and Catholics in the seventeenth century: schism or intercommunion?', in D. Baker (ed.), *Studies in Church History*, vol. 9 (Cambridge 1972), pp. 249–76 at p. 264.

name Andreah, and then six years later became Patriarch of Antioch. In 1684 the Coptic Patriarch Yuhanna XVI accepted the authority of Rome. Armenians were converted in large numbers, attracted by the quality of Catholic education. They became so numerous that an agreement had to be brokered by the French ambassador whereby the Catholic Armenians agreed to worship in the Armenian national Church, and the Church agreed to remove the condemnations of the teaching of the Council of Chalcedon from its teaching – a compromise that did not win the support of the Armenian national hierarchy. In 1808 it was estimated that of 32,000 Catholics in Constantinople and the surrounding areas, 30,000 were Armenians. In Ankara 75 per cent of the population was Armenian Catholic.

The policy led to muddle and division. Schism often arose between Catholic and non-Catholic Patriarchs. One of the most confusing episodes concerned the Church of the East. A schism between two factions led John Sulaqa to seek papal support, and in 1553 he was consecrated by the Pope as bishop, and Patriarch of a 'Catholic' Church of the East, to be called the Chaldaean Church. In due course his successors reverted to their Nestorian confession, rejecting papal authority, but meanwhile the Patriarchate of the Church of the East (as opposed to the Chaldaean Church) had became further divided, and by 1681 both parts of this Nestorian Church of the East made their separate submssions to Rome, becoming thereby Catholic. Then, to complete the muddle, in 1771 the successor of John Sulaqa, Shim'un XVI, followed suit. So now there were three Patriarchs of the once-proud Church of the East, all of them Catholic. In due course the Sulaqa succession once again affirmed the historic faith of the Church of the East.

This policy of individual conversions led to parallel Oriental Orthodox and Eastern Catholic Churches in all parts of the Ottoman Empire. There are today significant Armenian, Syrian and Chaldaean Catholic Churches, alongside the Orthodox national Churches, as well as Eastern Catholic Churches in other regions.

The policy of individual conversions worked best in the Middle Eastern parts of the Empire. In the Greek and Balkan areas the missions were less successful. There are plenty of examples of co-operation and conversion, especially in the Greek islands, but even there Greek attitudes hardened in the early eighteenth century. In 1755 the three Greek Patriarchs of Constantinople, Alexandria and Jerusalem pronounced that non-Orthodox baptism was invalid, and that a Catholic joining the Orthodox Church should be re-baptised, rather than chrismated as had been the case since 1484. This virtually ended co-operation, and has been claimed by some as the real beginning of schism between Catholic and Orthodox. At the same time Catholic attitudes were also hardening, and in 1729 the Papacy issued a directive prohibiting any common worship 'in terms of the utmost strictness'.

The alternative to this strategy of individual conversion was corporate conversion: the establishing of Church communities which preserved local liturgy and tradition but accepted the authority of the Roman see. This was an extension of the policy of individual conversion, but it differed in setting up a Church which was distinct and separate from the Orthodox parent Church, rather than encouraging converts to remain within their national Church. The basis of the existence of these Churches were the decisions of the Union of Florence, and Churches thus formed are sometimes called Uniate Churches, or Greek Catholic or Eastern Catholic Churches. The nature and history of these differ, but have the common characteristic of combining Eastern tradition with Roman authority.

The largest of the Uniate Churches in the Middle East is the Melkite Church. The name is derived from the Arabic *malek* or king, and had earlier referred to Byzantine Orthodox in the ancient Patriarchates of Antioch, Alexandria and Jerusalem, who were known as Melkites or the Emperor's Church – as opposed to the national non-Chalcedonian Churches. As a result of Catholic missionary activity, a number of bishops in the Patriarchate of Antioch became Catholic and succeeded in 1724 in electing a Catholic sympathiser as Patriarch Cyril VI. The Greeks promptly elected a rival, Jeremiah III, and the schism has persisted since then. The Melkites are now drawn from the Patriarchates of Alexandria and Jerusalem as well as Antioch, and form the largest Church in the Middle East.

The union strategy was carried out not only through conversion, as in the Middle East, but also through political changes which resulted in Orthodox communities suddenly finding themselves under Catholic rule. This happened especially in the area now called the Ukraine. This large country lay on the borders of East and West. Orthodoxy entered Russia through Kiev, the capital of the Ukraine, in 988, but after the area was conquered by the Mongols the centre of the Russian nation was slowly shifted north-east to Moscow, leaving the Ukraine open to dominance from the Catholic nations of Poland and Lithuania. There was a variety of different influences on the Church. Isidore, Metropolitan of Kiev, was present at the Council of Florence and so a supporter of the Union but, since he was unable to commend it successfully in Russia, he retired to Rome, where he was rewarded with a cardinal's hat. Later, in 1458, a schism took place in the metropolitanate of Kiev between the anti-Unionist Jonah and the pro-Unionist Gregory. Meanwhile both Poland and Lithuania were extending their power into the Ukraine, and at the Treaty of Lublin formed an alliance. The Orthodox Christians found themselves disadvantaged and decided, in 1596, to explore the possibility of union with Rome. They prepared a list of thirty-three conditions of union, and these formed the basis of the Union of Brest-Litovsk agreed in 1596. They retained their traditional creed, liturgy and customs, and became the Ukrainian Catholic Church.

This Church has had a turbulent history since its territory was ruled successively by Russia, Poland and Austria–Hungary. In 1807 an archbishopric of Lviv (Lvov in Russian) was created, a post later held by the remarkable theologian and nationalist Cardinal Andrej Szeptyckyj (1900–44), who has been called the 'father of the Ukrainian people'. The Church was abolished by the Soviet Union in 1946 and its members were forced to become Russian Orthodox. In spite of this, the Greek Catholics maintained an underground existence, and the Church was able to re-establish itself when conditions permitted. In 1975 Metropolitan Joseph Slipy unilaterally proclaimed himself Patriarch of Kiev, Halych and all Rus, and groups of clergy and faithful gradually joined him. In 1989 official permission was given for Ukrainian Catholic parishes to be registered. Around two-thirds of the population of the western part of the Ukraine is Catholic, while most of the east, including Kiev, is Orthodox.

Another Catholic Church set up in Eastern Europe was the Ruthenian Catholic Church, which came into being at the Union of Uzhgorod in 1646. The Ruthenians, or Rusyns, speak Ukrainian and live in the area south of the Carpathian mountains in Slovakia and neighbouring areas. They too have lived under foreign rule – Hungarian, Czechoslovak and Russian – but have kept their national consciousness alive. The hierarchy was re-established in 1991. Many emigrated to America, and of these about a half joined the Russian Orthodox missionary diocese.

The Greek Catholics sometimes claim to be a bridge between East and West, showing the shape of a possible unity in which Orthodox and Catholic can once again form one Church, true to the traditions of Orthodox theology and practice but in communion with the Pope of Rome. But Orthodox would point out that the claims of the Pope of Rome are incompatible with Orthodoxy, and so the form of union cannot be the true Church. It is no longer possible to reach back behind the controversies and re-create the Church of the first millennium, since developments in both East and West have resulted in two new entities which can no longer claim to be identical with the undivided Church. The Uniate Churches occupy an uncomfortable middle ground somewhere between the two, considered as neither Catholic nor Orthodox and forming a barrier rather than a bridge. Matters have now deteriorated further since the confused situation in the Ukraine and elsewhere has led to many disputes over the ownership of churches and other property. Instead of assisting reunion, they have inflamed the schism.

Not all Eastern Catholic Churches are the result of missionary activity or military conquest. Two claim an unbroken communion with Rome. The Maronites of the Lebanon and surrounding areas trace their origins to a group of disciples of St Maron, a holy man who lived in Syria in the fourth century and formed the monastery between Antioch and Aleppo which is known by his name. They were staunch supporters of the Council of Chalcedon, and by the eighth century had retired for safety to the remote mountain regions of what is now the Lebanon. In 1182 they affirmed their union with Rome through the Latin Patriarch of Antioch, installed by the Crusaders, but firmly stated that this was a re-affirmation of their communion with Rome, since they had never entered a state of schism. The Syrian and Orthodox roots of the Church were diluted at the Synod of al-Luwayzah in 1736, where the local traditions were suppressed and a series of canons introduced Latin customs, including the insertion of the *filioque* into the Creed. This contradicted the official papal policy that the Eastern Churches should preserve their traditions intact, and raises questions about the sincerity and coherence of the Uniate position.

A much smaller, but still significant, Church is the Italo-Albanian Church. This was built on the Greek traditions of Sicily and South Italy, which was under the jurisdiction of the Byzantine Patriarch from the eighth to the eleventh centuries and developed a lively monastic life. About three hundred years later this community was supplemented by emigrating Albanians, some of whom were Orthodox, and they were formed into a Eastern-rite community of the Catholic Church by Pope Clement VIII in 1596. They still preserve the important monastery of Santa Maria di Grottaferrata.

The existence of these Churches, especially perhaps the Maronites, raises the interesting question of how final the separation between East and West in fact was. Certainly Byzantium and Rome broke off communion, but these Greek Catholic Churches provide examples of its restoration, and the Maronites provide an example of more or less unbroken continuity, although communication lines were for a while broken off through geographical isolation. They are a further reminder that we have to be cautious about suggesting a state of union until 1054 followed by a state of schism afterwards.

ECUMENISM

The Pope has sometimes been described by Eastern theologians as the first Protestant. The assertion of papal power was a divergence from the truth of the Orthodox tradition which led inevitably, from an Orthodox viewpoint, to further fragmentation. All Western Christianity shares in the same errors of leaving the true Church. From a more historical viewpoint, it is clear that Western Christians of all persuasions shared in the same cultural and historical development. The controversies between them were couched in the same philosophical language and discussed the same issues. Meanwhile the Orthodox Churches occupied a different space, with priorities and concerns dictated by the need to maintain the glorious tradition to which they looked back and to maintain the life of the Churches in hostile political circumstances.

In spite of this suspicion of all things Western, the Orthodox did discover that there was some common ground with non-Roman Catholic Western Christians, especially Anglicans, Old Catholics, Lutherans and Calvinists. These shared in the characteristic of not being Roman Catholic. Since there has usually been a state somewhere between simmering tension and outright hostility between Roman Catholics and the rest, both Orthodox and Protestants have from time to time made overtures to each other to explore possible agreement. Within these early exploratory contacts lie the seeds of an alternative approach to reunion, that of ecumenism.

A group of Lutherans tested out Orthodox reaction to their Augsburg Confession by sending a copy to Patriarch Jeremias of Constantinople in 1573. There was an exchange of letters, in which the Patriarch expressed his reservations about some of the doctrines, and the correspondence petered out. However, Protestant theology continued to gain supporters in the East, especially the Patriarch Cyril Lucaris and Feofan Prokopovich. In addition to these somewhat notorious figures, there was some more balanced but friendly contact. The Greek priest Metrophanes Kritopoulos (1589–1639) made a lengthy sojourn first at Oxford and then in various German and Swiss universities, learning about Protestant doctrines and presenting Orthodox teaching in a sympathetic but clear manner. In spite of differences in teaching, recognised by most Orthodox, the Biblically based and economically buoyant Protestant communities had much to commend them. There was some co-operation.

An English political conflict led to another series of contacts. After the Protestant William and Mary acceded to the English throne in 1688, a number of High Church bishops refused to swear an oath of allegiance to the new monarchs, since this would be to dishonour the oath already sworn to the previous king, James II. Called the Non-Jurors, they were removed from their positions by the English Parliament in 1690. In seeking to develop their ecclesiastical status and being of a High Church persuasion, they hoped to establish communion with Orthodoxy, and entered into a correspondence with the Russian and other Orthodox Patriarchs. However, they were not prepared to accept the respect given to icons, nor the Eastern veneration of the Virgin Mary, nor the Orthodox doctrine of the Eucharist, and suggested that the Patriarchate of Jerusalem should be the leading bishopric – and so, not surprisingly, these explorations did not bear fruit.

Contact continued through travellers, students, diplomats as well as churchmen. These were often marked by cordial and equal relationships. Although they did not make progress towards unity, the warmer climate contributed to the rapid growth of ecumenical contact during the last hundred years. There has been growing contact between the Churches, sometimes with growing understanding and hopes of re-establishing communion, and at other times with a certain frigidity creeping in.

During the General Assembly of the World Council of Churches at Evanston in 1954 a delegation of the Coptic Church was welcomed as new members. This somewhat surprised the Coptic delegation as they considered that they had been involved in ecumenism since at least 451. Although there has been continual contact throughout the history of the Church, the growth of the ecumenical movement has led to a fresh round of discussion and prayer in which the Orthodox Churches have been present in continuing, creative and critical ways. There have been three approaches: through the World Council of Churches (an administrative structure within which relationships can be developed), through discussion on doctrine (called 'the dialogue of truth' by the Second Vatican Council), and through meeting and shared projects ('the dialogue of love').

First, international ecumenical contact has developed on an official level, leading up to the formation of the World Council of Churches. The Orthodox Churches were involved from the beginning of the last century. In 1902 Patriarch Joachim III of Constantinople raised the question of Orthodox contact with other Churches. Then in 1920 the Patriarchate wrote to the Churches as follows: 'Our own church holds that rapprochement between the various Christian Churches and fellowship between them is not excluded by the doctrinal differences which exist between them. In our opinion such a rapprochement is highly desirable and necessary.'[7] He went on to propose a common calendar for the great feasts, conferences to examine doctrinal issues and shared charitable work. This statement is sometimes seen as the start of the modern ecumenical movement.

Russians, newly arrived in the West, enthused by the still recent Council of 1917 and also deeply concerned for the future of Christianity following the Bolshevik Revolution, were a part of the ecumenical project from the outset. Among those present at the inaugural conference of the Life and Work movement at Stockholm in 1925 were Professors N. Arseniev (1888–1977) and N. Glubokovsky (1863–1937); and at the Faith and Order Conference at Lausanne in 1927 as part of a delegation led by Metropolitan Germanos of Thyateira. Metropolitan Germanos

---

[7] The Patriarch's encyclical is in G. Limouris, *Orthodox Visions of Ecumenism* (Geneva 1994), p. 9.

was Exarch of the Ecumenical Patriarch in Western Europe from 1922 until 1951, and so had an important leadership role during the establishing of the World Council of Churches. Orthodox delegations also took part in the 1937 Conferences, of Life and Work in Oxford, and Faith and Order in Edinburgh.

In 1948 the World Council of Churches held its first meeting. A number of Orthodox Churches meeting in Moscow decided not to attend, but the Churches of Constantinople and Greece did not attend or support this Conference, not least because it would suggest that Moscow had the right to convene a pan-Orthodox Council. These two Churches joined in the work of the WCC from the beginning. Later the Russian Church followed their example, but more as a result of political pressure (since both the Stalinist government and the Church were keen, for different reasons, to maintain what contact they could with Western Christians) than of commitment to the unity of the Church. Ecumenism turned out to be of vital importance to the Russian Orthodox Church in the huge struggle to survive under an atheist government. The interest which official visitors to the USSR showed in some of the monasteries and institutions of the Church helped them to stay open. In return the Orthodox representatives were required by the Communist authorities to make continued claims for the freedom of the Church, in the face of powerful testimonies to acute persecution from many sources.

The Orthodox have provided a valuable contribution to the work of the WCC and have been much respected by other participants. But Orthodox have expressed concerns. Partly because Roman Catholics have abstained from membership, the WCC has a largely Protestant membership, and, given their less precise understanding of the Church, Orthodox have suspected that the WCC might be seen as a kind of super-Church transcending denominational boundaries. The sharing in the Eucharist, which is for Orthodox the fruit of doctrinal agreement, is proposed as a means to achieve unity, while for Orthodox this is inextricably bound up with unity of faith as constituting the Church. Then there is the emphasis on social and political action at the expense of doctrinal discussion, and the representations from groups significant in Western Christianity but less so in Orthodoxy, such as women priests and gay Christians. All this has led to a general concern among Orthodox that they are being bludgeoned into following a Western ecumenical strategy.

In 1998, in advance of the quinquennial meeting of the World Council of Churches at Harare in Zimbabwe, a consultation of Chalcedonian Orthodox was held in Thessaloniki. It agreed that Orthodox should go to Harare but not vote or participate in worship, and should participate only in Orthodox themes. They also asked for a theological commission to discuss Orthodox participation in future meetings. So, with the exception of the Georgian and Bulgarian Churches which had already decided to withdraw, the Orthodox went to Harare, played a vocal and active part in discussion, and achieved agreement for the setting up of the commission. It is currently at work, and will report in 2008.

Doctrinal discussion

This growing contact also led the Churches to explore their different understandings of doctrine. As a result a series of commissions and informal discussions have been set up to explore points of disagreement and unexpected areas of agreement.

Orthodox and Roman Catholics have met in an International Theological Dialogue, which was set up in 1979. This followed a series of eirenical statements and actions by both sides, with each making some recognition of the other as an equal or sister Church. In 1965 Pope Paul VI and Patriarch Athenagoras I of Constantinople removed the mutual excommunications of 1054, which had remained in place ever since, and in a memorable moment, Pope Paul knelt down and kissed the feet of the Patriarch's representative.

The Dialogue has produced four agreed statements and was making good progress in overcoming many centuries of hostility. But a chill has entered into the discussions in the 1990s as a result of political changes in Eastern Europe. The Roman Catholic Church was able to benefit from relaxed conditions in Russia to re-establish its hierarchy of bishops, which was seen by the Russian Orthodox Church as an attempt to proselytise. Then the re-emergence of the Eastern Catholic or Uniate Churches has led to tension in many countries. At the meeting in 1990 the Orthodox representatives requested that the programme of discussion be interrupted in order to air the problem of the Uniate Churches. From the Orthodox point of view, the Uniate Churches are an attempt to bring unity by tempting Orthodox communities away from the Orthodox Church and incorporating them into the Catholic Church. This is an offence against the presupposition of the Dialogue that the two recognise each other as sister Churches. The next meeting at Balamand in the Lebanon in 1993 rejected the Uniate way both 'as a method to be followed or as a model of the unity our Churches are seeking', although it did recognise the right of the Greek Catholic Churches to exist.[8] Since then Orthodox complain that the terms agreed at Balamand have not been observed by Rome, and as a result the Dialogue is suspended. More productive have been a series of meetings in Vienna from 1971 to 1988 between the Roman Catholic and Oriental Orthodox Churches, which produced the Vienna Christological Formula. This is a shared statement of Christological belief between the two traditions.

Discussions have taken place between Orthodox and Anglicans, and have produced two agreed statements, at Dublin and Moscow. At first both sides expected great things of the discussions, perhaps even the establishing of some form of inter-communion, but Orthodox became increasingly unhappy at the signs of a liberal approach to theology and Church order in Anglicanism, especially over the ordination of women. The conversations were suspended and then re-started, but have sunk down the list of priorities of both Churches.

The most dramatic progress has been between the Chalcedonian and non-Chalcedonian Orthodox. The first meeting of the series was at Aarhus in 1964, which led to a Joint Commission on Theological Dialogue which by 1991 had come to a common mind, and was able to agree that 'fundamentally and essentially we on both sides have preserved the same faith in Our Lord Jesus Christ in spite of diverse formulations and resulting controversies'.[9] While this has led to the formal re-establishing of communion only between the Syrian Churches, in practice the two families of Churches often welcome members of the other to receive communion. It has provided an encouraging precedent in that unity of faith has been recognised without either side requiring the other to alter their view of the Council of Chalcedon. This could, in theory, be extended to the recognition of the faith of another Church without requiring formal agreement on disputed formulations. In addition, discussions have been going on involving the Church of the East,

---

[8] Balamand agreement section 12, in J. Borelli and J. Erickson, *The Quest for Unity: Orthodox and Catholics in Dialogue* (Crestwood, NY 1996).

[9] C. Chaillot and A. Belopopsky (eds), *Towards Unity: the Theological Dialogue between the Orthodox Church and the Oriental Orthodox Churches* (Geneva 1998), p. 36.

which has led to improved relations between that Church and both Roman Catholics and Oriental Orthodox.

Growing friendship

Behind this flurry of official negotiation lies a growing experience of meeting, friendship and mutual learning. The arrival of large numbers of Russians in the West again proved fruitful. Both the St Sergius Institute in Paris and St Vladimir's Seminary in New York have been centres of ecumenical contact. They have shared in theological work with members of other traditions, and have offered courses to non-Orthodox. The Holy Cross seminary in Massachusetts is also involved in ecumenical education, as is the recently established Institute for Orthodox Christian Studies in Cambridge, in England. The extensive publishing programme of St Vladimir's has helped to bring Orthodox history and theology into the forefront of the consciousness of Western thinking.

The Fellowship of St Alban and St Sergius was founded in 1927 by Nicolas Zernov and others in England. Its aim was to provide opportunities for Christians of different traditions to meet each other and explore their different insights. It has published a journal, *Sobornost,* and arranged an annual conference, among other activities, which have influenced Church leaders, theologians and many lay members too. In recent years it has begun to establish branches in Athens, Moscow and other Orthodox countries.

The starting-point for Orthodox involvement in this wide variety of ecumenical contact is that Orthodoxy is the faith of the apostles, lived and handed on by the whole Church. Other Churches have deviated, either through distorting the ordering of the Church by introducing authoritarian models of leadership (the Pope), or unilaterally altering the shared faith of the Church (the *filioque*), or developing individualistic or liberal versions of Christianity, which lead further and further from the faith of the apostles. On this basis unity can only take the form of non-Orthodox returning to Orthodoxy. And since the sharing of the communion is the action that defines and makes the Church, it should be enjoyed only after unity has been achieved – and not used as a method of doing this. Orthodox tend, therefore, to object to the practice of inter-communion as a part of ecumenical life, and to the emphasis on common action at the expense of doctrinal discussion.

Some Orthodox have questioned this clear and simple position. The question of whether and under what circumstances inter-communion is possible was discussed in the 1930s. Two approaches to this issue emerged. The first was associated with the figure of Sergei Bulgakov, Dean of the St Sergius Institute in Paris, who suggested that inter-communion was the way to achieve unity. He asked Orthodox to consider the question of whether Christians outside the Orthodox Churches should be considered to be also outside the One Holy Catholic Church affirmed in the Creeds, and also asked what Orthodox mean when they assert that full doctrinal agreement is necessary for communion in the sacraments – pointing out that the word 'full' is not defined and also that there is some variety of belief among Orthodox as well as among other Christians. The implications of his view were that inter-communion could be offered between Orthodox and others, and he advocated this practice in certain circumstances. His view did not receive favour either from official Orthodox circles, or from other Christians. In fact, at that stage, it was Anglican members of the Fellowship of St Alban and St Sergius (where he explained his ideas) who were more hostile to inter-communion than Orthodox. The other pioneer of Orthodox ecumenism was Georges Florovsky. In a speech at the opening conference of the World Council of Churches in 1948 he countered the view of many that the meeting together was a manifestation of the voice of a united Christianity. He stated firmly that 'Christian disunity is an open and bleeding wound on the glorious body of Christ' and argued for a programme of theological discussion within the context of personal relationships, as the means of seeking unity. Inter-communion should be looked forward to as the fruit of unity, not as the means to achieve it. The view of Georges Florovsky was followed by most of those Orthodox who took part in ecumenical discussion, including Alexander Schmemann and John Meyendorff, both of whom settled in the USA.

The moves towards improving relations became more cautious as the twentieth century progressed. Confidence in doctrinal discussion has declined, as the last hundred years have tended to lead Western Churches into greater liberalism, and a sense that the issues which confront Western Churches are different from those of concern to the East. Links of friendship, however, often remain warm.

The history of relations between the Churches of East and West is long and tragic. Division has been present from the day Diocletian divided the Empire, and has grown and extended on many levels. There is the level of estrangement, a process which begins when the two sides lose contact, living in different places, forgetting each other's languages, and losing sympathy for each other's needs, and is completed when ambition and greed leads to violence and hate. Then there is the level of doctrinal divergence, which springs out of estrangement, and becomes codified in credal statement. Then there is Church organisation, which is also a doctrinal divergence but then sets up forms of Church life that cannot accommodate the convictions and understandings of the other. These have a mutual influence and dynamism which lead to a growing distance that becomes ever harder to overcome. The many-sided nature of the process shows why it is so difficult to give a date to the Great Schism between East and West.

Attempts to find reconciliation and agreement have also been present from the beginning, although they have often been overshadowed by the more negative forces. They too are complex and need to address the different levels of disunity. In a world which has seen the effect of hate and conflict in the twentieth century and in a Church which believes in unity, it is reasonable to expect that, while there may be setbacks on some levels of the search for unity, the momentum towards agreement and friendship will continue on others.

11

Prospect: a cautious reforming

A NEW STAGE IN THE LIFE OF THE CHURCHES

We began this survey with a stroll down Straight Street, in the city of Damascus. The last chapter has brought us westwards, to the border between Orthodox and Catholic, and the line dividing Eastern from Western Europe. It has also brought us to the present day, with ecumenical relationships in an unresolved position, with the Churches still divided by prejudice and hostility, yet also discovering new friendships and co-operation. The task here is recognised to be to find ways that the very different Church traditions of East and West can relate and work together while respecting the different approaches of those involved. This pattern is repeated in other areas of Church life.

Much has changed. In 1971 – a generation before the close of the second millennium – there was little reason to hope for or expect a bright future. In Russia the pressure on the Church, which had began in 1917, was being carried on under Leonid Brezhnev. The number of open churches was continuing its remorseless decline (it sank to a low of 6,806 church communities in 1985), and there was the consecration of a new Patriarch, Pimen, who was described in a report to the Soviet government as 'mediocre, rude, passive, lacking any strong will but with a moving way of celebrating the liturgy' – all no doubt excellent qualifications from the point of view of an atheist government.[1] Throughout

---

[1] Attributed to the present Patriarch Alexis II; see D. Pospielovsky, *The Orthodox Church in the History of Russia* (New York 1998), p. 332.

Eastern Europe the Communist regimes were secure and settled in their discrimination against the Churches. In Cyprus tension was growing both within the Church and with the Turkish population, and the country was on its way to partition, resulting in exile for many hundreds of thousands of Orthodox, and also further weakening the position of the Greek community inside Turkey. In Egypt President Sadat was seeking to revive the Islamic movement and increase the use of Sharia law in cases involving Christians as well as Muslims, and the new Pope Shenouda III found that the old Church leadership was retiring from active life. Perhaps worst of all, in Greece monastic life generally and on the Holy Mountain in particular was in decline, with the numbers of monks on Mount Athos at its lowest level for over a century: only 1145 monks remained. A Byzantinist, John Julius Norwich, commented after a visit, 'Athos is dying and dying fast. The disease in incurable. There is no hope.'

Thirty years later the situation has changed. Most dramatic has been the fall of Communist governments across Eastern Europe and Soviet Asia, which has left the Churches there facing a volatile if more liberated future prospect. But in addition monastic life has revived, and all parts of the Church are showing some signs of new life. The changes have left the Church, especially in Eastern Europe, with two over-riding challenges to contend with, which are also two enormous tasks to be undertaken.

The first task is moral and spiritual. The twentieth century saw a series of persecutions of a ferocity unparalleled in any period in the history of the Church. While the West did not escape the pain of these years, the violence of persecution was directed almost exclusively against the Christians of the East. Many discovered a new life and strength through this. Metropolitan Antony of Sourozh was asked once, 'Is the Church in Russian free?' He replied, 'the freedom of the Church is to love until death.' The Churches have learned to survive, although most of the formal activities of the Church's life, with the enormously significant exception of the liturgy, were made illegal, and to show a heroism and sanctity which has been recognised as a true spiritual gift. It is a continuing paradox of the Christian life that difficulty, persecution and suffering often breed a vitality and renewal in direct contradiction to the effect desired by the persecutors. Bishop Kallistos Ware commented: 'Talking with the contemporary fathers in Romania who had lived through the years of persecution, I was impressed again and again by their non-judgmental attitude, by their realistic compassion, by their quiet joy.'[2]

Now, however, new trials are confronting the Orthodox Churches. There is the need for the renewal, nurture and re-conversion of societies undergoing economic and political disorientation, and for a response to the arrival of Western exports of secularism, consumerism and globalisation. Faced with a rapidly changing society, the Orthodox Churches may see their vocation as maintaining a pure and unchanging tradition and so become inward-looking, defensive and condemnatory of others. Or they may become committed to a new world order, responding to new demands and questions posed by science and technology and to the sheer presence of other Churches and faiths in an increasingly interdependent world. They may find it possible to be both true to the tradition of the past and open to the opportunities of the future. This will require a form of spiritual and moral re-orientation more far-reaching than anything required of the West.

The second task is similar to the first, but is transposed to the political and cultural arena. In the course of a long history, the Orthodox Churches have moved through several locations on the world cultural map. The process began with a thousand years of being the centre of culture, in the Byzantine Empire, with Islam and the Catholic West as increasingly assertive but still subordinate competitors on either side. In the next period Western Europe and Islam were the two major powers, with the Orthodox Churches functioning partly as a minority within Islam and partly as a Russian Empire which could be called, with some reservations, Orthodox. The question now is: where do the Orthodox belong?

Those in the Middle East are conscious of shared Semitic roots. They are closer than Western Churches to the Semitic roots of Christianity and so share some cultural common ground with both Judaism and Islam. This sense of shared Semitic culture enables the Middle Eastern Christians to live as loyal and active citizens in mainly Muslim states. As a minority they have little choice but to point to their commitment to the Turkish, Syrian or Egyptian state, but the shared cultural background

---

[2] K. Ware 'The witness of the Orthodox Church in the twentieth century', *Sourozh* 80 (May 2000), pp. 1–14.

makes it possible to join with others in the project of building a national identity.

For the Orthodox of Eastern Europe and Russia – the Chalcedonian community of Christians – the options are twofold. The Orthodox could become a separate cultural entity, part of a reconstituted Russian-dominated economic and cultural alliance. This is the view of the celebrated – or infamous? – theory of Samuel Huntington, set out in a book which touched a raw nerve among many Orthodox by suggesting that Orthodoxy belongs to a different civilisation from Western Christianity.[3] Or they could become part of a new Europe, culturally reverting to the Graeco-Roman synthesis of the Empire before it was torn apart by the embitterment of the Great Schism, and so developing an identity within a new enlarged Europe. This is a question which has long preoccupied Orthodox Christianity: in fifteenth-century Constantinople, with its debate over the acceptance of the Council of Florence; or in nineteenth-century Russia, with the division between Slavophils and Westernisers. In the past the Orthodox have decided against seeing themselves with the West, as part of European Christian culture, and any suggestion of rapprochement with Catholic or Protestant has been firmly rejected by the common mind of the Church. But now the new circumstances of the post-Communist era in the East, and the post-Christian era in the West, may lead both East and West to come up with different answers from those of the last millennium which approximate more closely to those of the millennium before, and to evolve a new Christian sense of common purpose and shared life within a unified European political and economic entity.

These questions are of urgent importance for the Chalcedonian Orthodox Churches. They may seem to be of lesser concern for the non-Chalcedonian Churches which are definitely outside Europe and are forced to work out a way of living alongside a newly confident Islam. But the prefixes of Chalcedonian and non-Chalcedonian are becoming increasingly out-moded as ecumenical discussion brings the two families of Churches into closer relationship, and so both will become more concerned with the same issues. But, still, there is a variety of experiences and not one single experience. Differences in the current situation of the Churches need to be recognised.

[3] S. Huntington, *The Clash of Civilisations and the Re-making of World Order* (New York 1996).

THE STATE OF THE CHURCHES

In Russia the period following the fall of Communism has been marked by the rebuilding of churches and re-opening of institutions on a massive scale. This is shown by these figures from the Moscow Patriarchate, suggesting a religious revival on a staggering scale.

	1990	2000
Monasteries	18	500
Theological schools	3	50 (at least)
Churches in Moscow	40	300 (at least)

The existence of this religious revival has, however, been questioned. Although accurate statistics are not available, those familiar with Russian society generally agree that between 1 and 3 per cent of the population of Russia attend church regularly. This level of attendance is less than in many countries in secularised Western Europe. But as much caution must be exercised over this more negative approach. For the West, with its post-Enlightenment individualism, belief is a matter of individual choice and the commitment of faith is expressed through attending church worship. The Orthodox East has inherited a more communal approach, with membership of a Church often being bound up with membership of a nation. Expression of faith is more finely nuanced and can be shown through keeping the fasts and sharing the celebration of feasts, the veneration of icons and visiting places of pilgrimage. People are likely to attend church on major festivals, rather than on Sundays. Such diverse forms of expression of faith are harder to assess, but there is plenty of evidence of firmly entrenched Orthodox practice. In 1999 the relics of St Panteleimon were brought to Moscow. There was huge interest: observers reported that around a million people queued for eight hours or more to venerate the relics. Such indicators suggest that religious practice is too varied and many-sided to be accurately captured in a survey.

A fuller picture of religious observance in Russia has recently been presented by a team of researchers who have travelled to all parts of the country. Rather than compiling statistics, they have chosen to produce a more descriptive survey of their findings. It provides detailed information about the state of Church life in different parts of Russia.[4]

[4] Some results of this survey are published in *Religion, State and Society* 28.1 (March 2000), pp. 7–69.

Compare, for example, the situation in two dioceses which the research team visited and described: Petrozavodsk, a diocese formed in the 1990s in the north-west of Russia; and Ekaterinburg, the former Sverdlovsk in the Urals, where the Tsar and his family were assassinated.

In Petrozavodsk the researchers found a lively and vibrant Church life. Bishop Manuil is from an intellectual St Petersburg background, enjoys good relations with Lutherans and Pentecostals, and uses a translation of the New Testament made by Finnish Pentecostals for his work among the Karelian-speaking congregations. The monasteries, especially the Muromsky monastery, are centres for this catachetical work. In the city itself the Zhuravka educational centre has been financed by the head of a building firm who is also the director of the centre. Its three-year course for catechists is taught by the bishop, leading priests and secular teachers. Some of its graduates have become priests. The bishop's press secretary however, is a leading conservative who regularly publishes nationalist articles that contradict the public statements of the bishop. The bishop values the variety of Church life in his diocese.

Ekaterinburg sprang into the news when it was learnt that in May 1998 books by the more open Orthodox writers – Alexander Schmemann, John Meyendorff and Alexander Men – had been burned in public. This was in fact the second book burning, as there had been an earlier occasion in 1994. The bishop who had ordered this was the young and upwardly mobile Bishop Nikon, who had been appointed to the diocese in 1994 while he was still in his early thirties. He turned out to be a keen fund-raiser for the diocese, raising money mostly from the parish churches, and also an opponent of foreign missions and heterodox sects. He built up good relations with the army and some of the local institutions, but was unpopular with many clergy. He cut off support for the Church's education programme, acted against liberal priests and aroused the opposition of some of the monasteries. He later denied to the Synod of Bishops that the book burnings had taken place, but was nevertheless eventually removed after numerous complaints against him had been received by the Patriarchate. He was then sent to the well-known, and conservative, Pskov Monastery of the Caves.

The leadership of the Church under Patriarch Alexis II is sometimes criticised for caution at a time when positive leadership is required. These two examples show just some of the range of Church life in Russia, and show the importance of the task of holding the Church together at a time of social change. Maintaining unity is one of the Patriarchate's priorities.

While the Russian Church is the largest of the Orthodox Churches, the historic centre of Chalcedonian Orthodoxy remains the city of Constantinople – since 1923 called Istanbul. Here Patriarch Bartholomew (consecrated in 1991) is in a completely different position from Patriarch Alexis. The number of Orthodox in Turkey has declined dramatically, and there are now fewer than 2,000 Christians in Istanbul. While the Patriarchs of other Churches have extensive diocesan responsibilities in their capital city, the main pastoral responsibility of the Ecumenical Patriarch is for the Greeks and others in Western Europe, America and Australasia. The Patriarch is recognised as the senior bishop in the East, but this is a primacy of honour and does not give power over the Churches. He is a bishop without a flock and a leader with no power to lead. From this paradox comes his unusual but creative position. The present Patriarch Bartholomew I said at his enthronement that he was 'a loyal citizen subject to the laws of his country' with a power 'which remains purely spiritual, a symbol of reconciliation, a force without weapons, which rejects all political goals and maintains its distance from the deceiving arrogance of secular power'. He convenes meetings of the heads of national Churches, presides over the Church in the West, meets with leaders of other Churches and faiths, and seeks to resolve disputes and difficulties. Ignatius of Antioch's image of the bishop and presbyters being in harmony like the strings of a lyre applies to the kind of authority which rests in the Patriarch. From 1961 successive Ecumenical Patriarchs have convened a series of meetings of the Churches, at which this ideal of harmony is expressed.

His position is not accepted by all. Conservative elements in the Church, including some of the monasteries on Mount Athos, over which he presides, do not recognise him because of his relationships with leaders of other Churches. His involvement in areas where there is disputed jurisdiction, such as Estonia and the Ukraine, has led to a tense relationship with the Patriarch of Moscow and others.

The Patriarch's continued residence in the ancient capital city of Constantinople remains uncertain. The Treaty of Lausanne of 1923 gave him the right to reside in Istanbul, and he will undoubtedly do so as long as possible. But the Greek community is decreasing in size, and, since Turkish law requires the Ecumenical Patriarch to be a Turkish citizen, it may prove impossible to find an acceptable successor. It may seem unthinkable that the Patriarch should leave the old imperial capital, but we have noted that the Patriarch of Alexandria resides in Cairo and three Patriarchs of Antioch are located in the city of Damascus. As well as the Patriarchate in the Phanar in Istanbul, the Ecumenical Patriarch has a variety of roles and responsibilities in the Church, and of centres which express them. There is Thessaloniki – near Constantinople and the old second city of the Empire – a centre for the leadership of Greek-speaking, ethnic Orthodoxy. Or the island of Rhodes, under the jurisdiction of Constantinople but in Greek territory, across the sea from the great city of Constantinople. Or Mount Athos, the spiritual centre of international Orthodoxy – and so the heart of the monastic and ascetic tradition. Or Geneva, the capital of the ecumenical movement – and so a place from where the Patriarch could be seen as a leader within world Christianity. Or New York, the centre of the large Greek archdiocese of America – and so of modern Western Orthodoxy. Wherever the Patriarchate may be based in the future, the development of a distinctive Orthodox form of primacy and conciliar presidency is an urgent priority, although the process is likely to be slow.

The Oriental Orthodox Churches continue to maintain a precarious existence within an increasingly militant and fundamentalist Muslim society. The Churches have become accustomed to life as a minority Church, and intermittently hostile conditions have become the normal condition of Church life. At present experiences vary. In Turkey the end of hostilities between Kurdish nationalist forces (PKK) and the Turkish army have brought some stability to the Syrian villages of the Tur Abdin. There are signs of slight growth in the Christian population, increased prosperity (especially in the town of Mardin), and even the re-populating of one formerly deserted monastery.[5] Just over the border to the south, the Syrian Orthodox centres of population in eastern Syria are vibrant and growing, with a healthy youth movement.

The most depressing places to visit are Israel and the Palestinian territories. In 1922 Christians comprised 10 per cent of the population of British mandate Palestine. Today they form less than 1 per cent of the combined population of Israel and Palestine, and the number is

---

[5] I am grateful to Stephen Griffiths, Anglican Chaplain in Damascus, who has sent me his reports on his six-monthly visits to the Tur Abdin.

decreasing continuously. Not only are the Christians Arabs, and therefore subject to Israeli attack, but also, being generally better educated than Muslim Arabs, there are more opportunities for them to emigrate. It is estimated that fifty Christian families are emigrating each week and if this continues the indigenous Christian population of the Holy Land will have virtually disappeared within a few years. The Holy Places of the Christian faith will become tourist attractions rather than places of living worship.

In Egypt the Coptic Church has been greatly strengthened by revival, but the community is subject to regular killings and other atrocities at the hands of Muslim extremists. More positive is the new independence of Armenia following the collapse of the Soviet Union and the successful war against neighbouring Azerbaijan for the control of the Armenian enclave of Nagorno Karabakh. This has given the Armenian Church a firm national base. The Armenian diaspora, on the other hand, has been almost eliminated in Turkey and reduced in Israel, but remains vigorous in the Lebanon and Syria. The large Ethiopian Church is numerous and powerful, but some are concerned at growing economic investment in Ethiopia from Islamic countries, especially Saudi Arabia, with the increasing influence which this gives to the Muslim half of the population of Ethiopia.

The situation of the Churches of the Middle East is a matter of grave concern and a reminder that persecution is still the continuing experience of many Christians. It should evoke massive support from the Churches of the West, rather than the indifference which is the more usual reaction of the world community. Compare the frequency with which Kurdish rights are reported in the Western press with the absence of references to the threat of extinction of the Syrian Christians in the same region of Turkey.

We should probably stop using the word 'diaspora' to describe Orthodox Christianity in the West. Members of the Churches in these countries are no longer scattered from their natural homelands. Many were born in the West, and are either second- or third-generation residents, or are Western converts to Orthodox Churches. There are more Chalcedonian Orthodox in most of the major Western capitals than there are in any of the cities of the five historic Patriarchates. In Great Britain, researchers note that, along with Muslims and Pentecostal Churches, the Orthodox are the only religious group that is growing. The experiences of Orthodox theologians, such as John Zizioulas, Metropolitan John of Pergamum, and Kallistos Ware, bishop of Diokleia, who work in the West, are watched with great interest by many Orthodox in the East, as guides as to how it is possible to retain fidelity to the tradition at the same time as being open to the secular world. The experience of Orthodoxy in the West will contribute to the shape and priorities of the life of the Orthodox Church of the future.

The main task facing Orthodox Churches in the West is the resolution of the present jurisdictional confusion. It is axiomatic for Orthodox ecclesiology that there should be one Church in one place, yet the Orthodox community is divided among several national Churches. It is clear that the correct solution would be a number of autonomous or autocephalous Churches covering Europe, America and Australasia. In Europe these would have to define their relationship with the Pope, since Europe is the area of the historic Patriarchate of Rome. This possibility is at present purely theoretical, and for the foreseeable future the Churches have to devise practical, even if imperfect, structures for developing an effective and coherent Church life. For many, the resolution of this problem of jurisdictional confusion is the most urgent challenge facing the Churches.

In 1993 a meeting of the Churches agreed that the proper method of attaining unity was to set up 'episcopal assemblies'. These would act as interim bodies to express the common life of the Church until such time as further organisational integration was possible. Such an assembly was founded in the USA in 1960 and was known as SCOBA, or the Standing Committee of Orthodox Bishops in America, and an Orthodox Episcopal Assembly met in France in 1997. The preferred procedure is to develop common initiatives as a method of exploring proper strategies for integration. This strategy allows a cautious exploration of the possibilities facing the Church in the West, which will undoubtedly gradually become a local Church. This would seem to be the way forward, but the will to embrace even this level of collaboration is as yet weak.

MONASTIC RENEWAL

The vitality of the life of the Churches is rooted in the faithfulness and resourcefulness of persons and communities living out their faith. While this happens in many contexts, the revival in monastic life is an indicator of a healthy state of Church life more generally.

The revival in monastic life has been unmistakable, unexpected and dramatic. It has affected most of the Orthodox Churches. Since Mount Athos is a centre of Orthodox monastic life, it is here that renewal is most significant, and from here that other monasteries have been founded or renewed.

The revival on Mount Athos has been widely reported. In 1902 there were 7,432 monks, with Russians outnumbering Greeks. Then followed a steady decline until 1971, when the number of monks sank to just 1,145. The magnificent Byzantine buildings of the monasteries were dilapidated and occupied often by just a few monks. But in some of the hermitages and *sketes*, or small communities, on the rocky cliffs in the south of the peninsula, a strong ascetic and Hesychastic tradition was being maintained. In 1972 the number of monks increased by one, and since then there has been a steady growth, with a total of 1,610 in 2000. Further encouragement is given by another figure, that of new monks coming to live on the Holy Mountain. Until 1987 there was an average figure of twenty-nine new monks per year, but since then this figure has increased to sixty-one, with a total of 609 new monks arriving between 1987 and 1996.[6]

There is a common pattern to this growth. Each of the monasteries has restored a coenobitic life-style, replacing the former idiorrhythmic way of life, in which each monk lived alone and decided on his own discipline. To assist in the restoration of a coenobitic life, a monastery invited an experienced spiritual father to come, with a group of disciples, to oversee this change and to ensure a rigorous and disciplined form of monastic life. The revival began in 1971 when the monastery of Stavronikita, then reduced to eight monks, invited a hermit and scholar, Fr Vasileios, to become its superior. He attracted new members and then, having built up the monastery, moved on to do the same at Iviron. Two years later a group of monks came from the mainland under Fr Aimilianos to Simonopetra, which remains a centre of study and is one of the more open monasteries. It is now full, and the monks are building more accommodation to house more members. They also look after a daughter house at Ormylia, where 125 nuns live a strict Athonite style of life. A similar renewal has affected all the monasteries, although

---

[6] I am grateful to Graham Speake, of the Friends of Mount Athos, for providing me with information about the revival.

growth at the Slav monasteries of Zographou and Hilandar, occupied by Bulgarians and Serbs respectively, is slow, not least because of the reluctance of the Greek authorities to allow non-Greeks to take up residence.

Whereas earlier generations of monks tended to come from peasant backgrounds and did most of the physical work themselves, new recruits are more likely to come from the city and to be well educated. As a result some of the work is done by contractors and workmen from the mainland. Also, since money is needed for rebuilding, the timber industry is expanding, with the problem of erosion of the forests, and introduction of roads and heavy vehicles for the extraction of the timber. Further pressure is placed on the traditional way of life by the number of visitors and the pressure from human rights groups to modify the discipline excluding women. The success of the Athonite revival has raised questions about the future of life on the Mountain, but there is every hope that the ruling council of the Mountain will find a healthy way forward.

Renewal in monastic life is not limited to Mount Athos, but is a feature of almost all parts of the Orthodox world. Since 1990 monasteries have been re-opened in Russia, Romania and elsewhere in Eastern Europe. The monasteries of Egypt have experienced a resurgence similar to Athos, with large numbers of young and well-educated monks developing existing monasteries, repopulating deserted monasteries and founding new monasteries.

Many monks are conservative, holding to the style of Church life which values a witness to the unchanging truth of Orthodoxy and is suspicious of anything hinting at compromise. Ecumenism is the archheresy, and even on the Holy Mountain, which is under the jurisdiction of the Ecumenical Patriarch, the monastery of Esphigmenou does not commemorate the Patriarch at the liturgy, thus showing its rejection of his authority. Monastic revival therefore tends to strengthen the conservative forces within the Church. The Athonite monk Fr Ephraim has established six new monasteries in the USA, all of which follow a traditional form of Orthodox life. Some monasteries follow a style of life more open to the world, such as the monastery of Simonopetra on Athos, and this gives encouragement to those who seek a fuller engagement with contemporary society.

The monastic zealots, as they are often called, combine precise adherence to the tradition of the Church, a rigid and ascetic style of life, and a rejection of ecumenism as a major heresy (I remember a sermon claiming that ecumenism was more dangerous to the Church than satanism, since it attacks the Church from the inside), and a hostility to those outside. To many, this form of Orthodoxy seems bigoted and narrow-minded, and potentially racist and anti-Semitic. Other Orthodox will sometimes use phrases like the 'struggle for the soul of Orthodoxy' to point to the danger they discern in the conservative tendency.

The inherent conservatism of the Orthodox Churches has often been referred to in earlier chapters. It has a legitimate and proper place in the spectrum of Orthodox Church life, and should not be judged too harshly. The need to adapt to new forms of social and Church life demands new reactions, which will develop slowly. One zealot monk spoke of the difficulty of knowing how to react to a non-Orthodox Christian, and of the conflict he felt between his instinctive affection for the guest and his determination not to compromise his Orthodox faith by allowing any accommodation to what is not truly Orthodox.

PATRISTIC REVIVAL

Alongside monastic revival is patristic revival. This has already been re-ferred to and continues. The theological groundwork for the revival had been laid through the careful and creative scholarly work on the patristic tradition by John Meyendorff, Basil Krivocheine, Vladimir Lossky and many others. This work has been going on throughout the twentieth century. A part of this project has been the translation of the *Philokalia* and with it the popularisation of the Jesus Prayer. Icon painters too have been working to reclaim the Byzantine tradition of iconography. Within a Church which had lived under the political domination of the Turks and the intellectual influence of the West, the last century has seen a determined effort to reinterpret the Byzantine heritage.

Christos Yannaras described Orthodox theology as 'not a metaphys-ical system but a formulation of the Church's experience'. Here the re-covery of Palamism with its emphasis on the experience of divine light and the renewed interest in the *Philokalia* with its harmonisation of doctrine, asceticism and Church life, all in a practical form, provide a solid base. Many, or most, Eastern theologians working today would see this tradition as forming the basis of modern Orthodox theology. The *Philokalia*, as has been said, is a somewhat unlikely source of theological renewal, being a lengthy and selective anthology produced as part of the nineteenth-century spiritual renewal movement, but it has been shown to have a continuing relevance to an altered society. It is in continuity with the past tradition, and also provides a basis for dialogue with those of other traditions, who find both points of convergence and stimuli to fresh thought in the interaction of the Philokalic synthesis with their own traditions.

Within this revival, liturgical renewal has taken place. This has been influenced by the Western rediscovery of the corporate nature of the Eucharist and the need to receive communion regularly. Orthodox would claim that this has been a part of the tradition of the Eastern Church, and especially of periods of spiritual renewal. Practice today is varied, with most Churches retaining infrequent communion, but regular communion is becoming more common.

The recovery of the patristic tradition is far from being an obscurantist historical exercise. The hallmark of patristic theology is a serious involvement with the issues of the day, a readiness to interpret the salvation of Christ in the terms of contemporary culture, while remaining true to the full faith of the Councils, and a sense of the human person as having a vocation to bring the whole creation to the vision and glory of God.

The potential of patristic thought is shown in the field of ecology. In 1989 the then Ecumenical Patriarch Demetrios declared the first day of the ecclesiastical year, 1 September, to be a day of prayer for the protection of the natural environment. Two years later a conference was held in Crete which was attended by representatives of all the Orthodox Churches, as well as theologians and scientists. The importance of this initiative has been to show that an approach based on the thought of the Fathers which firmly places humanity at the heart of creation, and calls us to work for a dynamic change within creation, can have a creative contribution to make to a contemporary political, scientific and technological debate. It places Orthodox theology within urgent concerns affecting the whole human race. To say it shows that patristic theology is relevant is a trite expression, but this is really why the Crete conference is seen as significant.

Following from this, it is hoped that Orthodox Christians, faithfully attending the liturgy, rooting their thought in the Fathers of the Church, and also committed to their individual involvement in medicine, scientific enquiry, psychiatry, or any other of the areas of research and development that are shaping our future, will find that they too have insights and initiatives which are rooted in the truth of the Christian faith. Here it is the influence of individuals which is likely to set the pace. However, the Councils of Bishops have also shown some interest and responsibility. The Russian Bishops' Council in Moscow held in 2000 adopted a document on social policy covering sexual and medical ethics and global economic concerns. The document was formulated over a period of six years through discussion and consultation with authorities in the relevant fields. It presents a varied approach: it condemns homosexuality as a sinful tendency and an example of human pride; it sets out cases where the Church sanctions divorce; it permits some forms of contraception; it rejects abortion and euthanasia. This document presents a blend of traditional teaching with views on new questions, and has been sent to all parishes and seminaries for consideration. It represents a very significant step in articulating a moral and ethical approach to some urgent questions, taking a clearly conservative position – by Western standards – but noticeably more liberal in some respects than, say, Roman Catholic teaching.

EDUCATION

Along with the revival of theology goes renewal of education. In Russia the first priority after the freedom of the Church was the rebuilding and re-opening of churches, monasteries and seminaries. But now the priority is shifting to education and, one might say, a spiritual rather than material rebuilding. Action is being taken to prevent the appointment of uneducated priests, and the state of the Church seminaries has given rise to some concern.

The interest in education has shown itself in the foundation of independent institutions of higher education. A group of Moscow clergy including Vsevolod Shpiller and especially Vladimir Vorobiev had been concerned about education before the fall of Communism. As soon as conditions allowed they launched a programme of study, at first in 1991 for around 300 students. This venture developed into the St Tikhon's Institute, which has continued to expand, with its present student numbers estimated as over 3,000, its courses validated by the national education authority so that its graduates are able to teach in the state education system, and a policy of training its own future teachers. It is increasingly undertaking the training of clergy in preference to the Church seminaries. It has a reputation for adopting a conservative theological position, although the teachers I have met have impressed me by their level of education, enthusiasm and openness to others. There are also other successful centres of education: St John the Theologian Orthodox University, organised by the Moscow Patriarchate; and the Open Orthodox University and St Andrew Biblical Theology Institute, both founded by the followers of the influential liberal preacher and teacher Fr Alexander Men, who was assassinated in 1992.

The ministry of laypeople is also often impressive. During a visit to Serbia in 2001 I attended a lecture at the Bishop Nikolai Spiritual Centre (named after Bishop Nikolai Velimirović) in Kraljevo, to the south of Belgrade. Here a group of laypeople had decided that, following a decade of wars and sanctions, Serbia needed spiritual renewal. The project operates from a hall in the town centre and is managed and financed by the group of laypeople who founded it. There are lectures (a lecture on liturgy which I attended attracted about 450 people on a cold winter's night), Church music, icon workshops, and a library. There are also close links with the local television studio, with regular religious broadcasts organised by the centre. While Serbia is often considered to have especially active lay and youth movements, such initiatives can be found in all parts of the Orthodox world. A focus for work among young people is found in an organisation called Syndesmos, which was founded in 1953, and brings together member youth organisations from all Orthodox Churches, including non-Chalcedonian. It organises conferences, training courses, publications, and a forum for discussion. Despite a sometimes precarious, and financially straitened, situation it has continued to encourage the active and creative life of Orthodox youth.

WOMEN IN THE CHURCH

An account of Orthodox Church life can give the impression of a patriarchal and male-dominated institution. Few women have been mentioned in these pages. The question of the role of women in the Church, and especially their ordination as priests, is a relatively new issue, and is an appropriate place to draw to a close. The understanding of the role of women in the Church has been brought into the foreground as a result of Orthodox participation in the ecumenical movement, and through encounters with Western Churches in the 1960s. It is not a question which would have arisen naturally in the Churches, nor in the societies in which most Orthodox live.

Arguments might earlier have been based on the traditional subordination of women to men (Paul's letters) or on the periodic ritual impurity of women which would make them unfit to approach the unbloody sacrifice (based on Leviticus 12 and 15; and it might be noted that in many circles a man who has cut himself and so has blood flowing from him would similarly be excluded from entering the sanctuary, although temporarily). Modern writers, such as Paul Evdokimov and Thomas Hopko, prefer to base the argument on the distinctions of persons within the Trinity which relate to complementarity of the roles of the sexes. So there is a kind of continuity between the Word of God, the figure of Christ and the man; and between the Spirit of God, Mary the Bearer of God and the woman. On this understanding, the West has blurred the distinction between the roles of the sexes, and this is related to the emphasis on unity in Western Trinitarian theology, which has overlooked the distinctions between the persons.

The Inter-Orthodox Commission held on the island of Rhodes in 1988 was made up of sixty theologians, including eighteen women. They proposed the re-introduction of the order of deaconess, which was clearly part of the life of the medieval Byzantine and Syrian Churches, where it seems from somewhat limited evidence that they were included within the clergy, although it remains unclear what exactly they did. The Commission also proposed the introduction of some kind of 'ecclesiastical act' which would provide recognition and empowerment for a woman's ministry of teaching or pastoral care. These remain on the level of suggestion and one cannot assume that these measures will be implemented.

An attempt to restore the order of deaconess took place in Egypt. The community of the Daughters of St Mary (*Banat Maryam*) was founded in 1965 in the diocese of Beni Suef under the innovative Bishop Athanasius. These are active nuns who work in education, medical care and community projects. This initiative was followed by the recognition of the state of the 'consecrated women', consisting of widows or unmarried women dedicated to a life of service. This informal state was adapted into an order of deaconesses when 180 deaconesses were ordained in 1981. The Church controls and regulates this order, requiring eighteen years of preparation as novice and sub-deaconess before a woman can be admitted. The deaconesses became involved in a wide range of ministries – medical care, work with drug addicts, care of unmarried mothers, literacy classes in rural areas, and much more besides. This development continues although the name 'consecrated women' is preferred to deaconess.

The ordination of women in other Churches is seen as an ecclesiological problem, rather than as heresy, but it has certainly led to a new difficulties in ecumenical relations – although, one might note, it is by no means the only difficulty.

FINALLY

We can expect the present trends to continue. A strong and determined conservative and traditional majority will remain, alongside an open and progressive minority, both of which will be held together by a cautious episcopate. This coalition of opinions, both of which are deeply rooted in and integral to Orthodox Church life, will continue to be involved with ecumenism and other Churches, but will challenge and re-shape the way that ecumenical organisations function. Specific tasks for the Churches are the building up of a local Western Orthodox Church of whatever form and the redefinition of the Orthodox role in the World Council of Churches. More general goals are a strengthening of theological education and the spread of the influence of monastic life. The Orthodox Churches will not conform easily or compliantly to Western expectations. But if the Orthodox do not withdraw and if the West allows them to be themselves, and if both are able to respect and value each other, then the Christian Churches could learn once again to breathe 'with both its lungs' and to find the life of all parts renewed as a result. Both the Christian Church and the world community will be enriched. This is surely the task which faces the Churches at the start of a new millennium.

Table of dates

1054	The Great Schism between East and West: mutual excommunications
1071	The battle of Manzikert: Saljuq Turks advance into Asia Minor
1204	Fall of Constantinople to the Crusaders of the Fourth Crusade
1240	Fall of Kiev to the Tartars
	St Sergius of Radonezh founds the Trinity Lavra
1341	Synod in Constantinople affirms Gregory Palamas and Hesychasm
1346	Establishment of Serbian Patriarchate by St Sava
1380	Battle of Kulikovo Field: the Russians defeat the Mongols
1389	Battle of Kosovo Polje: the Turks defeat the Serbs
1438–9	Council of Florence: an unsuccessful attempt at Union
1453	Fall of Constantinople to the Ottoman Sultan Mehmet II: the end of the Empire
1596	Union of Brest-Litovsk: founding of the Ukrainian Greek Catholic Church
1700	Peter the Great allows the Russian Patriarchate to lapse
1724	Schism in Patriarchate of Antioch: Melkite Greek Catholic Church formed
1775	The *Philokalia* published in Athens
1793	Paisii Velichkovskii's translation of the *Philokalia* into Slavonic
1794	The first Russian missionaries arrive in Siberia
1850	The Church of Greece becomes autocephalous
1872	The Russian Diocese moves its centre to San Francisco
1915–20	Genocide of Armenians in Turkey
1917	Council of Russian Orthodox Church, restoration of Patriarchate
1918	Separation of Church and state in Russia leading to Communist persecution
1923	The Great Catastrophe: exchange of population between Greece and Turkey
	New Calendar adopted by Constantinople and other Orthodox
1974	Partition of Cyprus
1988	Millennium of the Baptism of Russia, then the freedom of the Church in Russia

Bibliography

The bibliography contains a selection of the huge amount of literature available. It is divided into two sections. The first contains select translated primary sources for the life and theology of the Orthodox Churches, from all periods of their history. The second contains some of the more important historical and critical studies. For an annotated bibliography of works in English, see K.Ware, *The Orthodox Church*; and for further reading on individual subjects, see the *Blackwell Dictionary of Eastern Christianity*.

The abbreviation PG in the footnotes refers to the series Patrologiae Cursus Completus, Series Graeca, edited by J.-P. Migne (Paris, 1857–66).

1. Primary sources

Anna Comnena, *The Alexiad*, trans. E. Sewter (London 1969)

Athanasius (Patriarch), *The Life of Antony*, trans. R. Gregg (New York 1980)

Basil, *The Ascetic Writings of St Basil*, trans. W.K. Lowther Clarke (London 1925)

Brock, S. *The Syriac Fathers on Prayer and the Spiritual Life* (Kalamazoo, MI 1987)

Cyril Lucaris, *Confession of Faith*, in *The Acts and Decrees of the Synod of Jerusalem*, ed. J.N.W.B. Robertson (London 1899)

Cyril of Alexandria, *On the Unity of Christ*, trans. J.A. McGuckin (New York 1995)

Cyril of Scythopolis, *The Lives of the Monks of Palestine*, ed. and trans. R. Price and J. Binns (Kalamazoo, MI 1991)

Dionysius the Areopagite (Pseudo-Dionysius), *Complete Works*, trans. C. Luibheid (New York 1987)

Bibliography

Dositheus of Jerusalem, *Confession*, in *The Acts and Decrees of the Synod of Jerusalem*, ed. J.N.W.B. Robertson (London 1899)

Ephrem, *Hymns on Paradise*, trans. S. Brock (New York 1990)

Eusebius, *Ecclesiastical History*, trans. H.J. Lawlor and J.E.L. Oulton (London 1927)

Life of Constantine, in H. Wace and P. Schaff (eds), *A Select Library of Nicene and Post-Nicene Fathers*, vol. 1 (Grand Rapids, MI 1979)

Evagrius of Pontus, *The Praktikos and Chapters on Prayer*, trans. J. Bamburger (Kalamazoo, MI 1987)

Evagrius Scholasticus, *Ecclesiastical History*, trans. J. Bidez and L. Parmentier (London 1898)

Germanus of Constantinople, *On the Divine Liturgy*, ed. and trans. P. Meyendorff (Crestwood, NY 1984)

Gregory Palamas, *The Triads*, trans. N. Gendle (New York 1983)

Ignatius of Antioch, *Epistles*, in *Early Christian Writings*, trans. M. Staniforth (London 1968)

John of Damascus, *On the Divine Images*, trans. D. Anderson (New York 1980)

Writings, trans. F. Chase (Washington, DC 1958)

John of Ephesus, *Life of James bar-Addai*, trans. E.W. Brooks, Patrologia Orientalia, vols. 17–19 (Paris 1923–5)

John of the Ladder (Climacus), *The Ladder of Divine Ascent*, trans. C. Luibheid and N. Russell (New York 1982)

Life of Saint Pachomius and his Disciples, trans. A. de Veilleux, in *Pachomian Koinonia*, vol. 1 (Kalamazoo, MI 1980)

Macarius (Pseudo-Macarius), *Fifty Spiritual Homilies and the Great Letter*, trans. G. Maloney (New York 1992)

Michael the Syrian, *Chronicle*, ed. J.B. Chabot (Paris 1899)

Nicholas Cabasilas, *A Commentary on the Divine Liturgy*, trans. J.M. Hussey and P.A. McNulty (London 1978)

The Life in Christ, trans. C. deCatanzaro (New York 1974)

Peter Moghila, 'Orthodox Confession', in J.J. Overbeck (ed.), *The Orthodox Confessions of the Catholic and Apostolic Church* (London 1898)

Procopius of Caesarea, *On the Buildings*, trans. H.B. Dewing, Loeb Classical Library (London 1914)

Romanus the Melodist, *Kontakia. On the Life of Christ*, trans. Archimandrite Ephraim (San Francisco 1995)

Rufinus, *Ecclesiastical History*, in *The Church History of Rufinus of Aquileia, Books 10–11*, trans. P. Armidon (Oxford 1997)

Sayings of the Desert Fathers, trans. B. Ward (Oxford 1975)

Socrates, *Ecclesiastical History*, in H. Wace and P. Schaff (eds), *A Select Library of Nicene and Post-Nicene Fathers*, vol. 2 (Grand Rapids, MI 1979)

Sozomen, *Ecclesiastical History*, in H. Wace and P. Schaff (eds), *A Select Library of Nicene and Post-Nicene Fathers*, vol. 2 (Grand Rapids, MI 1979)

Symeon the New Theologian, *The Discourses*, trans. C. deCatanzaro (London 1980)

The Festal Menaion, trans. Mother Maria and K. Ware (London 1969)

The Lenten Triodion, trans. Mother Maria and K. Ware (London 1978)

Theodore of Stoudion, *On the Holy Icons*, trans. C.P. Roth (New York 1981)

Theodoret of Cyrrhus, *History of the Monks of Syria*, trans. R.M. Price (Kalamazoo, MI 1985)

The Philokalia, trans. G.E.H. Palmer, P. Sherrard and K. Ware (London 1979–95)

The Way of a Pilgrim, trans. R.M. French (London 1954)

2. Secondary sources

Alexander, S., *Church and State in Yugoslavia since 1945* (Cambridge 1979)

Atiya, A., *A History of Eastern Christianity* (London 1968)

Barker, E., *Social and Political Thought in Byzantium* (Oxford 1957)

Bat Ye'or, *The Decline of Eastern Christianity under Islam, from Jihad to Dhimmitude* (London 1996)

Behr-Sigel, E., *Lev Gillet, a Monk of the Eastern Church* (Oxford 1999)

Behr-Sigel, E. and Ware, K., *The Ordination of Women in the Orthodox Church* (Geneva 2000)

Binns, J., *Ascetics and Ambassadors of Christ, Palestinian Monasticism 325–641* (Oxford 1994)

Blackwell Dictionary of Eastern Christianity (Oxford 1999)

Bolshakoff, S., *Russian Mystics* (Kalamazoo, MI 1977)

Borelli, J. and Erickson, J. (eds), *The Quest for Unity: Orthodox and Catholics in Dialogue* (Crestwood, NY 1994)

Bourdeaux, M., *Gorbachev, Glasnost and the Gospel* (London 1990)

  Opium of the People: Christian Religion in the Soviet Union (London 1977)

Brailsford, H.N., *Macedonia, its Races and their Future* (London 1906)

Breck, J., *The Power of the Word in the Worshipping Church* (New York 1986)

Brown, L., *The Indian Christians of St Thomas* (Cambridge 1982)

Brown, P., 'A Dark Age crisis: aspects of the iconoclast controversy', *English Historical Review* 346 (1973), pp. 1–34

  The Body and Society. Men, Women and Sexual Renunciation in Early Christianity (New York 1988)

  'The rise and function of the holy man in Late Antiquity', *Journal of Roman Studies* 61 (1971), pp. 80–101

  The World of Late Antiquity (London 1971)

Bryer, A. and Cunningham, M. (eds), *Mount Athos and Byzantine Monasticism* (Aldershot 1996)

Bulgakov, S., *The Orthodox Church* (London 1935)

The Wisdom of God (London 1937)

Cavarnos, C., *Anchored in God* (Belmont 1955)

St Cosmas Aitolos (Belmont 1971)

St Macarios of Corinth (Belmont 1972)

St Nicodemos the Hagiorite (Belmont 1974)

Chaillot, C. and Belopopsky, A. (eds), *Towards Unity: the Theological Dialogue between the Orthodox Church and the Oriental Orthodox Churches* (Geneva 1998)

Chetverikov, S., *Starets Paisii Velichkovskii* (Belmont 1980)

Chitty, D., *The Desert a City* (Oxford 1966)

Chryssavgis, J., *Ascent into Heaven, the Theology of the Human Person according to St John of the Ladder* (Brookline, MA 1989)

Repentance and Confession in the Orthodox Church (Brookline, MA 1990)

Clapsis, E., *Orthodoxy in Conversation, Orthodox Ecumenical Engagements* (Geneva/Brookline, MA 2000)

Clement, O., *Conversations with Ecumenical Patriarch Bartholomew I* (New York 1997)

Coakley, J. and Parry, K. (eds), 'The Church of the East: life and thought', *Bulletin of the John Rylands Library* 78.3 (1996)

Congar, Y., *After Nine Hundred Years* (New York 1959)

Conomos, D., *Byzantine Hymnography and Byzantine Chant* (Brookline, MA 1984)

Cunningham, J., *A Vanquished Hope* (New York 1981)

Dalrymple, W., *From the Holy Mountain* (London 1997)

Davey, C., *Pioneer for Unity* (London 1987)

Day, P., *Eastern Christian Liturgies* (Shannon 1972)

de Beausobre, I., *Flame in the Snow, a Life of St Seraphim of Sarov* (London 1945)

de Mendieta, A., *Mount Athos* (Berlin 1972)

Dunlop, J., *Staretz Amvrosy, Model for Dostoevsky's Staretz Zossima* (Belmont 1972)

Dvornik, F., *Byzantine Missions among the Slavs* (New Brunswick 1970)

The Photian Schism, History and Legend (Cambridge 1948)

Ellis, J., *The Russian Orthodox Church, Triumph and Defensiveness* (London 1996)

Featherstone, J.M.E. (trans.), *The Life of Paisij Velyckovs'kyj* (Cambridge, MA 1989)

Fedotov, G.P., *A Treasury of Russian Spirituality* (London 1950)
   The Russian Religious Mind, 2 vols (Cambridge, MA 1946, 1966)
Fennell, J., *A History of the Russian Church to 1448* (London 1995)
Figes, O., *A People's Tragedy, The Russian Revolution 1891–1924* (London 1996)
Florovsky, G., *The Collected Works* (Belmont/Vaduz 1972–87):
   vol. 4, *Aspects of Church History*
   vols 5–6, *Ways of Russian Theology*
   vol. 7, *The Eastern Fathers of the Fourth Century*
   vol. 8, *The Byzantine Fathers of the Fifth Century*
   vol. 9, *The Byzantine Fathers of the Sixth to Eighth Centuries*
Forest, J., *Praying with Icons* (New York 1997)
Frazee, C., *Catholics and Sultans. The Church and the Ottoman Empire 1453–1923* (Cambridge 1983)
   The Orthodox Church and Independent Greece (Cambridge 1969)
Frend, W.H.C., *The Rise of the Monophysite Movement* (Cambridge 1972)
Garrett, P., *St Innocent, Apostle to America* (New York 1979)
Gill, J., *The Council of Florence* (Cambridge 1959)
Glenny, M., *The Balkans 1804–1999* (London 1999)
   The Fall of Yugoslavia (London 1992)
Golitzin, A. (ed.), *The Living Witness of the Holy Mountain* (New York 1996)
Gorodetsky, N., *The Humiliated Christ in Modern Russian Thought* (London 1938)
Gregorios, P., *The Human Presence, Ecology and the Age of the Spirit* (New York 1987)
Gregorios, P., Lazareth, W. and Nissiotis, N., *Does Chalcedon Divide or Unite?* (Geneva 1981)
Hackel, S., *A Pearl of Great Price. The Life of Mother Maria Skobtsova 1891–1945* (London 1982)
Hadjiantoniou, G., *Protestant Patriarch: the Life of Cyril Lucaris (1572–1638), Patriarch of Constantinople* (London 1961)
Hammond, P., *The Waters of Marah* (London 1965)
Haugh, R., *Photius and the Carolingians, the Trinitarian Controversy* (Belmont 1973)
Herrin, J., *The Formation of Christendom* (Oxford 1987)
Hill, H. (ed.), *Light from the East* (Toronto n.d.)
Hirschfeld, Y., *The Judaean Desert Monasteries in the Byzantine Period* (New Haven 1992)
Hitti, P., *A History of the Arabs*, 10th edn (London 1979)
Hollerweger, H., *Tur Abdin, Living Cultural Heritage* (Linz 1999)

Huntington, S., *The Clash of Civilisations and the Remaking of World Order* (New York 1996)

Hussey, J., *The Orthodox Church in the Byzantine Empire* (Oxford 1986)

Jardine Grisbrooke, W. (ed.), *Spiritual Counsels of Father John of Kronstadt* (London 1967)

Jones, A.H.M., 'Were the ancient heresies national or social movements in disguise?', *Journal of Theological Studies* NS 10 (1959), pp. 280–98

Kaplan, S., *The Monastic Holy Man and the Christianization of Early Solomonic Ethiopia* (Wiesbaden 1984)

Keleher, S., *Passion and Resurrection: The Greek Catholic Church in Soviet Ukraine 1939–1989* (Lviv 1993)

Khalidi, T., *The Muslim Jesus* (Cambridge, MA 2001)

Kontzevitch, I. (ed.), *The Northern Thebaid, Monastic Saints of the Russian North* (Platina, CA 1974)

Krivocheine, B., *In the Light of Christ* (New York 1987)

Lang, D.M., *Armenia, Cradle of Civilisation* (London 1970)

Levine, D., *Wax and Gold. Tradition and Innovation in Ethiopian Culture* (Chicago 1966)

Limouris, G., *Orthodox Visions of Ecumenism* (Geneva 1994)

Lossky, V., *The Mystical Theology of the Eastern Church* (London 1957)

Louth, A., *Denys the Areopagite* (London 1989)
  Maximus the Confessor (London 1996)
  The Origins of the Christian Mystical Tradition. From Plato to Denys (Oxford 1981)

Lowrie, D., *St Sergius in Paris: the Orthodox Theological Institute* (London 1954)

McPartlan, P., *One in 2000* (Slough 1993)

Malcolm, N., *Bosnia, A Short History* (London 1994)
  Kosovo, A Short History (London 1998)

Malone, E.E., 'The monk and the martyr', *Studia Anselmiana* 38 (1956), pp. 201–25

Maloney, G., *A History of Orthodox Theology since 1453* (Belmont 1976)

Mango, C., *The Homilies of Photius, Patriarch of Constantinople* (Cambridge, MA 1958)

Matthew the Poor, *The Communion of Love* (New York 1984)

Meinardus, O., *Monks and Monasteries of the Egyptian Deserts* (Cairo 1961)

Meyendorff, J., *A Study of St Gregory Palamas* (London 1964)
  Byzantine Theology, Historical Trends and Doctrinal Themes (New York 1974)
  Byzantium and the Rise of Russia (Cambridge 1981)
  Christ in Eastern Christian Thought (New York 1975)

Gregory Palamas and Orthodox Spirituality (New York 1974)

The Orthodox Church (New York 1962)

Rome, Constantinople and Moscow (New York 1996)

Meyendorff, J. (ed.), *The Primacy of Peter* (New York 1992)

Meyendorff, P., *Russia, Ritual and Reform* (New York 1991)

Moosa, M., *The Maronites in History* (New York 1986)

Murray, R., *Symbols of Church and Kingdom: a Study in Early Syriac Tradition* (Cambridge 1975)

Nichols, A., *Light from the East* (London 1995)

Rome and the Churches of the East (Edinburgh 1992)

Theology in the Russian Diaspora: Church, Fathers and Eucharist in Nikolai Afanas'ev (1893–1966) (Cambridge 1989)

Obolensky, D., *The Byzantine Commonwealth, Eastern Europe 500–1453* (London 1971)

Oleksa, M., *Orthodox Alaska. A Theology of Mission* (New York 1992)

Ostrogorsky, G., *History of the Byzantine State*, 2nd edn (Oxford 1968)

Ouspensky, L., *Theology of the Icon*, new edn, 2 vols (New York 1992)

Ouspensky, L. and Lossky, V., *The Meaning of Icons* (New York 1982)

Pain, J. and Zernov, N. (eds), *A Bulgakov Anthology* (London 1976)

Palmer, A., *Monk and Mason on the Tigris Frontier: the Early History of the Tur Abdin* (Cambridge 1990)

Pelikan, J., *The Spirit of Eastern Christianity* (Chicago 1974)

Popović, J., *Orthodox Faith and Life in Christ* (Belmont 1994)

Pospielovsky, D., *The Orthodox Church in the History of Russia* (New York 1998)

Rinvolucri, M., *The Anatomy of a Church. Greek Orthodoxy Today* (London 1966)

Roberson, R., *The Eastern Christian Churches, a Brief Survey*, 3rd edn (Rome 1990)

Rousseau, P., *Basil of Caesarea* (Berkeley, CA 1994)

Runciman, S., *The Eastern Schism* (Oxford 1955)

The Great Church in Captivity. A Study of the Patriarchate of Constantinople from the Eve of the Turkish Conquest to the Greek War of Independence (Cambridge 1969)

Russell, N., *Cyril of Alexandria* (London 2000)

Saloutos, T., *The Greeks in the United States* (Cambridge, MA 1964)

Sarkissian, K., *The Council of Chalcedon and the Armenian Church* (London 1967)

Saward, J., *Perfect Fools* (Oxford 1980)

Schmemann, A., *For the Life of the World. Sacraments and Orthodoxy* (New York 1973)

Introduction to Liturgical Theology (London 1966)

The Eucharist, Sacrament of the Kingdom (New York 1988)

The Journals of Father Alexander Schmemann 1978–1983 (New York 2000)

The Historical Road of Eastern Orthodoxy (London 1963)

Ultimate Questions. An Anthology of Modern Russian Thought (New York 1965)

Seraphim [Rose], *Blessed Paisius Velichkovsky* (Platina, CA 1976)

Sherrard, P., *Athos, the Holy Mountain* (London 1982)

Constantinople, Iconography of a Sacred City (London 1965)

The Greek East and the Latin West (London 1959)

Shulz, H.-J., *The Byzantine Liturgy: Symbolic Structure and Faith Expression* (New York 1986)

Sophrony (Archimandrite), *Saint Silouan the Athonite*, trans. R. Edmonds (Tolleshunt Knights, Essex 1991)

Staniloae, D., *Orthodox Dogmatic Theology. The Experience of God* (Brookline, MA 1994)

Theology and the Church (New York 1980)

Stokoe, M. and Kishkovsky, L., *Orthodox Christians in North America 1794–1994* (no place of publication 1994)

Taft, R., *A History of the Liturgy of St John Chrysostom*, vol. 2, *The Great Entrance*, 2nd edn (Rome 1978)

The Byzantine Rite (Collegeville, MA 1992)

Tamrat, T., *Church and State in Ethiopia 1270–1527* (Oxford 1972)

Tarasar, C. (ed.), *Orthodox America 1794–1976* (New York 1975)

Thomson, R.W., *Studies in Armenian Literature and Christianity* (Aldershot 1994)

Thunberg, L., *Man and the Cosmos: the Vision of St Maximus the Confessor* (New York 1985)

Microcosm and Mediator: the Theological Anthropology of Maximus the Confessor (Lund 1965)

Ullendorff, W., *Ethiopia and the Bible* (London 1968)

van Doorn-Harder, Vogt, K. (eds), *Between Desert and City: the Coptic Orthodox Church Today* (Oslo 1997)

Vasileios (Archimandrite), *Hymn of Entry. Liturgy and Life in the Orthodox Church* (New York 1984)

Vischer, L. (ed.), *Spirit of God, Spirit of Christ* (Geneva 1981)

Walker, A. and Carras, C. (eds), *Living Orthodoxy in the Modern World* (London 1996)

Ward, B., *Harlots of the Desert* (London 1987)

Ware, K., 'Orthodox and Catholics in the seventeenth century: schism or inter-communion?', in *Studies in Church History*, vol. 9, *Schism, Heresy and Religious Protest*, ed. D. Baker (Cambridge 1972)

'The Church: a time of transition', in R. Clogg (ed.), *Greece in the 1980s* (London 1983), pp. 208–30

The Orthodox Way (London 1979)

The Power of the Name. The Jesus Prayer in Orthodox Spirituality (Oxford 1986)

'The witness of the Orthodox Church in the twentieth century', *Sourozh* 80 (May 2000), pp. 1–14

Ware, T., *Eustratios Argenti. A Study of the Greek Church under Turkish Rule* (Oxford 1964)

The Orthodox Church (London 1963)

Wellesz, E., *A History of Byzantine Music and Hymnography*, 2nd edn (Oxford 1961)

Williams, R.D. (ed.), *Sergii Bulgakov. Towards a Russian Political Theology* (Edinburgh 1999)

Wybrew, H., *The Orthodox Liturgy* (London 1989)

Yannaras, C., *Elements of Faith: an Introduction to Orthodox Theology*, trans. K. Scram (Edinburgh 1991)

Philosophie sans Rupture (Geneva 1986)

The Freedom of Morality (New York 1996)

Zernov, N., *The Russians and their Church* (London 1945)

The Russian Religious Renaissance of the Twentieth Century (London 1963)

Zizioulas, J., *Being as Communion* (New York 1985)

Index

Index